This deeply personal devotional guide probes the heart with human stories and profound honesty. Thad shines a light on the depths of God's love in all our relationships. This is the way true love transforms those who humbly live in life's messy, everyday world.

—JOHN ARMSTRONG, president, ACT3 Network

Barnum has done it again. He has given us another volume in his Deeper Devotions series that will bless the soul of any person who seeks to know our Lord Jesus better and love Him more. This rich book—perfect for deeper daily devotional discipleship—at once enriches the mind and opens the eyes of the heart. I pray it finds a wide audience of real discipleship.

—LYLE W. DORSETT, Billy Graham professor of evangelism, Beeson Divinity School, Samford University; senior pastor, Christ the King Anglican Church

It's so refreshing to hear someone ask the hard questions about God, life, and loving others, which Thad so aptly does while encouraging us with the news that the answers are out there.

—JULIA DUIN, former religion editor, *The Washington Times*; author of *Quitting Church* and *Days of Fire and Glory*

In *Real Love*, Thad Barnum demonstrates what we need to follow Jesus well: putting our true hearts on the table before God. When we do, the Bible comes alive and God's grace is seen for the unspeakable power that it is. There we find the gentle, loving change we so desperately search for.

—TODD HUNTER, bishop; author of *Christianity Beyond Belief* and *Our Favorite Sins*

In this inspiring and very real devotional, Barnum leads us toward the heart of Jesus in brilliant and compelling ways. Each reading calls for further thought and reflection. The result is no less than a deeper love for ourselves, for others, and for our Lord.

—JO ANNE LYON, General Superintendent, The Wesleyan Church

The distance between knowing *about* love and actually *living* it is infinite. In wonderfully readable prose, my friend Thad Barnum helps us see what it means to know love and authentically live it, as God intended for us when He made us. It's actually possible! And since it's also one of the most important things in our lives, I'm thrilled to recommend this book.

—ERIC METAXAS, *New York Times* best-selling author of *Bonhoeffer: Pastor, Martyr, Prophet, Spy* and *7 Men and the Secret of Their Greatness*

Thad Barnum is a man who lives at the intersection of the Bible and daily life. In *Real Love*, he invites us to join him there. Thad writes about the highs and lows of life and everything in-between and how God's Word reveals God's love to us wherever we are. *Real Love* is a book about real life and the love we can experience if we have ears to hear and eyes to see.

—DAVID ROSENBERRY, dean and rector, Christ Church, Plano, TX

Real Love makes the biblical application in our contextual life a spiritual diagnosis. Bishop Thaddeus exposes and connects the truth of the Scripture to our life experience. Highly recommended for Bible study in groups.

—JOHN RUCYAHANA, president of National Unity and Reconciliation Commission; author of *Bishop of Rwanda*

Real love is something for which we all long and secretly doubt we will ever find. Thad Barnum renews our hope by showing us how a day-by-day relationship with Jesus pours real love into us so that it overflows from us to really change our love-parched world. Read this book and find what you long for in the One who longs for you.

—STEVE TREASH, senior pastor, Black Rock Congregational Church, Fairfield, CT

Barnum brings life to sacred texts and throws sacred texts on life as people live it in the midst of their own personal turmoil. I cannot recommend this book too highly.

—DAVID W. VIRTUE, president of Virtueonline, an orthodox Anglican Online News Service

Here is what you will find in these pages: Like the best of friends, Thad will be with you in your pain, tease you a bit if you are simply trying to put on a nice face, and invite you to enjoy and act upon a vision to love deeply from the heart.

—EDWARD T. WELCH, author, seminary professor, and counselor at CCEF in Glenside, PA

REAL LOVE

WHERE BIBLE AND LIFE MEET

THADDEUS BARNUM

wphonline.com

Copyright © 2014 by Thaddeus Barnum
Published by Wesleyan Publishing House
Indianapolis, Indiana 46250
Printed in the United States of America
ISBN: 978-0-89827-914-6
ISBN (e-book): 978-0-89827-915-3

Library of Congress Cataloging-in-Publication Data

Barnum, Thaddeus.
 Real love : where Bible and life meet / Thaddeus Barnum.
    pages cm
 ISBN 978-0-89827-914-6 (pbk.)
 1. Bible. Epistle of John, 1st--Meditations. I. Title.
 BS2805.54.B37 2014
 242'.5--dc23
                          2014008442

To Gregor

Other books by Thaddeus Barnum include:
Never Silent, *Remember Eve*, *Where Is God in Suffering and Tragedy?* and *Real Identity*.

For more information about these and other discipleship resources, visit the call2disciple ministry website at www.call2disciple.com.

Thad's first devotional in this Deeper Devotion series, *Real Identity*, is available at wphonline.com.

CONTENTS

Use *Real Love* devotions to accompany group
Bible studies or preaching in 1 John.

Free discipleship resources are available for download at
www.wphresources.com/reallove.

ACKNOWLEDGEMENTS

Erilynne and I are having the best run. We're married thirty-three years this year—all of it has gone by so fast. But even now, as we look back, we realize we've always had the privilege of being in the heart of Christian community. It's how we started. We belonged to the best of churches where we experienced the wonder of the Lord's presence in worship, teaching, mission, and fellowship. It was led by a remarkable man, the Rev. Dr. Everett "Terry" Fullam, whose excellence in Bible teaching spanned the globe. He mentored us—like he did so many—strengthening our walk in Jesus and preparing us for a lifetime in His service. We can't imagine these devotions without Terry's signature on our lives.

Terry went to be with the Lord on March 15, 2014. We felt the best way to honor him was to introduce you to him. If you're longing for great Bible teaching, go to www.lifeonwings.org.

Fast forward, and we are surrounded by the fellowship of so many. Thank you Dad and Elena, Barry and Kate, for your unending love and prayers—especially for these writing projects. Teresa, my brother's widow—you're the best! Krissy, Susan, Jill, Jan—our daughters, their husbands and children—you brighten our life beyond measure. To Ken, David, Steve, and Quigg—thank you for holding me accountable. To our staff, parish council, and church family at Church of the Apostles, Fairfield, Connecticut—these devotions would never be possible without your kind encouragement.

We're also grateful to be part of "call2disiple"—a ministry encouraging every Christian to become conformed to the image of His Son (see Rom. 8:29). Thank you Susan and Jan for overseeing the office and helping me every week with these devotions. For Sandy, as well as our board: David and Nancy, Ralph and Beth, Barbara and Lou. You are all the dearest of friends.

Wesleyan Publishing House did an incredible job on *Real Identity*. I am so grateful they have welcomed me back for this new volume. I want to especially thank Rachael Stevenson who masterfully copyedited and proofed the text; Lyn Rayn, for the cover and interior design; as well as Dane Benton and Jeff Ray who oversee the marketing and sales of this book.

Craig Bubeck—who acquired, edited, and directed the publication of *Real Love*—you are a great writer, teacher, and friend. Thanks for pushing me. If it's OK with you, don't stop!

To the Lord be all praise and glory.

INTRODUCTION

*Come to Me, all who are weary and heavy-laden,
and I will give you rest.*

—MATTHEW 11:28

After Mom died in October 1973, my older brother, Gregor, and I entered our adult years rarely crossing paths. We simply couldn't find common ground. He gave himself to psychology and philosophy with as much passion as I gave myself to the Lord. Early on, we ended up butting heads nearly every time we talked. The two of us—well, it just didn't work.

As much as we tried to connect, superficial was about the best we could do. Weather, health, family, work. We always promised to talk soon. Always said we loved each other. But nothing ever came of it. And somehow years passed between us. For reasons of his own, he distanced himself from many in our family. He rarely came around. We'd see each other once or twice . . . a decade.

Until we entered our fifties.

We talked a little more. He came to some family events. The things that separated us didn't seem to separate us as much. The bond between us was real and strong. He loved us—me, our dad, our sister Kate, and our families. And we loved him.

Surprisingly, he not only came to our dad's eighty-fifth birthday party in January 2012, but he and his wife actually stayed with Erilynne and me at our home for a night. It may sound small, but it was big to us. And what concerned us most that night was his health. He wasn't feeling well. He had all kinds of doctor appointments set up, and he looked scared.

So I called him more. He called me more.

Then the news came. On May 17, the doctors said he had metastasized cancer and months—maybe a year or more—to live.

After that, we talked or texted every day.

"I want to talk Bible," he said, not long after. "Where do we start?"

It took me my complete surprise. "How 'bout tomorrow, late morning?" I asked, pushing him off.

"Cool," he said.

And immediately I felt this pit in the center of my stomach. I was scared this conversation would hurt our relationship. It would spark debate between us and we'd quickly fall back to old patterns of butting heads. Arguing. Building walls between each other, and I didn't want that. Not now, especially now.

How do I do this?

So the next day I called him and admitted I was nervous. "I want to take this slowly, if you don't mind. And if it doesn't go well, let's stop, OK?"

"Yeah," he replied, "but I really want this."

So off we went. "There's one place we have to start," I said, taking him to Matthew 11:25–26. "It's a passage where Jesus prayed to His Father and said, 'I praise you, Father, Lord of heaven and earth, that You have hidden these things from the wise and intelligent and revealed them to infants. Yes, Father, for this way was well-pleasing in Your sight.' This is important," I interjected. "He's setting ground rules. This has nothing to do with how brilliant we are."

"No, I get that," he came back.

"It means we can't, with our own minds, understand God. Or the Bible. We need His help. He reveals Himself— if we come to Him as little children. It may sound unfair. But He doesn't care if we're scholars or simple-minded. People in the Third World living in poverty, who have no access to universities, have as much access to Him as we do. That's the story."

He surprised me. He was all in.

"Agreed, I like it. Now keep going," he insisted.

So I asked him what he thought of verse 28. He read it out loud: "Come to Me, all who are weary and heavy-laden." And he stopped. There was silence on the phone between us. I waited until he finally read, "For I am gentle and humble in heart" (v. 29). I heard him take a deep sigh and say, "I've never seen that before."

And here we were. The two of us. At the hardest place of all.

"Gregor, this is it," I said to him. "This is everything. It's the entire Bible in just a few words. Can you see it?"

"I'm not sure."

"From the beginning, God created us to be in relationship with Him. We messed up. That's why He came. It's why He went to the cross—to right our wrong; so He could look us in the eye and say, 'Come to Me. Be in relationship with Me. Real, dynamic, intimate relationship.' This is His heart for us."

"Say more," he pressed.

"You and me—we're not coming to a philosophy, a theological doctrine, a worldview of some kind. We're coming to God Almighty. We are coming to His Son. He wants us to know Him and love Him with all our heart, mind, soul, and strength. He wants this relationship with us. That's the beauty of it."

I stopped and said nothing more. Not then. I knew I had stepped on sacred ground. Nothing plagued my brother more in life than broken relationships. It had always been hard—with women in the past, with his own family.

Between us.

"You OK?" he asked, wondering why I stopped.

"Yeah, kind of," I said honestly.

"Why, what's up?"

Part of me didn't want to go on. I didn't want to tell him the next piece of the story—that is, if we step into this relationship with Him, He requires that we step into relationship with each other. These two inseparable pieces are the exact reason I started writing devotions on 1 John. I knew, at the heart of John's message, stood the royal law. That is, if we truly love God, if we believe in Jesus Christ as our Savior, then we must—by God's decree—love one another.

And if we don't, John said we are liars and the truth is not in us (1 John 2:4).

In my world, especially in 2012, I witnessed great Christian leaders break from each other. Churches split apart. Marriages ended in divorce. Long-time Christian friends took sides against each other. Things were done, were said, that should never be named among those who belong to Jesus. But it was.

It is. Division in the body of Christ—it's everywhere. And I was just as much to blame. Even here—starting here—with my own brother.

So I told him everything. About broken relationships in the church, among pastors and leaders, between churches right across the street from each other, among Christian denominations who hold the same creedal faith in Christ. The breaks in my own life.

"It's not acceptable," I said. "He doesn't allow us to love Him and then refuse to make it real in the relationships in our lives. This is why I'm going through 1 John. It's why I write devotions like I do. I believe with all my heart that He wants to take us to the place where Bible and life meet. Where what we say and how we live are one and the same. It doesn't matter if we believe something is true. It matters whether it's real in our lives. And if we're going to say we love the Lord, then we have to do what He says and love each other with as much passion as He, in Christ, has loved us."

"I agree," he shot back quickly.

And then he surprised me—again.

"I want to do this with you," he thundered.

"Really?"

"Yeah. You OK with that?"

"Yes, absolutely!" I agreed. And suddenly, the two of us—well, it just worked. Runners in stride for the first time since the days of our youth.

"We should've done this a long time ago," he said later.

And more than anything—in these days of his sickness—I wanted all those years back, with decades more to come.

PART 1

BEHIND THE TREE

1

LET'S TALK RELATIONSHIPS

Reflections on Matthew 5:21–23

*Search me, O God, and know my heart; try me and know
my anxious thoughts; and see if there be any hurtful
way in me, and lead me in the everlasting way.*

—PSALM 139:23–24

I sit at my desk holding a letter in my hand. The man
who wrote it is my friend. We've known each other the better
part of twenty years. And, if I were honest with myself, he's
family to me, like a brother.

I trust him. I love him.

But the last few months have been hard between us. What
can I say? In my opinion, he made a wrong decision. He fell
hard into a world of church politics and chose the way that
brought him acceptance and favor. For as long as I've known
him, that's not been his story. He's always stood for what is
right and true and honorable when it comes to our Lord.

Better than me.

He's always been there, at my side, the moment I waver.
Poking and prodding. Sometimes gentle, sometimes not,
because that's what we do for each other in Christ. Though
it's been hard on occasion, we've grown stronger over the

years. We've been iron sharpening iron in the best way possible (Prov. 27:17). Until now.

The letter is three months old. I keep it in my journal so I never forget, day after day, to beg God to heal the break between us. And again, for the umpteenth time, my eyes fall on the words that hurt the most:

I never thought this day would come. How dare you judge me for what I've done. You stab me with your words having no idea you're in the wrong. Not me. And you're too blind to see it. You've broken trust. You've torn the bond between us that I can't imagine will ever be repaired. Not easily. Not unless the Lord steps between us. But even then . . . I wonder.

He asks me not to call. Not write. Not for a while.

You have heard that the ancients were told, "You shall not commit murder" and "Whoever commits murder shall be liable to the court." But I say to you that everyone who is angry with his brother shall be guilty before the court; and whoever says to his brother, "You good-for-nothing," shall be guilty before the supreme court; and whoever says, "You fool," shall be guilty enough to go into the fiery hell.

—MATTHEW 5:21–22

In the days following his decision, I strongly opposed him. I was fully convinced I could change his mind. I gave him everything I had—just as he'd done with me countless times. But it didn't work. The more I pressed, the more he dug in.

He said the same of me.

I got angry with him. Why push me away like this? Am I nothing to him? And why couldn't he see the consequences of his decision? People were hurt. All kinds of relationships were being torn apart—just like ours. But still he stood his ground and turned it all back on me. I found myself reacting in the worst kind of way. I started to quietly distance myself from him emotionally, pretending I didn't care—when I did.

Our last phone call scared me. Not in what he said. But rather, in the way he said it. The tone in his voice disarmed me completely. I lost the fight to argue. Or defend. Or re-posture. I was suddenly aware I was losing—or had just lost—my dear friend. This story was changing us. Something I never dreamed possible. So rather than mounting my next assault, I stopped the conversation.

I told him I loved him. I told him I was sorry for the way I'd handled these past weeks.

He sighed and quietly agreed. We ended the call on a semi-peaceful note. But that was it. We wouldn't talk again for months.

A few days later, his letter came in the mail.

As the weeks passed, I prayed for him every day. At first, it was all about him. I kept saying the same thing: "Lord Jesus, correct his wrong, bring him around, and make our relationship right again. Like all this never happened."

But eventually, the Lord stepped in and shifted my prayers. It wasn't all about my friend anymore. I couldn't escape the conviction that I'd broken the most important of all God's commands. The one He gave us at the dawn of time. The same one perfectly modeled by all the Lord Jesus Christ said and did.

Because it's Him. It's His law—the royal law (James 2:8). We are to love one another.

So what was I doing living in a broken relationship with a friend as close as a brother? What was my part in it? Why did I let it happen? How am I supposed to balance the tension between hating his decision and yet not compromising either my love for him or for the Lord and His command? Who does this well?

This isn't easy.

And so I started praying King David's prayer: "Search me, O God, and know my heart. . . . And see if there be any hurtful way in me" (Ps. 139:23–24). I also started working my way through the epistle of 1 John realizing, at every turn, the apostle's message thunders with unmistakable strength and power: Relationships are *everything* in the kingdom of God. And that means we can't love God and hate our neighbor. If we do, when we do, we call Him a liar. We walk in darkness (1 John 2:4, 9).

But real love, when it comes down from heaven and fills our hearts by the Holy Spirit (Rom. 5:5), we do differently. We live differently.

He has work to do in me. And He has work to do in us, His church. For "if we walk in the Light as He Himself is in the Light, we have fellowship with one another" (1 John 1:7) and that fellowship, that light, has the power to turn the world upside down.

For Him, and for His glory.

A few more months passed.

In my office, one late afternoon, the phone rang. I looked at the caller ID and it was him. I froze. I could feel my heart start to race. I didn't want to answer it simply because I feared another setback.

"Hey," I said softly, my guard down.

"Have you got a few minutes?" he asked, his voice sounding troubled. He was driving home after a day of meetings that didn't go well and wanted to talk. He told me there were a lot of things in his life that weren't going well and, slowly, he began to share. Piece by piece. Opening his heart to me, trusting me again. Talking like we used to talk. As if this horrible mess between us was over.

"I haven't had the peace of Christ in me. Not since we broke," he said.

"Me too," I confessed.

"If you don't mind, I don't want to go back over it all again. Not right now. Is that OK?" he asked.

"Yeah. We will, in time."

"I'd like that," he said quietly. And somehow, at that moment, we began to find our stride again. As if we'd both learned what we thought we already knew. Yes, in Christ, we're allowed to disagree with each other. Sharply. Strongly. But there are rules that govern us. Kingdom rules that can never be broken. Ever.

He commands us to love each other. As Christ loved us. This is His story. It's meant to be our story.

And I want it with all my heart.

QUESTIONS FOR REFLECTION*

What would happen in your life if you made Psalm 139:23–24 your prayer? How would it affect you if you applied it to broken relationships in your life?

How are we supposed to balance the tension between disagreeing with someone and the command to love them in Jesus Christ? How would we do relationships differently if, no matter the issue, we let the royal law govern our hearts?

---

* *The reflection at the end of each devotion is designed to encourage prayer, journaling, and conversation in small group settings. It's easy to read and go on. It's better to read, stop, and engage in dialogue and prayer.*

2

BROKERING

Reflections on Matthew 5:20–24

Therefore if you are presenting your offering at the altar, and there remember that your brother has something against you, leave your offering there before the altar and go; first be reconciled to your brother, and then come and present your offering.

—MATTHEW 5:23–24

Leave. Go. Be reconciled. Come and present—got it.

I knew this as a young child.

My mother would see me push someone smaller than me and make them cry. She would march over, swat my rear, and say, "Now go over there and say you're sorry. And mean it!" Of course, I didn't want to. I'd stomp my foot, shake my head, and say, "No."

She'd tell me, "Fine, if you don't, you're in bed by 7:30 for a week." And that, in front of my older brother and sister, would be humiliating.

I didn't have a choice. I wasn't doing the 7:30 thing.

So I'd go over to the sniffling little brat I hurt and grunt "Sorry" in that "I don't really mean it" kind of way and then walk off. Mom would see and holler, "You know that's not what I meant; now go back there and do it right."

I'd think to myself, "OK, so you want me to do it right? I can do it right. I can put on the actor's face, play pretend, and tell this little runt, 'How it pains me that I wrongfully pushed and hurt you.' Then, with a bow, exit stage right."

Big smile on my face for Mom.

For I say to you that unless your righteousness surpasses
that of the scribes and Pharisees, you will not
enter the kingdom of heaven.

—MATTHEW 5:20

Adult relationships are far more complicated, but the simple rules learned as a child still apply.

Most of us know we're not supposed to hurt each other. We know that if we do, we need to take the initiative, and say sorry. A real sorry, from the heart. We also know, if we're honest, that it has a lot more to do with us than with them. Not because Mom's watching, but because God is.

And He's harder to fool. He tends to see and hear *everything* and play acting only works if—get this—we fall for our own act.

Which I'm actually good at.

I remember picking up the phone a few years ago surprised to hear the voice of an old friend. He and his wife had moved to another state, and we'd lost touch. Intentionally. We didn't end on good terms. I'd faced him with some issues, and he countered back, hard. Neither of us budged. We cordially, in a good Christian manner (play acting), parted ways.

"Thad!"

He called to say sorry. He'd gone through the Ash Wednesday service and began the season of Lent fully convicted by the Lord that he had to get right with me. And here he was, on the phone, extending kindness.

A real sorry, from the heart.

All these years have passed, and I still love telling the story of that phone call. We did everything we were supposed to do. Each of us confessed we were wrong. We asked each other for forgiveness. We prayed for each other on the phone and, after a long talk of catching up, we ended the call fully at peace with each other. In the Lord. All things put right. Everything perfect.

It all felt so good—like I could feel the Lord smiling down on me.

Until a few years ago. I told the story one too many times. A person finally asked the question, "So how's your relationship now? Is it still going well?"

Hmmm. Not really. We haven't talked since.

For I say to you that unless your righteousness surpasses . . .

—MATTHEW 5:20

He demands more. Not just because God said so but because it's who God is. And we get the tiniest glimpse of this as we come to know the love and fellowship of the Father for His Son, the Son for His Father, with the Holy Spirit, one God, forever and ever.

Relationships are everything in the kingdom of heaven.

It's why the Father sent His Son to us. It's why our Lord suffered on the cross. This, in God's eternal wisdom, was the only way to reconcile what was broken. Us with Him. Him with us. Us with each other. At the highest cost imaginable.

And He will not allow relationships to be treated lightly. Superficially. At no personal cost to our hearts.

I know this. But I don't want this.

I want the law. I want rules. I want the quick-fix, five steps to unbreaking what's broken. Give me: (1) initiate, (2) confess, (3) say sorry, (4) ask forgiveness in Jesus' name, and (5) extend the Lord's peace; and I'm happy. I can do that. I want to do that. It keeps everything superficial, and it doesn't mess with my heart.

It doesn't make me face *me*. The real, broken me.

And better yet, it can all be done on Facebook and Twitter! Getting right with others gets me right with God and gives me a righteousness that makes me all warm inside.

You will not enter the kingdom of heaven.

—MATTHEW 5:20

The fact is, I don't want to do the hard work of kingdom relationships. I want to be in the kingdom. I just don't want to do the kingdom stuff.

My heart's been hurt enough. I already have too many scars layered with too many big, fat callouses. Good calluses—since I don't hurt as much when people stomp on me, or leave me, or call me things I never dreamed they'd call me. Bad calluses—because it makes me so uncaring, so insensitive, so cold of heart and blind to the people I love so much and hurt so easily.

Just let me keep everything light. Simple. Easy. Superficial.

And if something happens, if I get hurt or if I hurt somebody, then I promise I will say sorry, a real sorry, from the heart, with play acting that even fools me. And I'll do what I do best.

I'll broker what's broken so I don't break in the process.

QUESTIONS FOR REFLECTION

If we fall for our own act, how do we wake up, get off stage, and start being real with ourselves? The Lord? Each other?

In what areas of your life are you brokering? With whom and why? Are you ready, in and with the Lord, to do something about it? What first steps can you take today?

3

GOD IS LIGHT

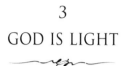

Reflections on 1 John 1:5

*This is the message we have heard from Him and announce
to you, that God is Light, and in Him there is no darkness at all.*

—1 JOHN 1:5

I live in two very different worlds.

The majority of the time—normal time—this great statement, "God is Light," has little or no impact on my daily life. It's not that I don't believe it's true. I do. But I relegate it completely to my mind. It's safe there. Safe because I'm able to transform the "Light" into a concept I can think about and not experience. God forbid the "Light" breaks through. That would completely mess up my life.

Like it or not, I live by a simple rule: Everything has to be safe and protected. That's why I shield my heart. That's why my mind is trained to filter the world around me. It has a job to do, a very specific job, to keep everything ordered 24/7/365. No big changes. No rocking the boat. Everything stays the same.

So, for example, every Sunday in church we begin our worship from *The Book of Common Prayer* with these words: "Almighty God, to you all hearts are open, all desires known, and from you no secrets are hid: Cleanse the thoughts of our hearts by the inspiration of your Holy Spirit, that we may perfectly love you, and worthily magnify your holy Name; through Christ our Lord. Amen."[1]

This prayer is almost identical in thought to the words of Hebrews 4:13: "And there is no creature hidden from His sight, but all things are open and laid bare to the eyes of Him with whom we have to do."

Together we say "Amen!" and then march right on with the service. I'm always glad for that. I fear one day these words will actually make sense, and we'll find ourselves faced with the "Light." Our massive defense systems gone. No big, thick walls between us and God, us and each other, us and ourselves. All of it gone, all of it true: Our hearts open, desires known, secrets exposed. Who can handle that?

Very unhelpful and way too emotional. I'd suddenly be forced to see myself for who I am and not who I pretend to be. I'd have to deal with things I've refused for years to deal with or talk about. I'd be suddenly tossed into the world of "messy," and I don't like messy. I don't want messy.

Just say the prayer and press on. Stick with the routine. Make the simple decision to stay in control. Nothing impacts my life today. No big changes. No rocking the boat. Do everything to turn the "Light" of God into a theological concept that never finds its way to my heart.

My broken heart.

Everything has to be safe and protected.

I remember as a little boy I was afraid of the dark. At night, Mom and Dad kept the hall light on and my bedroom door open a crack. I had just enough light to feel safe. And just enough dark to sleep.

I like that arrangement.

I want just enough "Light" to feel safe. And just enough dark to live my sleepy little Christian life in peace and quiet.

For God, who said, "Light shall shine out of darkness," is the One who has shone in our hearts to give the Light of the knowledge of the glory of God in the face of Christ.

—2 CORINTHIANS 4:6

Every once in a while I slip into "God-time" and enter the kingdom world where the Light shines bright in my heart.

Sometimes it's His doing. I'm driving so hard, so fast with my busy life and I suddenly see His police lights in my rearview mirror. I hear the sirens. I get that horrible feeling of guilt in the pit of my stomach and get mad at myself that I've done something wrong. That I was caught. That I needed to be caught.[2]

But most times, it's my doing.

I can't sustain the image. I do everything I can to manage my world and, most times, it works. But sometimes it doesn't, and I come crashing down. I become instantly aware of the people I've hurt, the things I've said and done which have offended God and others, and worse—I've known it for a long time. I've pushed it farther down, refusing to deal with it. Refusing to admit my own rebellion.

And I find myself on my knees. Turning myself in. Slipping out of "normal time" into "God-time."

He speaks, and the Light shines in my darkness to give me the knowledge of the glory of God in the face of Christ.

This is where it all began. Years ago, when I was in my late teens, when I first came to know Jesus Christ as Lord of my life, as the Light of the world (John 8:12; 9:5). I knew He knew me. I knew my heart was open, my desires known, my secrets fully exposed—and I loved it. I loved it because the fight to be somebody I'm not was over. The burden of carrying the weight of my sins was off of me.

And I knew what I didn't know before. The secret of the kingdom of God is found right here.

"For thus says the high and exalted One Who lives forever, whose name is Holy, 'I dwell on a high and holy place, and also with the contrite and lowly of spirit in order to revive the spirit of the lowly and to revive the heart of the contrite'" (Isa. 57:15).

In humility. In confession. In repentance.

This is where He dwells with us. This is where He has ordained the stuff of relationships to begin and to be lived out day by day, year by year, in this age and in the age to come. This is the place, the only place, He is in fellowship with us. We with Him and each other.

And I lived here for a while. I went back over all the relationships I'd messed up over the years and I went to them. Or called them. Or wrote to them. Just to say sorry and to own my part in what went wrong. I was learning to be and walk in the Light, not just with my past. Doing right-now relationships with an open heart. Desires known; secrets exposed. In humility. In confession. In repentance.

Where nothing is safe and protected.

Until I got hurt. Once, twice. And then watched others get hurt. Not by people of the world but by the people of the Light. I didn't understand it. I didn't know what to do. So I did what I've always done. I ran back to my other world.

And quietly slipped into "normal time."

QUESTIONS FOR REFLECTION

How would life change for you if your heart was open before the Lord, desires known, secrets exposed?

We often love darkness more than light (John 3:19–21). What do you need today to help you be and walk in the Light of Jesus Christ? With Him? With others?

NOTES

1. *The Book of Common Prayer*, red ed. (New York: Church Publishing, 1979), 355.

2. This is the work of the Holy Spirit who convicts us of our sin (John 16:8). It is also called "the discipline of the Lord" who "disciplines us for our good, so that we may share His holiness." See Hebrews 12:5–11.

4

THOSE LITTLE ANNOYING NIGGLES

Reflections on 1 John 1:3

*And indeed our fellowship is with the Father,
and with His Son Jesus Christ.*

—1 JOHN 1:3

Over dinner, in casual conversation with a few good friends, I stepped on a land mine. Even after it went off, stupid me, I didn't get what happened; so I asked about it. Bad decision. Should have kept my mouth shut.

"What you did was really hurtful," one guy said. A few others nodded their heads. And they told me, frankly, straight to my face, that I'd been part of a decision-making process a few years back that caused them real hurt.

"Are you kidding me?"

They weren't kidding. They looked at me curiously, wondering if I'd engage the conversation, dig into the story of the past, say what needed to be said then—maybe just maybe—own the wrong I'd done. Make my confession. Clueless me. The best I could offer was, "Gosh, I'm sorry, I had no idea."

Which didn't help at all.

Within seconds, we were back to the casual, friendly ban-
ter of friends. I put on the mask, rolled with the evening, and
acted like I wasn't devastated by this news. But I was. In my
mind, I tried to race back to what had happened. How had I
hurt them? What did I do? They had clearly made the decision to welcome me back into their friendship despite what
I'd done. Why? How long had they been talking about this?
About me? Did they think I intentionally hurt them?

We parted that night as if the land mine never went off.
But it did, and we all knew it. I think everyone also knew
I couldn't handle it. And they kindly let me sweep it under
the rug.

I immediately called a colleague who was part of making
the decision that, now I knew, caused so much hurt. It brought
great comfort for me to hear that he was as shocked as I was
that we'd hurt a number of people. We rehearsed all the
details of the events leading up to the decision and encouraged each other to press on, trust the Lord, and not look back.

I must say, I like being with people who agree with me.

Of course, I pretend the Lord agrees with me too. I
know, by His mercy, I am rescued in Christ. I have fellowship "with the Father, and with His Son Jesus Christ."

That's all that matters.

Everything else is just stuff. Life is hard. Relationships
are hard. We all try and do the best we can. And for me, I
cling to this one essential truth: I love the Lord. He loves
me. This is the only relationship that counts—right?

I convince myself of that as I continue to think through
what I did to hurt my friends in Christ whom I love and

trust. I go back over the details of the events one more time. I ask myself, "What led me to take the decision I took? Why did I do it? Did I think through the consequences of the decision on others?"

Two themes emerge. First, I work diligently on my defense. I start with the premise that what I did was exactly the right thing to do. Now I need to prove it again, build my case, and justify how I did what I did, why I did it, and why I'd do it again if faced with similar circumstances.

Second, it's helpful to think through how my dear, close, good friends are actually to blame for their own hurt. I simply need to lovingly prove it's not my fault; it's theirs.

All the while, as I deal with this most difficult situation, I continue to find comfort in the fellowship I enjoy "with the Father, and with His Son Jesus Christ." Me and Him. Him and me, and the few who agree with me.

What we have seen and heard we proclaim to you also, so that you too may have fellowship with us; and indeed our fellowship is with the Father, and with His Son Jesus Christ.

—1 JOHN 1:3

No matter how deep, how strong, how convincing I am in my defense, I can't stop those little annoying niggles— like little pinchers—pricking my conscience.

My friends are hurt.

And I know, deep down, the Lord doesn't play my game. He never has, though I convince myself every time I come to a moment like this that He does. He takes sides— my side. He helps me build my case. He helps me blame others. And I know that's not true, though I spend most of my days believing it is.

The fact is, I know too much. I know the Lord makes it impossible for me to claim that my relationship with Him is the only relationship that matters. It's not true, and I know it. Fellowship with Him is forever bound to the fellowship we have together in Jesus Christ.

My friends are hurt.

I have to do something about it. Something far greater than going to them and saying, "I'm sorry for hurting you." Of course, I like that because it allows me to say sorry and still think I'm right. But I know that won't work for them, and it won't work for the Lord. I have to do what I don't want to do.

I have to dismantle my defense. I have to deal with the drive inside me both to be right and to blame others. I've got to find out my part in this story.

And own it, really own it.

So that you too may have fellowship with us.

—1 JOHN 1:3

But then, it suddenly dawns on me. Why listen to those little annoying niggles? After all, my friends are still my friends. They've obviously dealt with the fact that I hurt them. They've accepted me back into their friendship. They told me I hurt them. I said I'm sorry.

So why not forget about it and move on? Just turn the niggles to mute. Make a concerted effort to be a better friend. Do what I can to never do what I did ever again. Stop working so hard. Stop condemning myself. Don't make a big deal of this. "Fellowship" in the kingdom of God isn't meant to be perfect. I mean, isn't it true of all of us?

But it doesn't work. Not for me. I find, at the oddest times, when I least expect it—the niggling comes back louder, stronger. Pinching me, urging me, to do what's right.

QUESTIONS FOR REFLECTION

What issues are you sweeping under the rug? Where are the places of conflict with others that you work hard at avoiding?

The dictionary defines *niggle* as "a persistent annoyance." When the Lord begins to niggle your conscience, what do you normally do? How do you react to it?

5

DOING THE DISS

~~~

Reflections on 1 John 1:1–6

What was from the beginning, what we have heard,
what we have seen with our eyes, what we have looked at and
touched with our hands, concerning the Word of Life.

—1 JOHN 1:1

I get out of bed, look into the mirror, and sigh. I look the way I feel. A full day of meetings ahead. No, not meetings. If only they were meetings. Meetings are great. I complain about them all the time, but, to be honest, they're task-driven, outcome-based, goal-filled, and satisfying. Meetings actually are perfect.

There's little time for too much relational stuff.

Today is full of people meetings. Real people, real hurts, real relationships, real exploring of things that really matter. Deep down, I love this. It's what I do. But sometimes I want to go back to bed.

This is the entire problem with the gospel. Give me a meeting-driven church that excels in biblical training for the mind, accents living the good old-fashioned moral life, majors in sharing the gospel and serving the poor in the local community and all over the world—and I say *perfect*! Then let gifted pastors do the "pastor" thing while the rest of us do the "doing" thing.

And I find my comfort zone.

The fact that He came — and the way He came — messes it all up. It's like He announced to the whole world: "Relationships are everything to me! Let me show you!" So He does the one thing that would drive us absolutely crazy. He comes fully Him, but also fully us. Sits down at the table, eats, drinks, looks us in the eye, and immediately deals with the forbidden matters of the heart.

I mean crazy! We're talking God the infinite, God the creator of solar systems we can still barely see, God the enormous, unfathomable, huge — sitting down at my table to eat with me? With us? Looking me, looking us, in the eye and talking real?

And why? Because relationships are *everything* to Him.

I can't escape it. The apostle John was thrilled by this. He said in effect, "We've heard Him! We've seen Him! We've touched Him! It's all about being in relationship with the Lord Jesus Christ, with His Father, with each other!" Can you imagine the joy?

Double ugh.

This, today, is not my comfort zone. If only Jesus Christ hadn't come, the relationship thing wouldn't be so front and center. Important, yes. But not *everything*. Then I could go off to a day full of meetings. Really good meetings where we set an agenda, assign tasks, and actually get things done for the kingdom.

And I can completely bypass the matters of my heart.

If we say that we have fellowship with Him and yet walk
in the darkness, we lie and do not practice the truth. . . .
The one who says he is in the Light and yet hates
his brother is in the darkness until now.

—1 JOHN 1:6; 2:9

It's hard to think of myself as a liar, walking in darkness.

My first meeting of the day was with a man I deeply
admire and respect. We haven't spent much time together
recently so I was actually looking forward to seeing him.
And it all went well until we stumbled into a conversation
about a mutual friend of ours. Someone I'd lost touch with
a few years ago. Someone he refused to lose touch with.

My mind flashed back to the last time I'd seen our
friend. We had spent years together in church, in ministry,
at dinners in our respective homes, on mission trips around
the world. No, not years—decades. And for whatever reason, one of the last times we were together, he snapped at
me. Really hard.

More like bit my head off.

I let some time pass. I reapproached to make things
right, to see what was wrong, to extend kindness to him. I
wanted to know if I'd done anything wrong to hurt him
and, if so, to say sorry. I thought I took a very humble
approach but with that very me-centered—is your problem
all about me?—kind of humility.

He bit again. And again, every time I approached. I finally went to others who knew him and asked for their counsel, but they didn't have any idea what was wrong with him either. So the next time I tried, and he dissed me again—harder than before—I got the message loud and clear. I threw my hands up in the air, walked away, and never called again.

I dissed him right back.

As much as it deeply pained me to lose his friendship, I felt I'd exhausted all possibilities to be right with him. In fact, I harbored a quiet little smugness that I'd followed all the biblical "right" things to do to reconcile with him and he'd refused. Plain and simple: This was his problem—not mine.

I think the old expression is, "I washed my hands of him."

Well, the man I met with today didn't wash his hands of him. In fact, he made it quite clear to me that he'd been dissed too. Worse than me. And even now, he kept saying, "It's still happening from time to time," and, "He's not out of the woods yet." He told me the story behind the story. Several years ago, our mutual friend had been severely wounded and heartbroken. Betrayed deep in his soul. Though I'd heard rumors of this, I had no idea of the depth of the pain he'd suffered.

"It crushed him. It turned him into the man he is now. If you don't mind the analogy, it reminds me of our beautiful golden retriever, Lexie, when she got hit by a car. The moment I put my hand out, she bit me. But that didn't stop me from picking her up, getting her to the vet, making sure she was alright, and loving her back to health."

Triple ugh.

I hate meetings like this. Why couldn't he have said something like, "Yeah, he bit me too. Tried a bunch of times to circle back but every time I did, he bit again. So I dissed him like you."

Just like me. Mr. Clean Hands.

God is Light, and in Him there is no darkness at all.
If we say that we have fellowship with Him and
yet walk in the darkness, we lie.

—1 JOHN 1:5–6

Sometime in these verses, I hear the sounds of my childhood: "Liar! Liar! Pants on fire!"

I caught a glimpse of the Lord's compassion today. I saw no matter how messed up I am, no matter how hurt I become, or how betrayed, or how run over by the car of life and tossed on the side of the road, how lost and forgotten I get—the Lord won't leave me like I did my friend. He won't "do the diss."

So, tell me, why did I?

QUESTIONS FOR REFLECTION

What does it mean to you that God Himself made relationships so important He came as one of us? Do you know the depth of His desire to be in relationship with you, and you with Him?

If He relentlessly doesn't give up on us, why do we give up on each other? What can you do today to take the compassion He has given you to someone you've given up on?

6

ME AND MY TREE

Reflections on 1 John 1:7

But if we walk in the Light as He Himself is in the Light . . .

—1 John 1:7

A friend of mine stopped by the office yesterday, sat in my chair, and grinned from ear to ear. "Two months, three days!" he smirked. He and his wife are going on the vacation of a lifetime.

An almost untouched Caribbean island. Bleach white sands. Clear, see-through water. Deep blue sky. Miles of beaches with no one in sight. Eight days, seven nights. Five-star hotel. The best restaurants imaginable.

I told him to get out of my office immediately.

"Jealousy looks good on you!" he bantered, with a child's delight in his eyes. He couldn't wait. This year, of all years, was the hardest on their marriage. They'd come through so much, weathering what most don't weather. And now here they were, past the worst of it, excited silly about their second honeymoon.

"I'm telling you, it's like being in paradise," he mused.

"Well, that's a bit scary," I said, a little more seriously. "I don't think I could handle a week in paradise right now."

He stood up, shook my hand, and took a last jab. "I think it's the other way around. I don't think paradise could handle you!" And with that, he was gone.

OK, not helpful. I closed my eyes and saw myself standing on the perfect beach in the real paradise of God. The sun—or the Son—at high noon in perfect strength. Give me the Caribbean. That would be great. But not this. Not today.

My life is too much of a mess.

The sun I can handle. It hits the skin. The Son, not so much. He hits the heart and exposes it. All of it. Not as a quick EKG or MRI done in rare times of need. But as a way of life. Everyday life.

He wants me to "walk in the Light."

This is the playing field of the kingdom of God. Like a baseball team taking the field, so Christians are called to step onto the playing field of the kingdom. Into the "Light."

And live here. And what's amazing, startling in fact, is that He Himself does exactly the same thing. He steps onto the playing field with us. He too walks "in the Light"— even though, get this, He actually *is* the Light.

But that's how relationships work in His kingdom. He is, always is, relational.

I think of Adam and Eve. They had no problem being on the field of light, walking with the Lord who chose to walk with them in the garden of Eden. No problem, that is, until they sinned. The moment evil and darkness flooded their souls, the sound of Him coming closer, and closer, and guess what? They found a tree. And hid.

Good move. That's exactly how I feel today.

This is the judgment, that the Light has come into
the world, and men loved the darkness rather
than the Light, for their deeds were evil.

—JOHN 3:19

I grab a soda from the fridge and head down to the basement. I pull up a chair, take a few boxes off the shelf, and begin to dig into my past. They're full of old letters, photos, service bulletins, and old keepsakes.

"Take time and go back," a Christian friend said. "What happens is we keep repeating what we've done in the past, over and over. We live so much in the present. We handle our relational problems, justify our decisions, and have no idea that what we're doing to people now is exactly what we've done to people before. Old, sinful patterns that hurt relationships in the past now hurt relationships in the present and we are too blind to see it."

"Go back and look," he challenged.

I embraced his counsel on this because, frankly, I am seeing too many broken relationships among Christians and Christian leaders that I don't know what to do about it.

And it's personal. This past week I received a letter from an old friend, who with incredible ease, wrote me off. How does that happen? Why does it happen? And what's my part in it? How am I supposed to respond to him if I refuse to do the work of looking at me?

That choice to step onto the playing field of "Light."

Search me, O God, and know my heart.

—PSALM 139:23

Spending an hour with my old self isn't actually a ton of fun. Had I done this with no agenda—be intentional, look for the patterns of sin—it would have been great. Seeing old friends. Remembering celebrations. Reading letters and cards I've held on to. A selective jaunt "counting my blessings one by one."

It didn't take long.

A face in the photos here. A face there. People, stories, lives shared and then gone when things didn't go well between us. Why did I let that happen? Why didn't I take initiative and, at the very least, extend kindness to them? Why was it so easy to turn my heart away, let them go, and press on into life? Leaving things between us unresolved.

Not once. Twice. Not twice . . .

Why is it still so easy?

I close the boxes, put them back on the shelf, hating that I've done this little exercise. There are patterns in my life I don't want to look at. Things I've done, things I'm doing, that I want to keep buried in the darkness.

But actually that's helpful. My guess is that my old friend who sent me the letter is no different. Same with other Christians who are suffering from broken relationships. We've all decided the same thing.

We're staying on the playing field of "Light." We're kingdom people. We take great comfort in knowing that. Saying that. Believing that. And the moment we hear someone we don't like coming closer—someone we've decidedly pushed away—we run, find our tree, and hide. Convinced we're still in the "Light" and still in the right.

Me and my tree. That's exactly where I am today.

QUESTIONS FOR REFLECTION

Too often, we choose to be superficial as a way of life. But He doesn't want a superficial relationship with us. Are you aware of that? What will it take for you to step away from the tree and enter fully into the light of His love for you?

Going back, looking at patterns in your life of broken relationships and allowing the Lord to step into those patterns and change them is a big step. What would you find if you did this?

7

OUT FROM THE SHADOWS

~~~

Reflections on 1 John 1:7

*But if we walk in the Light as He Himself is in the
Light, we have fellowship with one another, and the
blood of Jesus His Son cleanses us from all sin.*

—1 JOHN 1:7

I wrote in my journal:

I wonder, has this verse ever been read before?

*I mean, come on, what if it said, "This is the cure for cancer"?
Don't you think every Christian would know this verse by heart?
Don't you think the world would beat down our doors just to get
the cure? Cancer would be gone forever—the suffering and pain
of a disease that took both my mother and my brother.*

*And that's exactly what this verse does. It shouts, "This is the
cure for all broken relationships for all time. Come and taste! It
never fails."*

Never.

*Of course, the world mocks as it passes by our church doors.
And well it should. We are a divided, broken people. We worship
in separate churches. We're split into thousands of denominations.
Our marriages sealed in Christ end in divorce just as much as the
world around us. Brothers and sisters who love Jesus and hold
to His gospel fight and can't even talk to each other.*

As if this tiny superpower verse didn't exist.

Great movements have tried and failed to unite the Christian church. Even now, a younger generation is rising up and demanding that Christians, who are Christians indeed, holding to the ancient faith, come together in Jesus every once in a while. For fellowship. For worship. For mission. They know what we all know. Something is wrong, really, really wrong.

Well, here is the cure. Right here.

I don't think the problem is that we haven't read the verse. Or that we haven't understood it. Or that we don't realize the power that's available to us.

I think the problem is that we don't want to do it.

But if we walk in the Light as He Himself is in the Light,
we have fellowship with one another.

—1 JOHN 1:7

I put down the journal and stared at the verse again.
I immediately rewrite it:

But if we walk in the Light as He Himself is in the Light, we have fellowship with . . . HIM!

Doesn't that make more sense? I mean, if we walk with Him, we have fellowship with Him. Right? Isn't it that simple?

And isn't that what it means to be "saved"? At some point, the light of the Lord Jesus Christ penetrates our hard, cold hearts. We know our sin, confess our sin, and believe in the free-flowing grace of Calvary that washes, forgives, and sets us free in new life. Isn't that the whole gospel message?

Fellowship with Him. Just me and Him.

Then I stumble on the little tiny word—*walk*. That makes it tough. Being saved isn't a one-time step into the Light. We're meant to step . . . and stay.

So here's the deal. I do what Adam did. I hide behind his tree in Eden and every once in a while, I step out. Little steps. Baby steps. Sometimes huge steps—depending if I'm really in need or if I've really messed up. And then, first chance I get, I run back into the shadows—quick. And stay as long as I can.

How's that for a summary of the Christian life? Years and years of stepping out, running back, stepping out, running back. Until the day we die. All of it real simple, focused on just me and Him. It's not about you. Got that? Which, by the way, is why I have no problem being separate from you.

And—little secret—that's why I needed to rewrite the verse.

But if we walk in the Light as He Himself is in the
Light, we have fellowship with one another.

—1 JOHN 1:7

The cure.

It's not complex. It's not riddled with legal loopholes or impossible moral demands. It's not designed for the elite, intellectual, sophisticated mind more than the simple and uneducated. It's available to all. The rich and poor. Young and old. The saints who have their acts together and the sinners who don't. It's not complex. That's the wonder of it. Its simplicity has only one demand.

Just step out from behind the tree.

Then stand there, before the Lord, in His presence.

It won't take long for us to be on our knees in worship before Him. Nor will it take long to know the condition of our hearts as He begins to peel back the layers of hurt and hate, pride and rebellion, self-will and self-reliance, a heart of stone rather than a heart filled with His Holy Spirit. This is what He does, gently leading us to repentance, humility, and brokenness.

If we could just stay here for a little while and not run back behind the tree, we'd find there's something wonderful and holy that happens: "The love of God has been poured out within our hearts through the Holy Spirit who was given to us" (Rom. 5:5).

The love of God fills our hearts by the Holy Spirit. There's cleansing in and by the blood of Jesus. And that's the cure. As long as we stay in the Light, as He is in the Light, "we have fellowship with one another" (1 John 1:7).

But we have to make the choice to come out from the shadows and step into His presence. We have to choose the path of humility and brokenness. That's where it all starts. And if we start there, He will turn our hearts toward each other and we will see each other differently—love each other differently.

If we do it together, we will find the cure together.

And more. We will have a new compassion for those who love the Lord and refuse to come out from the shadows—stuck deep behind the shadow of their tree. We will also have a new heart for people who aren't in the kingdom, lost in the darkness of this world. It's here where we taste the kind of miraculous superpower love that prays for those who hate us, abuse us, and stomp on us.

If we could just stay here . . .

But if we walk in the Light as He Himself is in the Light, we have fellowship with one another, and the blood of Jesus His Son cleanses us from all sin.

—1 JOHN 1:7

The problem isn't that I don't know this. The problem is that I do.

And every once in a while, I find myself in church with a company of people who have stepped out of the shadows, into His presence, and I'm overwhelmed by it all again. By the worship in the Holy Spirit. By the fellowship of the people. And I find the cure pours deep into my soul so that, in me, compassion starts welling up for those I never thought I'd have compassion for. But I do.

And it makes me want to stop hiding. And take a few steps . . . just out from the shadows.

QUESTIONS FOR REFLECTION

Can you imagine what the Christian church would be like if we who belong to Jesus apply this verse to our relationships together? Start with you. Here's the cure; do you want it?

And can you imagine how we'd win the hearts of those outside the church? Again, start with you and someone who does not believe in Christ. How would you be different, act different, toward them?

8

I GOT THE POINT

~~~

Reflections on 1 John 1:7

*But if we walk in the Light as He Himself is in the
Light, we have fellowship with one another, and the
blood of Jesus His Son cleanses us from all sin.*

—1 JOHN 1:7

I saw my big brother do what he shouldn't have done.

So I ran and told my dad. Mr. Tattletale at the ripe old
age of five. My finger wagging in the direction of my
brother.

Got him!

My dad decided to get my brother's version of the story.
Bad move. At age ten, my brother had far more experience
in debate, finger wagging, blame, and—of course—winning.
The moment I saw the tide turn, I got out my finger . . .

And burst into tears.

The next thing I saw was the smirk on my brother's face,
the swift hand of my dad moving toward my hind quarters,
and the inside of my bedroom with the door shut for an hour.
I think I said something profound like, "It's not fair . . ."

Me and my finger. I point and shoot and get the point
right back. I had to do better. Practice makes perfect. And

I got better. Especially as I grew older, the competition heated up, and I found that everybody's really good at this.

I mean, everybody! It's what we do. Find a target. Point, shoot, and say, "You are to blame. Not me."

The man said, "The woman whom You gave to be with me, she gave me from the tree, and I ate."

—GENESIS 3:12

The point and shoot began behind a tree in Eden. A half second after the Lord confronted Adam with his sin, the finger came out and wagged.

Point—at Eve. Shoot—"The woman . . . she gave me from the tree."

Point—at God. Shoot—"The woman whom You gave to be with me."

Adam didn't need lessons. He did it as an instinctive impulse. It came all too easy—blame Eve; blame God; defend self, and do it with authority. Eve was just as good.

Point—at the serpent, or at least where she last saw him. Shoot—"The serpent deceived me, and I ate" (Gen. 3:13). And the finger wags.

It's a gift. It comes from deep within the sin-sick soul. A half second after we're found out, before we give it any reasonable thought, the defenses go up. The arm goes in motion. The finger comes out. Not because somebody taught us. But because we belong genetically, spiritually, to the fallen family of Adam and Eve.

It's called "life" behind the tree.

I do it when I'm guilty. I do it when I'm not. I do it when everybody else is doing it just because it's cool to do it. Just give me a day when nothing's going my way: the bills are too high; the weather isn't right; my head is hurting; my pants are too tight. Somebody is always to blame.

Just point and shoot.

Then give me friends, family, and people I trust and we will solve the problems of the world. Because somebody is always to blame. And doing it together is fun. It fills the heart with a strange joy. We feel better about ourselves.

Like maybe, we really aren't to blame.

But if we walk in the Light as He Himself is in the Light, we have fellowship with one another, and the blood of Jesus His Son cleanses us from all sin.

—1 JOHN 1:7

It happened so fast yesterday.

I "got the point" in an e-mail. I read it once and was incredulous. A second time and was angered. I was actually typing an e-mail in response—fast, harsh, and outraged— when the phone rang and rescued me.

"What's going on with you?" a friend asked after I'd told him the story. I said I had no idea why I was being wrongfully accused for things I didn't do. I went into great length, pointed my finger, and told him I felt deeply insulted.

"And well you should," he sided with me with a hint of sarcasm. "But I still want to know what's going on with you?"

What's he talking about? I told him I didn't understand.

"I'm more concerned about your reaction than this guy's e-mail," he said.

He forced me to see myself doing what Adam and Eve did—the point and shoot from behind the tree. He said emphatically, "Don't you dare respond until you've taken it to the Lord. You've got to figure this thing out."

I got the point. This time, in a good way. He helped me turn my finger toward myself and examine, not the content of the e-mail, but my emotional reaction to it. Why was I firing back, hot and passionate in my self-defense, without taking time to pray? Or consult others? Or see the wrong in me first?

Me. My finger still wagging in the air.

After all these years, I'm still doing it. I did it as a child. Now I do it as an adult and, worse, as a Christian. Always right. Always pointing away from me to blame others. And doing it because I believe I'm walking "in the Light." As if He is with me. He agrees with me. As I point, He points. As I shoot, He shoots. We do it together.

In my little world of pretend.

What was I thinking?

We have fellowship with one another,
and the blood of Jesus His Son.

—1 JOHN 1:7

Down through the years, I've seen what I shouldn't
have seen. Strong, mature Christians who have walked
with the Lord for years and years. Men and women who
love their Bibles and who've served in faithful, fruitful
ministry. Doing the point and shoot.

It gave me confidence to do the same. "If they can do
it, well, so can I."

But these days are different for me now. I slowly got
the point. I've realized that every time I do the point and
shoot—every time—I'm doing what I shouldn't be doing.
It's a sign of my own brokenness and sin.

Me not "in the Light" but standing behind the tree. Me
in desperate need of the "blood of Jesus His Son" to cleanse
me from my sin.

If I'm going to do relationships well in the kingdom of
God, I have to come out from behind the tree, step into "the
Light," stop pointing my finger in blame, and run to the
only tree that matters—the cross of my Lord and Savior,
Jesus Christ.

Help me, Lord, to stop blaming others, even those who are against me. Help me love them as You do and pray for them as You call me to pray. I need You to do a profound work in me that makes me see the sin in my life. So that I get the point. No matter what comes my way, let me get the point. Amen.

QUESTIONS FOR REFLECTION

Go back to the last time you did the point and shoot. What do you learn about yourself?

There is power in the blood of Jesus to cleanse. But we have to be willing to do the work of knowing what in us needs to be confessed for cleansing. What will it take for you to be willing?

PART 2

THE FACE
OF HYPOCRISY

9

DUPLICITY

Reflections on 1 John 1:8–10

*If we say that we have no sin, we are deceiving
ourselves and the truth is not in us.*

—1 JOHN 1:8

The apostle John wrote like a dad. And I need that sometimes.

This entire letter is like a big highway billboard sign saying, "Relationships are everything in the kingdom of God. I mean, everything!"

He wrote because there are forces—evil forces—determined to undermine those relationships. First, the fellowship we have "with the Father, and with His Son Jesus Christ." And second, the fellowship we have with each other (1 John 1:3).

It's been this way from the beginning.

The Devil breaks us apart. He splinters the local church. He divides the wider church into thousands of denominations. He wants us to deny that the cross of Jesus Christ is the only means of reconciliation with the Father. He wants us to turn on each other so that we fight, quarrel, and divide.

It's why John wrote. We are not to allow these divisions in Jesus.

But the Devil is not done. He wants to work that same break inside of me. So that who I am on the outside is at odds with who I am on the inside. So that I believe one thing but do another. Say another. Live another. There are times I'm aware of the split. Other times not. Times I have me figured out. And times I don't.

And that makes life more difficult. If I'm not right with me, how am I going to be right with you? Or with God?

It's why I run to John's letter. I need these words to wash over me again and again.

It reminds of me of a story a friend of ours told years ago. Planting season had come and she went out to her front yard and planted a row of bushes. The rains came. The sun shone. Time passed and nothing happened. Exasperated, she went out, got on her knees, and began to gently dig around the area where she'd planted the first bush.

Expecting to see nothing, she was surprised to see the most beautiful, complex root system imaginable. This bush was ready to break ground and come out into the sunshine. Everything was in perfect order.

She quickly replaced the dirt, praying her little peek hadn't damaged it. Weeks later, the bushes rose out of the ground, flowered, and became all she'd hoped they'd be.

All but one.

The first bush, well, our friend called it "beautiful and deformed." She was devastated to know her little peek had traumatized it beyond repair.

And that's just it. That's our story. We can go back to the garden of Eden and say the same thing: When the Devil, sin, and death came into the world, we were traumatized beyond repair with no hope of change. Or we can look back at our own lives and see how people and circumstances hurt us. Deformed us.

Shaping how we see ourselves. Defining how we push ourselves to be what we know we're not—one thing on the outside. Another on the inside.

All of it should make us fall on our knees and seek the face of God. He is the only one who can repair us and make us right. He can reform what has been deformed. But instead, we keep believing the lies. We allow the divisions in our souls to continue. Believing one thing, but doing another.

Ripping us apart. So that we, in turn, can rip each other apart.

If we say that we have no sin, we are deceiving ourselves and the truth is not in us.

—1 JOHN 1:8

John knew these forces—these evil forces—were cunning and deceitful. Like the serpent of old dressed in the disguise of an angel of light (2 Cor. 11:14). Tricking us to deny what we know is true. Making us believe, for example, "we have no sin."

That we're really not deformed.

Like the funeral I attended a few weeks ago. A Christian man in his late forties had died. He'd been fighting cancer for some time, but his "home going" service was still marked by the shock that he'd left us too soon. The church was packed and the grief was palpable.

The message from the minister was the same one given by a dozen people who rose to give eulogies of the man's life. Over and over, I heard that he was a saint. He never did wrong. He never spoke an unkind word. He always helped those in need. He was the best dad, the best husband, the best friend.

"The world has lost a great man today!" one person said tearfully. "Heaven's doors have been opened wide for him!"

I was sort of hoping the casket lid was going to pop up. The man I knew would hate this. He knew better than anyone that he was a sinner redeemed by the blood of Jesus Christ. If there was any sainthood in him, it came because Jesus was Lord of his life, Lord of his heart. And he knew that so well.

But for whatever reason, he decided not to pop out of his casket. And that left me with the cold hard facts.

The apostle John was right. The forces—the evil forces—are still at work in our hearts. We say we believe in Jesus. We make the confession with our lips. But, in truth, is there something stronger inside us?

Tearing us apart?

Down deep, don't we believe we're good enough? We're not deformed? Heaven is waiting for us—though we may have done wrong from time to time, that wrong does not outweigh the right we have done. We are good people and the Lord our God smiles down on us as the saints we know we are. Isn't that right?

If we say that we have no sin, we are deceiving ourselves and the truth is not in us. . . . If we say that we have not sinned, we make Him a liar and His word is not in us.

—1 JOHN 1:8, 10

This is why I run to Jesus. He can repair me and make me right. He can reform what has been deformed. It's why I run to John's letter. He reminds me over and over again that it's time for our divisions to cease. And that begins with me. I want to be on the outside what I am on the inside. I want to believe one thing and do it. Say it. Live it. So that the peace of Jesus Christ inside of me can be the peace I extend to you.

And there's only one way to start this process. On my knees. Before the Lord. But I don't do it alone. John said we have to do it together. It's why he wrote these words in the plural *we*: "If we confess our sins, He is faithful and righteous to forgive us our sins and to cleanse us from all unrighteousness" (1 John 1:9).

This is where it all begins.

QUESTIONS FOR REFLECTION

Every time we minimize the sin within us, we minimize our need for a Savior and what He did to pay for it on the cross. How are you deceiving yourself today? If you think you are not, are you sure?

Do you see yourself in 1 John 1:8 and 10? Be real, honest, and true. What prevents you from running to verse 9 with all your heart and soul?

10

DUMB AND HAPPY

Reflections on 1 John 2:1–4

The scribes and the Pharisees sit on Moses' seat,
so do and observe whatever they tell you, but not the
works they do. For they preach, but do not practice.

—MATTHEW 23:2–3 ESV

They say one thing. They do another.

I love the word *they*. Like it was meant for somebody else—everybody else—and not me. I know it wasn't. And I know it wasn't meant just for me either. This is what sin does to all of us. It breaks us on the inside.

It breaks us deep.

It breaks us so we become actors on a stage. Players who slowly, methodically, work into our roles. We mold them to those who share our stage. We play them for so long and do it so well that there comes a time when we can no longer separate who we are on stage from who we are off stage.

We are that good.

The break is that deep.

The Bible word for this phenomenon is *hypocrite* or *pretenders*. It means we step onto life's stage with a mask fit perfectly over our faces so people see who we pretend to be and not who we are. That's exactly the picture of these men in Matthew 23. They wore preacher masks and preached the Bible brilliantly.

So brilliantly, in fact, Jesus told us to do what they say.

But then these men stepped off the stage. They took off their masks and became different people. They lived in opposition to their own preaching and they did it together, as if doing it together made it right somehow. And they did it, oddly, so people could see, so God could see, that they don't do what they say.

Mask on. Mask off. And when the mask is off, there's another mask right behind it. Making me wonder if the real face can ever truly be found.

The one who says, "I have come to know Him,"
and does not keep His commandments,
is a liar, and the truth is not in him.

—1 JOHN 2:4

I saw it played out as a young Christian in my twenties. A group of us loved to get together after church and just hang out. It came so easily, so naturally, for us to talk about other people in the church. People we liked, people we didn't, people we opposed. Over time, all we had to do was say a person's name.

Wink. Wink.

No need to say more because we all had the person pegged and branded. And not just people in the pews, the elders too. The ministers. The good ones (well, they often joined us after church) and the not-so-good ones.

We talked openly, freely. The more we trusted each other, the more our words and judgments against others grew in strength. It was like an inside secret. We were doing it together and doing it together somehow made it right.

Perfect us.

Of course, the moment we were back in church, we slipped on a mask. We'd find ourselves face-to-face with people we talked about. And, of course, we greeted them with Christian kindness. We took Communion beside them. We spoke as if nothing stood between us because we were good at what we do. The perfect pretenders when the spotlight hit our face.

Never thinking of ourselves as actors on a stage. Never imagining that we were doing what was wrong in the sight of God. And sadly, never realizing that even when we were together, after church, in our safe little group, we still weren't able to see each other's face.

The one who says, "I have come to know Him,"
and does not keep His commandments,
is a liar, and the truth is not in him.

—1 JOHN 2:4

These people, the apostle John wrote, who've infiltrated the church with their strange teachings say they "know God," but they don't. And here's how you know: They say what He said but don't do what He did.

I remember vividly when I got caught.

I was a pastoring a church in the Midwest and had been asked to serve on a committee with other clergy. In one of the meetings, a pastor mentioned a man who might be of great service to our work together. "Oh no," I said to him quietly. "You don't want him." And then I proceeded to tell him why, using words that were not kind. Worse, that spoke ill of the man's character.

I thought I had freedom with this pastor to speak like I used to speak in our small group back home. I thought he was safe, a friend, somebody who knew that Christians speak one way out loud and another way in private. But he wasn't safe. He immediately turned on me.

"Who are you to judge this man?" he asked, waiting for a response. But I was so caught off guard, I stood there speechless.

"Never do that again," he warned and walked off. And not just walked off; from that day on, he held me at arm's length. Never allowing me to get close. Never trusting me.

At first, I didn't think I was caught. I thought I'd simply made the mistake of confiding in the wrong person. But later, the memory of this brief encounter haunted me. I couldn't shake it. It slowly dawned on me that I'd risked using this harsh language because I wanted him to be my friend. Somebody I could trust. I'd been missing that in my life and thought this was a perfect opportunity to reach out to him.

And what better way to do it? The test of real friends is whether we can talk real talk, not the Christian talk. That's what we do in public. But the kind where we take off the Christian mask and just be ourselves. Right?

Our real selves.

Wearing masks that we don't know are masks at all.

And if anyone sins, we have an Advocate with the
Father, Jesus Christ the righteous; and He Himself
is the propitiation for our sins; and not for ours only,
but also for those of the whole world.

—1 JOHN 2:1–2

Eventually I got it.

I came to realize that I was a true, bona fide actor. Both on stage and off. And that my language off stage about others was both wrong and sinful. I'd become the exact kind of person Jesus talked about in Matthew 23 and the apostle John talked about in 1 John 2: a person who'd say one thing, but do another.

The break inside me is that deep.

I sometimes wish I still lived in a world of masks. And every once in a while I slip back into the game without realizing it. It lasts for a while and I find myself like I used to find myself.

Dumb and happy.

Until somebody comes, rips off one mask and then another, and maybe another after that, and sends me running to Jesus, my "Advocate with the Father" and propitiation for my sins, who's in the business of finding my real face.

QUESTIONS FOR REFLECTION

We're not allowed to say we know Christ and not obey Him. Can you see this break in you? Can you feel your own masks?

When knowing and obeying Him come together, real and true, our Lord begins to remake us in His image (Rom. 8:29). What's the next step for you? Are you willing to ask the Lord Jesus to come help you with that step?

11

A SELF-PORTRAIT

Reflections on 1 John 2:1–4

My little children, I am writing these things to you so
that you may not sin. And if anyone sins, we have
an Advocate with the Father, Jesus Christ the righteous.

—1 JOHN 2:1

I saw myself the other day through the eyes of someone I hurt. Their words painted a portrait of me in front of a number of people who—for the first time—saw me in a new light. Or maybe, a new dark.

Hearing the words, seeing the portrait, was hard. A hideously horrible-looking me.

It wasn't like the feeling of heartache a parent gets when their child screams, "I hate you! I hate you! You're the worst parent ever!" and runs to his or her room, slams the door, and yells words that he or she doesn't really mean. All because you made a decision the child didn't like.

Because family is family. These storms come and go. Soon enough, the child comes out of the room and eventually, as emotions calm, conversations happen. The child comes to understand the reasons why the decision was made. And all quietly returns to normal.

This was different.

I made a decision that this person (and a number of people) didn't like. For a host of reasons, before the Lord, I could make no other. It was one of those decisions in my job as pastor of a church where I knew—no matter how I decided—it would bless some and hurt others.

It's part of life. Moments like this come all the time as we choose careers, schools, spouses, or make hard decisions at work or in health care. I saw it just a few weeks ago as I cared for a family having to make the difficult choice of turning off life support for their elderly father. As you might guess, some were in favor. Some were not.

These are impossible moments.

For those we hurt, we become foul, ugly creatures of contempt. The portrait they now paint with their words goes on display for any who will listen. And though it's hoped that it's only for a short time—that soon the storm will pass and all will be miraculously forgotten—it suddenly becomes all too real that what has happened feels permanent.

I saw my portrait the other day. I saw it and recoiled. Everything inside of me became defensive, shaking my head, saying, "But that's not me!"

Or at least, I pray that's not me.

The one who says, "I have come to know Him,"
and does not keep His commandments,
is a liar, and the truth is not in him.

—1 JOHN 2:4

A friend of mine called. He'd seen the portrait and raced to my defense.

"It's like they're rewriting history," he said appalled. "They're twisting your words and assigning to you motives you never had. This is just wrong."

"But it's how they feel," I said. "They believe I've made the wrong decision. All these years they've trusted me both as a Christian and as a pastor and now they think my mask has come off and they're seeing the real me—exposed."

"Yeah, well, you know it's not true. Everybody does." And with that, he spent the next fifteen minutes trying to distract me from staring at my new portrait. He did his best to toss buckets and buckets of encouragement all over me.

I loved it. There's nothing like a trusted friend.

"It's hard, you know," I told him frankly. "To see yourself as others see you. To think that people think you're a Christian actor, playing a role, but really inside you're being governed by the world, the flesh, and the Devil. That you're one thing on the outside and another on the inside."

"You have to stop listening to them," he ordered.

But I couldn't get my eyes off the portrait.

To face the hard, ugly fact, it stirred in me an ungodly desire to defend myself. I wanted to rip it off the wall and burn it. I wanted to stand on my self-appointed soapbox and paint the real portrait for all the world to see. The real me. The real story.

Not the other.

And actually I really do want my friends to gather around—all those who believe in me and believe what I did was right—because they shield me from seeing the portrait. They tell me things I want to hear. They pour down the grace and blessing of God that strengthens and soothes my soul.

So that I won't look.

But I do look. I have to look.

Because people I know, people I love, are hurt by my actions. If I walk away, if all I do is defend myself and surround myself with people who agree with me, I will never be able to see—or understand—their perspective.

And I want to.

If for no other reason so I never forget what my actions have done to them. Or what I look like to them. This way I can remember them. Pray for them. And maybe even learn from them. Because maybe part of what they're saying is right. Maybe I really do look like that a little.

In God's eyes.

My little children, I am writing these things to you
so that you may not sin. And if anyone sins, we have an
Advocate with the Father, Jesus Christ the righteous.

—1 JOHN 2:1

I don't need a mask with Him. He sees me. The real me.

Nor do I need friends and family to distract me from seeing these horrible, ugly portraits of me. I love that they want to. And I know I do the same for them. But what I actually need is for them to stand there with me in front of the portrait and take it all in with me.

Because I'm not always right. Because I don't always make good decisions. Because I don't ever need to come to the Lord with my good face on. My happy face. My "I'm always right, they're always wrong," self-justifying face. He didn't come and go to the cross and die for me because I'm cute, perfect, and good.

He came because I'm not.

And for that reason, this horrible portrait of me isn't something to run away from. It's something to take to Him—my Lord, my Savior, my "Advocate with the Father."

Lord, if any part of this is me, help me.

Because He doesn't ask me to change my face so I'm pleasing to Him. He wants me to let Him do that. In His power. In His love and mercy.

In Jesus' name.

QUESTIONS FOR REFLECTION

We have a promise given to us when we sin. But how are we supposed to go to our Advocate and make our confession if we're not willing to truly face our sin?

The promise is forgiveness by His blood. It's also a new heart to know, love, and obey Him, and the joy that He changes us day by day. Do you want that? If so, pray. Ask. Seek. And never stop.

12
LOVE PERFECTED

~~~~~

Reflections on 1 John 2:5

But whoever keeps His word, in him the love
of God has truly been perfected.

—1 JOHN 2:5

"He told me I have to dig deeper."

"But what does that mean?" I asked the young man. We were at a local coffee shop. He'd been having dating troubles. In the last eighteen months, three women had broken up with him, all saying he had commitment problems.

He finally decided to go to a counselor. After a few sessions, he felt something wasn't right. After church, he asked me to have coffee with him.

"I think I know exactly what it means. I'm to dig deeper into my past. I come from a broken home. My dad and mom separated when I was six. Both eventually remarried. I was tossed between homes every other weekend and holidays. My dad got divorced a second time and remarried a couple of years ago. Plus, on my mom's side, my grandparents also divorced and remarried. So commitment problems are like a virus in my family."

"And you think that's what's impacting your relationships now?" I asked.

"Yeah, I think so. But this counselor is confusing me. It's like every time I share some part of my life, a memory from my childhood, he's looking for something else. He's waiting for me to get something—and I don't know what it is.

"And then," he sat up, really animated, "like out of nowhere he turns to a verse in the Bible, reads it, looks at me, and waits for me to respond to it. It's really weird. It's like we're in two different worlds. I'm talking about one thing and he's talking about another. We're just missing each other."

"OK, wait," I said, intrigued. "Give me an example."

"Alright, two days ago, he read the first part of John 15. You know, Jesus is the vine, we're the branches, apart from Him we can do nothing. I nod my head and tell him I know all that but have no idea how it relates to what I'm talking about. I'm spilling my guts and he's quoting the Bible at me."

"So what did he say next?"

"He told me I have to dig deeper."

I smiled. I told him it sounded like he had a great counselor.

"What?" he said, disappointed.

"Yeah, well, I had a counselor just like that. Only, in my case, the story was wildly different. There was a couple in our church many years ago who had gotten quite upset with me. The more we talked, the worse it got. So we decided to ask a mutual friend of ours, a Christian counselor, to be part of our next meeting. It was the best thing we could have done.

"And just like you, I was so confused!

"Of course, we started the meeting in prayer. This couple then stated their case. I stated mine. Then we started getting into the nitty-gritty details of the problem between us. A half hour goes by and the counselor raised his hand and quoted a Bible verse that seemed completely out of left field."

"Don't you hate that?" this young man exclaimed, rolling his eyes.

"Yeah, actually I do! Or, at least, I did.

"But here's the kicker. This counselor knew exactly what he was doing. And this couple got it way before I did. You see, all we cared about was the problem between us and how to resolve it. The counselor, well, he basically wanted to change the subject. He wanted to put the Lord at the center of our conflict. And if He was at the center, he believed it would change our conversation."

"So, you're saying, it worked?" my young friend asked.

"Yeah, and here's why. We were digging deep in the wrong place. And I think that's what your counselor is saying to you too. You want to dig into your past and find out the source of your commitment problems. If you can figure it out, you can do something about it. You can make real changes in your life. Right?"

"Yeah, absolutely."

"Then why not go to a secular counselor?"

He looked at me surprised, wondering why I'd ask the question.

"You see," I stepped in, "you're a Christian man. Something is different about you. Before you and I go digging into our pasts or digging into our problems, we need to remember who we are first. Something happened to us when Jesus Christ came into our lives. Something that changes everything.

"If we're going to dig deeper," I smiled, "we have to dig here first. Before we dig anywhere else. Do that, and all the puzzle pieces eventually come together."

The young man sat back in his chair and I could tell he needed more.

But whoever keeps His word, in him the love
of God has truly been perfected.

—1 JOHN 2:5

"By the way, if it's any help, I found my counselor totally irritating!" I mused. "He wanted to talk Jesus. We wanted to talk conflict. But he persisted and completely won the day."

My friend, listening intently, asked, "How?"

"Because Jesus Christ changes the story. He always changes the story. He demands one thing from us. Only one thing. We have to love each other first. Not just because

He loves us so much that He died and rose for us. You know that. It's more. He puts that love inside us. He inscribes it on our hearts.

"And that changed two things for me. First, I saw my own selfishness. I was far more concerned about standing for the principles I hold dear than about loving and caring for this couple in the midst of our differences.

"Second, this counselor helped me see patterns of self-ishness that go way back in my life. He helped me dig deeper into my past only because he first helped me dig deeper into who I am in Christ.

"I may be—no, actually I really am—the king of self-ishness. But here's what I know. The love of God in Jesus Christ is perfected in my heart and He wants me to live into that more and more every day.

"So, I took the first step. I looked at this couple and con-fessed my own selfishness. I told them I was sorry. They did the same thing, confessing things from their own lives. It did everything to get us back on the right path."

"You think that'll happen to me?" he asked, really want-ing to know.

"Yeah, I do."

"So why didn't the counselor just come right out and tell me that?"

I shook my head, took a sip of my coffee, which was now cold, and told him that Christian counselors can some-times be really, really weird.

And with that, he burst into a fun, playful laugh.

QUESTIONS FOR REFLECTION

We have to start at the beginning: Is the love of God abiding in you? If Christ dwells in you, you have all you need to love others in your life. Do you know that? Do you believe that?

The love of God is perfected in us when we let His love for us be His love through us. Again, it's a choice. Can you take the step and put Him first—even in times of conflict?

13

THE MARK

Reflections on 1 John 2:5–6

By this we know that we are in Him: the one who
says he abides in Him ought himself to walk
in the same manner as He walked.

—1 JOHN 2:5–6

I went out late at night to walk our sheepdog. My soul in anguish.

The scene played over and over in my head. I'd thought the conversation had gone well. My friend and I had a lot to talk about, and I'd felt quite free to speak my mind because we've known each other so long. We trusted each other.

But I somehow, mistakenly, crossed that invisible line. That sacred boundary that touches matters of the heart.

And he quietly erupted.

His face flushed. The veins in his neck stuck out and pulsated. His words were controlled and measured, almost eerily calm, as he profoundly objected to what I'd said. It caught me by surprise, and I found myself in a defensive posture, restating my position and refuting each of his objections.

Thinking it would help.

It didn't.

I'd offended him. He quickly, wisely, ended the conversation. We agreed to see each other in the morning. And then he was gone. The matter completely unresolved.

Leaving me, late at night, in anguish. I didn't mean to offend, but I did. I didn't know we were in such sharp disagreement, but we were. I didn't know it was a personal matter, but it was. I'd hurt his heart and it grieved me.

At the very least, I should have said I was sorry. Before he left.

> By this we know that we are in Him: the one
> who says he abides in Him ought himself to
> walk in the same manner as He walked.
>
> —1 JOHN 2:5–6

There's an old phrase in the Bible: "Do not let the sun go down on your anger, and do not give the devil an opportunity" (Eph. 4:26–27).

Late at night is no fun.

I find myself easily tormented. I hate what conflict does to me. Like a swift kick to the stomach, I ache. I want to shake it. I want to push it out of my mind but I can't. The moment I try, it pops back, the scene replaying—again.

Remembering what I said. What I should have said. What I could say tomorrow when we meet. For reasons beyond me,

I find I'm still defending my position. Why am I doing that? All that matters, all that should matter, is that I hurt him.

And by hurting him, I hurt the Lord.

I do what I always do. I run to the promises of 1 John. I know I have an "Advocate with the Father, Jesus Christ the righteous." I know if I confess my sins, "He is faithful and righteous to forgive us our sins and to cleanse us from all unrighteousness." I know He has said, and I believe it's true, "The blood of Jesus . . . cleanses us from all sin" (1 John 2:1; 1:9; 1:7).

Forgive me, Lord. Be with my friend tonight.

I hate this window of time. In a perfect but broken world, all conflicts would be settled before the sun goes down. Or at least before bed. Everything neatly wrapped, simple, perfectly in order, so we can rest at night in peace.

Tonight is not peaceful. Not for me. I wonder if it is for him.

Is he in anguish over this like me? Maybe not. Maybe he's better at all this than I am. Maybe he's able to compartmentalize, push tomorrow's problems into tomorrow, and sleep like a baby. I admire that. I'm not like that.

Or maybe it's the exact opposite. My mind races to the "what-ifs"—the very place, I find, the Devil takes opportunity. What if my friend's anger against me is growing, taking root? What if he's not willing to reconcile with me? What if the chasm between us is becoming insurmountable the more the hours pass? Could this one conversation do that? Divide us for a time? Divide us for good?

Late at night is no fun.

By this we know that we are in Him: the one
who says he abides in Him ought himself to
walk in the same manner as He walked.

—1 JOHN 2:5–6

First John is more than a letter of promises. It's full of
tests that poke, prod, challenge, and demand. And nothing
is more demanding than the test of whether or not we're
keeping—obeying—His commandments.

Or rather, one commandment in particular. The one in
which all others find their fulfillment. The command to love
one another as Christ Jesus has loved us (John 13:34–35).

If that command is in us, if we are living that love every
day, it's proof that "the love of God has been poured out
within our hearts through the Holy Spirit" (Rom. 5:5), who
has been given to us. That, said John, is how we know we
are in Him and that we abide in Him and that we know that
we know Him (1 John 2:3–6).

If we love one another.

It's the mark that tells us we're Christians. A mark branded
on the heart.

And when Christians break the command of God, that
mark comes to life. Like a hot-iron searing of the soul, pricking of the conscience, bringing the conviction of the Spirit,
that mark speaks, hurts, demands, tests, and proves forever
that we are in Christ. Christ is in us. We're not walking as

He walked and now's the time to do something about it. Can we hear Him? Urging us to do what is right.

Love one another. As He loved us. As He loves us.

And if we're not Christians—this is the test—the mark isn't there. Broken relationships are part of life. It's what we do. And we just keep on doing it.

> By this we know that we are in Him: the one
> who says he abides in Him ought himself to
> walk in the same manner as He walked.
>
> —1 JOHN 2:5–6

I woke up grouchy. Fitful sleep.

I didn't want to see my friend again. Selfish me. I was convinced that we'd have another confrontation and, no matter what I said and no matter what I did, it would only fan the flames of discontent. I didn't want that. Not again.

Such little faith.

From the corner of my eye, I saw him come into the room with a spring in his step and a brightness in his face. As I turned to him, I saw him heading right for me. I stood there, so confused, as he put out his hand to shake mine.

"You are so messed up," he said, his face almost serious.

"Well, you're not so bad yourself," I bantered back.

"Yeah, well, we disagree about all this. But we'll work through it, right?"

I nodded, said I was sorry, as the waves of my friend's love and gentleness washed over my anxious heart and made it light again. I should have known the Lord's kindness would win this story. I should have known—because my friend has the mark. For as long as I've known him, I've known that. I should have trusted it.

The mark—it's a must.

And when you don't have it, it's because you never had it.

But if you do have it, it's yours forever.

QUESTIONS FOR REFLECTION

We cannot love God and break from each other. To walk as He walked is to love as He loves—passionately, relentlessly. Is His mark in you? How do you know?

Every time we face broken relationships, we face choice. Do we face it, run from it, avoid it, or ignore it? Or do we turn to Him and ask Him to teach us how to love this person? What choices are you making in your life?

14

NO LONGER STONE

Reflections on 1 John 2:7–8

Beloved, I am not writing a new commandment to you,
but an old commandment which you have had from the beginning;
the old commandment is the word which you have heard.

—1 JOHN 2:7

She sat by herself at a table in the church fellowship hall. People were still getting their food at the buffet table and settling into their chairs for a meal.

I spotted her, went to her, and asked if I could join her. Even though I was a visitor that night, she did her best to be gracious and welcome me, asking about my family and my health. I did the same with her and when the time was right, I broke the ice.

"I'm sorry for all this," I said, knowing the grief that must be weighing down on her.

She nodded her head and didn't talk for a minute.

Eventually, she said, "I've been part of this church for over forty years. We've had a few bumps along the way but nothing like this. I fear we're headed for a major split and there's little I can do about it but pray."

She stared down at her plate, lost in thought. I knew she might be right. A group of people in the church were fighting to bring back their former pastor. Another group was sticking with their current pastor and people were choosing sides and holding meetings where things were spoken out loud, in anger.

Things that should never have been spoken.

Not by those who bear the name of Christ.

"You know, I stood up at the last meeting," she said, looking toward me, her eyes still downcast. "I told them this was all wrong. We had no business fighting each other. I came to this church because Jesus Christ is preached here, and loved here, and His command is lived here. Forty plus years, up to now. But this bickering has nothing to do with Him. It's personal and it has to stop."

She raised her finger and tapped it on the table.

"Christ commands us to love one another. That's it. It's a nonnegotiable. If we do, the Lord will bring us back together and He will resolve the differences between us in His time and in His way. If we do not, we will be torn apart. That's all I said. And then I sat down."

"You did the right thing," I replied.

She put her hand on my arm and said, "No one listens to an old woman. My words fell on deaf ears. A few minutes after I sat down, people again erupted in debate, voices raised, it was terrible and I know it grieved my Lord's heart. Even now, I keep shaking my head in disbelief. These people should know better."

"I'm sure they do."

"Well, then, it's a test. Are we going to do it or aren't we? Is it still an Old Testament command written on stone? Or has Jesus Christ written it on our hearts? If He has, then we stop all this immediately. But if He hasn't and we continue to behave like this, then I have to wonder if we're Christians at all."

She said it so softly, gently. Her eyes compassionate but sad, like she could already see what I didn't want to see, what I wasn't ready to see—the church splitting into pieces. I didn't dare respond. Not with her. Not in her present state of sadness. I simply nodded in agreement.

"It's here," she said finally, her hand resting on her heart, "it has to be here."

On the other hand, I am writing a new commandment to you, which is true in Him and in you, because the darkness is passing away and the true Light is already shining.

—1 JOHN 2:8

She told me her husband had left thirty years ago. They'd hit middle age. Both their kids were in college. He fell in love with someone at work, packed up, and moved out. She'd never dreamed of life without him. She never gave a thought to what she'd do if she had to work. He'd always promised to take care of her—and now he was gone.

She leaned heavily on her church family in those days to get through. She prayed he'd come back. She prayed he'd meet Jesus. Of course, she'd always prayed that. Church meant nothing to him. Never had. Still, she'd hoped. She wanted nothing more than for him to see a glimmer of Jesus' love for him.

And she knew if that were to happen, it had to begin with her.

"It took a while," she admitted. "But not too long."

"What did?" I asked,

"To forgive him. To love him even though he rejected me."

He never looked back. Less than a year later, the divorce was finalized. He quickly married the woman from work. It lasted three years. They divorced. Eventually, he remarried again. Moving to Chicago. Then to Boston.

And still, thirty years later, she speaks of him with kindness and care.

"I pray for him every night. Every couple of months I send him a short note. I'll include an article I found that I think might interest him. Or I'll see a little nick-knack in a store that I think he'll like, and I'll send it along. And I'll always include a little prayer, just so he knows there's somebody praying for him."

"I don't know how you do it," I marveled, "after all he did to you."

And then she did it again. She rested her hand against her heart and said, "Oh dear boy, you know full well I could never have done this by myself. A few months after he left, I asked Jesus to love him through me and He answered my prayer. After all these years, He still does."

For just a moment, I felt sorry for her. All these years alone. Having suffered the anguish of lost dreams, of what life should have been, could have been, and never was for her. But that moment quickly vanished as she repeated the simple words that made her painful life possible to live.

"It has to be here," she said, pointing to her heart. "It has to be here."

The darkness is passing away and the
true Light is already shining.

— 1 JOHN 2:8

A few months later, the church split into two.

The former pastor started Sunday services a few miles away. About 40 percent went with him; 60 percent stayed.

I called my new friend and asked her how she was doing.

"We're doing what we're supposed to do," she said, sadly. "Those of us who've stayed are praying for those who left, and we're asking for the Lord to teach us something we seem to have lost along the way."

"What's that?" I asked.

"We've forgotten how to love each other. And if we don't have that," she said again, for the thousandth time, "we've don't have Him."

"Because He writes it on our hearts," I said, repeating her words back to her.

"That's right! Why, I can't believe it," she said, teasingly. "You can actually remember the words of an old woman!"

QUESTIONS FOR REFLECTION

How is it possible to know the love of Jesus in our hearts and divide, hurt, separate, and break from each other? What can you do to make a difference?

When we love one another and keep His old, yet new, command, the light shines. The darkness passes. What will it take today to walk in the light with the relationships in your life?

15
LIGHTEN UP

—⁓⁓—

Reflections on 1 John 2:9

*The one who says he is in the Light and yet hates
his brother is in the darkness until now.*

— 1 JOHN 2:9

I finished the afternoon meeting, got back to my hotel
room, and collapsed in the chair by the desk, exhausted.
Everything inside me wanted to pack my bags, head to the
airport, and go home. But I couldn't. I had to study. I had
to pray.

I was preaching in a few hours.

But how could I? I felt strangely violated. Like I'd been
forced to see things, hear things, feel things I wanted nothing
to do with. Things that should never have been spoken out
loud and were—with mocking laughter. But not just that.
There was more. Somehow I was part of it all, and I didn't
like it.

This story has been my story too. In the past.

But not like this. Or, maybe, too much like this.

I saw a pen on the desk and a pad of paper. I decided I
needed to get up, take a shower, clear my head, and turn

my mind to the service that night. But before I did, I picked up the pen and wrote down the words piercing my heart.

"We are a violent people—it's what we do."

———

The one who says he is in the Light and yet hates
his brother is in the darkness until now.

—1 JOHN 2:9

———

A pastor from a Methodist church had invited me to preach the opening service of a conference. I asked if I could fly in early and interview him and a few of his clergy. He agreed and took us all out to lunch.

From the moment we sat down, I felt like I'd been welcomed into an elite circle of good, close friends. The talk between them was seamless, a fluid motion moving from topic to topic, all in a language that could only be spoken after years spent together. There was trust here, loyalty, respect.

With one driving passion: being a church that reached a lost world.

"We have no other goal," one of the pastors told me, "than to bring Christ to our city."

During lunch, they talked freely. Every once in a while they looked at me, the odd man out, and teased me into the conversation. I was glad to join in. I told them my interest was in how they—as clergy—did relationships together.

They didn't pick up on it right away.

They wanted to talk mission. It's what excited and thrilled them: when and where to start the next new church; how to raise up leaders in different parts of the city to host home groups; what hot topics the twenties and thirties crowd care about most so they could sponsor an event, bring in a speaker, start a conversation, and gently lead people to Christ. Like they'd done before.

Every once in a while a name popped up. A name I didn't know. Then another. Then another. And with these names, came words. Harsh, vulgar words.

"He's such a jerk," or, "The man's a freak," or, "He's got an IQ of zero. Not exactly playing with a full deck."

And they'd laugh, making fun of them in quick side comments, with rolling eyes and odd expressions they've probably done a hundred times together. And within seconds, they'd be back on topic. Not missing a beat.

It happened once. And twice. And ten times in a half hour.

I finally raised my hand and got their attention.

"Who are these people?" I asked. I'd written their names down and read them off. "You mock these people and make fun of them. Who are they? What do they do?"

"Great question!" one of them said and sat up and posed, distorted his face, and did, apparently, a perfect imitation of one of them. It was like a skit from *Saturday Night Live* and it sent the table full of pastors into hysterics. One after the other jumped in, the senior pastor leading the pack.

Somehow, perversely, as it always does, deepening their bond together.

I stood up from the table and excused myself. I could feel my heart pounding, a crazed anger inside that had sparked and burst into flame. I could feel my face hot to the touch, and I knew it was best just to go. To the men's room. Cold water splashing freely on my face. I was half bent over and waiting for my heart to calm when I heard the door behind me open and I saw, in the mirror, the senior pastor coming in.

"You OK?" he asked.

I looked at him with a blank stare, having no words to respond.

"You looked pretty upset back there. I don't know what you got yourself all worked up over but if you want some personal advice from me . . ." he said in a low, southern accent and then hesitated, maybe so I'd hear him loud and clear. "You need to lighten up a little bit."

The one who says he is in the Light and yet hates
his brother is in the darkness until now.

—1 JOHN 2:9

I don't know how I got through the opening address that night. I'm just glad I did. The Lord was kind to help me put the upset of the afternoon aside and let me do what I love best—to speak the Word of God, by the Spirit of God, for the people of God.

But I was a mess inside.

I'd walked into a world that frightened me. An inside world of close colleagues that I had no business being part of, not even for a minute. They let me see what I shouldn't have seen and hear what I shouldn't have heard. And I wanted to stop them. I wanted to tell them what they were doing was wrong. Completely wrong.

We are not allowed to speak of others like that—ever.

We cannot say that we, ourselves, are walking with Jesus, walking in the Light, in communion with the Father, filled with the Holy Spirit, passionate about reaching the lost, while with our tongues, our hearts, we hate. We trash. We violently rip apart people with screams of laughter and a volley of fist-pumps.

But I said nothing. Not then. I waited until the conference was over. And then, alone with the senior pastor, I told him my story.

I've done the same thing. In my past. I still do from time to time without even knowing it. In my little, close-knit world of colleagues, friends, and family, where it's safe. Where we're bonded together, loyal and true. Where we can talk freely about people—and do what they don't know we're doing.

Laugh and mock, slander and hate.

I told him the afternoon scared me.

How could I "lighten up" when, in being with these pastors, I saw a picture of myself—of what I've done—of what I should never have done or do? How is it possible to love the Lord with all my heart and then speak of others this way? Just to be welcomed into the group? Just to join the camaraderie and fun?

It's hypocritical. It's wrong. It's completely wrong.

"That's your problem, not ours," he shot back. I looked at him, saddened, and said out loud the words that still pierced my heart. But this time, I think it was meant for me.

"We are a violent people. It's what we do."

QUESTIONS FOR REFLECTION

With our tongues, we speak against people for whom our Lord died. Why do we do this so freely? How can you—and how can you help others—do what's right in the Lord's sight?

John's passion is to take what we believe and make it real in our lives. His imagery contrasts light and dark. What do you need from the Lord to help you break from patterns that belong to the dark?

16
THE SOUND OF LIGHT

Reflections on 1 John 2:10–11

*The one who loves his brother abides in the
Light and there is no cause for stumbling in him.*

—1 JOHN 2:10

When the plane crashes in the ocean and sinks to the bottom of the sea, the "emergency locator pinger" is activated.

Like a beacon blasting sound through deep, cold, dark waters with a simple but clear message, "Here I am. Find me!" to all who know how to listen.

Ping.

Heard at the depths of twenty thousand feet for a minimum of thirty days. Mounted on top of the aircraft's black boxes— which actually are a bright safety orange—that house the flight data recorder and the cockpit voice recorder. Both telling the story of what went wrong. And for how long. And if the pilots really knew.

The nearly indestructible black boxes.

Ping.

The one who loves his brother abides in the Light
and there is no cause for stumbling in him.

—1 JOHN 2:10

"I want to read something to you," he said, grabbing the letter off his side table. "It's to an old friend."

I nodded my head but wondered why. In today's world, we don't send letters to old friends. We call them. We e-mail them. We text them. Letters are more formal these days and, if I were to guess, I'd bet this was to an old "lost" friend—somebody he needed to reach out to while he still had time.

You see, Nicholas was dying. He'd been diagnosed with leukemia two years back. He'd done well with treatments but, two months ago, the doctor told him the medicine was no longer helping. Both he and his wife of forty-two years drove home that day, hands intertwined, tears running down their faces, devastated by the news. They'd thought, they'd always thought, they'd have more time.

Nicholas caught my puzzled look. "What?" he growled.

"Why are you writing an old friend?" I asked. "Why don't you just call?"

"Can't. It's been too long."

"That never stopped you before."

"It's easier this way," he said, shaking his head. "We were friends for some thirty-five years and what happened between us is no one's business but ours. Maybe if I felt better, I'd call. But I don't. I don't have the strength to drudge up the whole story and get into a long conversation. So this is what I decided."

"Makes sense," I agreed.

"You have to understand something," he said softly, his eyes piercing straight into mine. "This was my fault. I was the reason our friendship broke. Not him. Not because he didn't have a part in it. He did. What he did hurt me more than I can say. But he did everything he could to make amends and say sorry."

He paused, looking down at the letter. "But I wouldn't hear it. He'd call, and I wouldn't return it. He'd write, and I wouldn't answer. I shut him out. Fourteen years. That's how long it's been. What I did wasn't right, and I've got to do something about it. That's why I've written this letter. You wanna' hear it?"

Ping.

"Yeah, I do."

Kelly,

   I've learned something about myself these last two years. I'm the best two-faced liar this side of the Mississippi. Funny how things change when you know you're dying. And I am. I was diagnosed with leukemia in the summer of 2010, and for eighteen months, I laughed at it. Never gave it a second thought. There was no way I was going to lose this battle. But about six months ago, I began to wonder. And come February, I knew.

   It's been hard saying my prayers recently. I keep thinking about you. I convinced myself a long time ago that pushing you *out of my life was the right thing to do. It's why I had no problem holding my head high in church. No problem serving as an elder, or teaching a men's Bible study, or taking Communion. The Lord understood and, I thought, agreed with me.*

But I'm not so sure about that anymore. I always thought hypocrites were God-fearing on the outside and Devil-worshiping on the inside. That's why I never thought of myself as one. But I do now. I've come to see that real, bona fide Christians can be hypocrites too. We can love the Lord on the outside and hurt those we love on the inside by pushing them away.

I'm writing to say I'm sorry. These fourteen years have been my fault. You've been my closest friend, closer than a brother, and I realize now I never stopped loving you. When I look in the mirror these days—and I see what this disease has done to me— I can see what my own hardened, bitter heart has done too. So I ask you to forgive me. In Jesus' name. And don't you think for one minute that I haven't forgiven you too.

You're the best man I've ever known, Kelly. You made me better just by being with you. I know you may be reading this after I'm gone. So I want to say this just the way it needs to be said.

I love you, old friend.
Nicholas

He looked up at me, expecting me to comment. "What do ya think?"

I said nothing. I couldn't even if I tried.

But the one who hates his brother is in the darkness and
walks in the darkness, and does not know where he is
going because the darkness has blinded his eyes.

—1 JOHN 2:11

The apostle John made it impossible to love the Lord, walk in the Light, and hate our family in Christ. We're not allowed to push each other away. And when our relationships break in mid-flight, come crashing into the sea, the remains scattered on the ocean floor, there comes a test.

Ping.

Are we Christians? Is the light of Jesus Christ really abiding in us? Has His love, given to us in its full expression on Calvary's hill, come to dwell inside us? If so, we are not allowed to treat each other this way. He's given us a command: We are to love each other.

Ping.

The sound of light coming from the ruins.

Ping.

"Here I am. Find me!"

But if we push away the sound and close our ears, if we pretend what happened never happened, or if we convince ourselves that we're right in treating our brothers and sisters in Christ this way, then—said the apostle—we are living in hypocrisy. Light on the outside. Dark and cold on the inside.

Ping.

QUESTIONS FOR REFLECTION

Too often, it takes some kind of crisis to make us put things right. Why do we wait? Are there pings in your life you've silenced long ago?

It is the work and ministry of the Holy Spirit to convict us of sin. He breaks through the darkness blinding our eyes, and when He does—we need to respond. Are you ready?

PART 3

PARENTS
IN THE FAITH

17

LITTLE CHILDREN

~~~

Reflections on 1 John 2:12

*I am writing to you, little children, because your sins
have been forgiven you for His name's sake.*

—1 JOHN 2:12

Reading 1 John is like bursting into a family meeting only
to find they're dealing with real dangers that have come
against them. Dad has stood up to address those dangers and
to bring encouragement, counsel, and caution.

He calls them "children" and "little children."

Nine times.

He is Papa. The church is family. There is love here.
Love because Jesus Christ has done what no one dreamed
or expected. He rescued a people for Himself and made
that people a family with dads, moms, grandparents, aunts,
uncles, cousins, teens, children, and babies. All called by
His name. All bonded by His love. And by His direction,
there is order here. Order and structure.

John was the papa. And the people gathered in Jesus
were his "little children."

Does that language work in our First-World culture?

I'm guessing the answer is no. The world around us has taught us that we're all equals. Give me family. Give me love. Give me something to do that's helpful, but don't put anybody in authority over me. Don't counsel me. Don't discipline me. Don't tell me what to do or what not to do because if you do, I'm out.

I'm out because it doesn't work like that anymore. No papas. No mamas. No obedience to godly elders. Those days are long gone. New days have come.

And by the way, I am not your "little child."

I am writing to you, little children, because your sins
have been forgiven you for His name's sake.

—1 JOHN 2:12

"Yeah, we're excited," the young pastor told me on Skype.

"OK, I want to know the whole story. Start from the beginning," I urged. He and his family were about to move to the heart of a Midwest American city to start a new church. It was a huge step of faith for him. He was leaving behind a great position, a nice home, a secure salary, and stepping into the big unknown.

"This all started about a year ago," he said. "The senior pastor took me out for coffee and asked how I was doing. I told him I loved being a pastor. I loved the people in the church and the opportunity to serve them. I told him I couldn't imagine being anywhere else or doing anything else.

"It was a great conversation. He was really honest with me. He told me he thought I was doing great. So great, in fact, that he thought I was ready."

"Ready for what?" I asked.

"Ready to be a senior pastor somewhere."

I tried to read his face but couldn't. So I prodded him a bit. "So how did you take that? Was it encouraging to hear or did it feel like a kick in the gut?"

"Both, I guess. But I'd say, at first, it felt more like a kick in the gut."

"What did you do?"

"My wife and I talked and prayed a lot. It wasn't easy because we love it here. Our kids love it here. But the more time passed, the more I kept going back to a principle that shaped my life. My dad always taught me, 'In the Lord, you'll find that blessings come when we submit ourselves to godly authority.'"

I nearly fell off my chair.

"OK stop!" I said, waving my hand in the air. "Say that again."

"Yeah, I don't always like it," he admitted. "But I've found it to be true in my life that when I listen, really listen, to those in authority over me in Christ—"

"You realize," I said, interrupting him, "no one says that anymore. Not in today's culture. I'm constantly talking to pastors who struggle with this issue. They try and bring godly discipline to Christians in their church but it hardly ever works. People don't want it. And worse, I find Christian leaders are the same way. They'd no more submit to authority over them than fly to the moon."

"Well, it worked here!" he said, smiling.

"You've got a great dad," I admired.

"And a great senior pastor," he added. "My wife and I finally realized that he loved us enough to speak into our lives. Once we were able to hear that, and really know that, the Lord began to do amazing things with us. We never dreamed we'd be planting a church in the city—and now look at us!"

I sat there amazed by him.

He'd been given the most beautiful gift—a treasure right from the heart of God. A principle of life and blessing that our Lord Jesus Christ modeled with His Father during His days on earth. Something I'd thought had been utterly lost in my day. And just for a moment, I had the urge to look him in the eyes and say what I think the apostle John might have said at a time like this: "Well done, little child. Well done."

I am writing to you, little children, because your sins
have been forgiven you for His name's sake.

—1 JOHN 2:12

I slipped down the aisle of the church unnoticed. People were scattered throughout the sanctuary, mostly lost in conversation with others.

The casket was still open. The service hadn't started yet.

I paused some feet away to pay my respects to this dear man who had, in a thousand ways, shaped my life. He was the first priest who'd taken me under his wing and challenged me to step into the call the Lord had in my life. He pushed, challenged, corrected, trained, and encouraged me.

Like papas do.

As I stood there, I instantly remembered the time he kicked me under a table at a restaurant. I was still in my twenties. We were having lunch with a senior pastor from another church. At some point in the conversation, this pastor said something that irritated me—that I thought was contrary to the Bible—and I quickly spoke my mind. Just as I was about to argue my position, I was kicked!

"You never speak to your elders that way. Not with that tone. Not without the honor and respect they deserve," he later said to me.

I didn't know it then. I didn't know it for some time. But the Lord had given me a rare gift in this man. And because of him, I caught a glimpse of what it means to be part of the family of God. To know structure. Structure and order. To know respect and honor. To know what it means to submit myself to godly authority and, because of it, to find the blessing and grace of Jesus Christ in my life.

Because this man loved me enough to be a papa in the faith to me.

And because, for a while, I got to be his "little child."

QUESTIONS FOR REFLECTION

Too often, culture shapes the structure and order of our Christian lives. But what about you? Have you ever had a papa or mama in the faith? What do you know about submitting yourself to godly authority?

Sometimes elders abuse this principle and we run from it—rightly. But the family imagery of the church in the Bible is meant for our good; for our encouragement, discipline, and growth in Christ. What positive examples can you give where it has worked? Are you willing to pray for it in your life?

18

TAKES TWO MINUTES

Reflections on 1 John 2:12–13

*I am writing to you, little children, because your sins
have been forgiven you for His name's sake.*

—1 JOHN 2:12

"I'm just so confused," she sighed. "Everything here is
a mess."

For the next half hour, she unpacked the story for me.
Staff meetings at church have become a nightmare. People
she loves are at odds with each other. One side argues—and
it makes sense. The other side argues—and it makes sense.

"I think something's wrong with me," she insisted.
"Everybody's saying the Lord is on their side. They hold up
the Bible. They give Scriptures. They tell stories of what they
think the Lord is doing. One minute, it looks like one side has
His favor. The next minute, it's the other side. And, get this,
both are trying to win me. What's up with that? Like I am
some prize at a raffle!" She sounded exasperated.

"I just want out. I want to leave the church. Every time
I walk into the building, it's like somebody hit me in the
stomach. I can't stand it anymore."

"So let's start at the beginning," I said. "Tell me what you know."

"I don't know what I know anymore," she blurted back fast. "Except, I know that Jesus Christ is my Lord and Savior. And that He loves me. That I know."

"Good answer," I said, quietly applauding.

I am writing to you, little children, because your sins
have been forgiven you for His name's sake.

—1 JOHN 2:12

Years ago, an older Christian woman gave me simple advice.

"It takes two minutes," she said. "If the Lord puts somebody on your heart, pick up the phone and call. Tell them God loves them. Encourage them. Build them up. Two minutes, that's all it takes. Why don't we do that more often?"

Good question; great advice. Over the years, as I've tried to take this counsel to heart, I've found it can be a little more complicated than it sounds.

But not at face value. Being an encourager can actually be crazy fun.

Especially the surprise attack—out of nowhere. A card. A call. A gift. An e-mail. A text. A Facebook message. A bundle of flowers. An unexpected visit. A volley of words that says everything you want to say—just to lift the person's heart. To tell them you care. Their Father cares. They're loved, right now.

My friend was right. It takes two minutes.

But there's a kind of encouragement that goes deeper. The kind that takes more time. Time to listen both to their story and to their heart.

There are times I've done this so poorly. I've listened and then rattled off a true but trite phrase like, "Don't worry. You'll be fine! The Lord is faithful. He's not going to let you go through what you can't handle!" And I'd get this glassy-eyed stare back. I didn't exactly get it until it was done to me, and then I got it.

A pat on the back. A high five. A thumbs-up with a big smile and a quote from the Bible that misses the heart can actually do more harm than good.

There's an encouragement that goes deeper. That loves deeper.

And I decided a long time ago that I wanted to learn how to do that.

I am writing to you, little children, because your sins have been forgiven you for His name's sake. I am writing to you, fathers, because you know Him who has been from the beginning. I am writing to you, young men, because you have overcome the evil one.

—1 JOHN 2:12–13

"What do you mean, 'Good answer'?" she said, puzzled.

"I mean, what you're going through is massively confusing. People you know, people you love, people you've trusted in the Lord for years are forcing you to choose sides. If I were you, I'd need to step back and get perspective."

"But everything here's so out of whack. I don't know how to do that."

"Yeah, but you just did," I suggested.

"I'm not so sure. My husband and I talk about this all the time. Every time we try and step back and focus on the Lord and what He wants from us, we get sucked right back into the mess. Somebody calls and says, 'Did you hear what so-and-so said or did?' And that sends us into a tailspin for two or three days."

"But you both do this all the time as parents," I said.

"What do you mean?"

"Your two sons. They're constantly getting into tailspins and you know exactly what to do. You pull them aside. You look them in the eyes. Sometimes you just hold them and other times you speak right to their heart. Sometimes it takes all of two minutes and other times it takes a little longer."

"Yeah, well, with my boys it generally takes a lot longer!" she laughed.

"It's the same thing now for you and your husband," I said, flipping open my Bible to 1 John. "You know this passage so well but I think it's exactly what the apostle John—the papa—was doing. In the midst of a hard, strong attack against the church, he pulled them aside, spoke to their hearts, and said, 'Your sins have been forgiven you for His name's sake. You know Him who has been from the beginning. You have overcome the evil one . . . '"

"He's telling them who they are in Jesus Christ," she commented.

"Repeatedly. Like medicine to the soul."

She sat back in her chair, quiet and reflective. "It's so funny," she said a few minutes later. "Over the last two months it's like the peace of Christ has been ripped right out of my heart. But every once in a while, I feel it again. Like right now. And every time it happens, I know one thing."

"What's that?" I asked.

"It's not what this side is saying or what that side is saying. What matters is the result. And the result is confusion and division among brothers and sisters in Christ. And that is wrong. It's not of the Lord. It's got to stop."

Then she smiled. Like something heavy had been lifted from her heart. As if, for just a minute, or maybe two, the Lord Himself pulled her aside and did what He loves to do best—and what He wants us to do for each other always.

A surprise attack!

I am writing to you, little children, because your sins
have been forgiven you for His name's sake.

—1 JOHN 2:12

My friend of years ago asked the question so simply, "Two minutes, that's all it takes. Why don't we do that more often?"

And I wonder how things would be different if we did.

If we, if I, would ask the Holy Spirit Himself, the encourager, to pour His gift into us. Then through us to each other. Every day. Especially our children. Especially the people the Lord has entrusted to our care—those we pray for, those we love. Friends and family and foe alike.

And then to a lost and needy world.

Just two minutes. And even more . . .

QUESTIONS FOR REFLECTION

In 1 John 2:12–13, John helped us know who we are in Christ—no matter what we're going through. Will you step back from all that's going on in your life and let these verses wash over your soul?

Notice the repetitions. Encouragement is like that. How will you start responding to the Lord's promptings in your life—two minutes!—and take to others the gift given to you?

19

SING IT AGAIN AND AGAIN

Reflections on 1 John 2:12–14

*I am writing to you, little children, because your sins
have been forgiven you for His name's sake. I am writing
to you, fathers, because you know Him who has been
from the beginning. I am writing to you, young men,
because you have overcome the evil one.*

—1 JOHN 2:12–13

She first wrote this poem in her journal in her senior year at college. Then again, after her second daughter was born. And now, in her mid-thirties, she writes it again. It never seems to go away.

*I have the greatest gift a woman could ever dream
A host of people who love me strong and hold me tight.
But a song in my head, buried deep in my heart
Somehow always steals it from sight.
"You never get it right, little girl. You never get it right."
As my daddy closed the bedroom door every night.*

She and her husband have three children now. They vowed, while their first was still in the womb, to never do what her father did to her. They'd sing blessings over their children, night after night, for Jesus to be theirs forever.

They'd lift them up and not push them down. Help them and not harm them.

Every night, a song. A prayer. Before the lights went out.

But it confuses her every time. Why can't she get past it?

Two months ago, she put a report on her boss's desk, two days before it was due. It was bold, innovative, risky, and shot straight. A week later she was gently reprimanded — in front of three of her colleagues no less. She was told to do it again but this time just facts, no editorials.

"Not good enough," she thought to herself. "Never good enough."

Then three weeks ago, she and her husband had a teacher's meeting. Their second child, Madison, had fallen behind in her schoolwork and wasn't behaving well with some of her classmates. It came as a total surprise. She'd thought her sweet Madison was doing so well at school. She seemed so happy.

"It's my fault," she blurted out to the third grade teacher. "I'll work harder with her at home. This won't happen again, promise."

Then, last Saturday, it came to a head. The kids were out playing in the yard when her husband wandered into the kitchen and quietly whispered, "Honey, you've got to back off on the kids. You're pushing them too hard."

"I am not!" she yelled back.

"I think you know that's not true," he volleyed.

She came strong against her husband. The last thing she needed was one more person telling her she wasn't good enough. How she raised her kids wasn't good enough, how she worked at the office wasn't good enough. She was doing her best, and if her best wasn't good enough, tough. It was all she had.

"I'm not backing down," she vowed to herself. "I can't. I won't."

The conversation ended abruptly. But late that night, she couldn't sleep. She went and sat in the bedroom chair, turned on the night light over her head, grabbed her Bible and journal, and began to write. But all she could write, over and over again, was the song screeching in her head, buried in her heart.

"You never get it right, little girl. You never get it right."
As my daddy closed the bedroom door every night.

It's hard to hear the songs in the Bible. We read the lyrics but when the lyrics have lost the melody, the harmonies, the sound of the voices, and the passions behind the voices, the mystery of the song is lost and the gift of music missed.

Songs were meant to be sung and sung again. Repeated and repeated again until they dig deep into every fiber of who we are and take root, marking our soul, shaping our lives, building our character, impacting our choices.

And this is exactly what the apostle John did.

The moment the church was in trouble—being attacked by an enemy gospel and leaders who brought confusion, division, arrogance, and pride into the heart of the Christian community, John wrote and in writing began to sing.

I am writing to you, little children, because your sins have been forgiven you for His name's sake. I am writing to you, fathers, because you know Him who has been from the beginning. I am writing to you, young men, because you have overcome the evil one. I have written to you, children, because you know the Father. I have written to you, fathers, because you know Him who has been from the beginning. I have written to you, young men, because you are strong, and the word of God abides in you, and you have overcome the evil one.

— 1 JOHN 2:12–14

Read it fast and you'll miss it.

Sing it once, sing it twice. Sing it until you know it and then sing it again. Sing it until the song leaps from the mind to the heart, the heart to the soul, and then do it for a week, a year, a decade, a lifetime. And when the time comes and you know the song is true, really true for you, you'll know from the Lord, by His strong and mighty hand, a new freedom has come.

Because all the songs that came before it will have finally, forever . . . disappeared.

She cried when she first read Kathryn Stockett's novel *The Help*. When the movie came out, she cried again. It struck too close to home. It's exactly what she didn't have growing up and it's exactly what she vowed she'd give her children until the day she dies.

A song, simple and clear, written on their heart.

"You is kind. You is smart. You is important."[1]

It's why she signed up to teach the children at Sunday school. It's why she's part of a weekly Bible study. She's learning to sing the "songs of Zion" (Ps. 137:3). She's taking the promises of God to heart. And the more time passes, the louder these songs are becoming inside her as a person, as a woman.

She writes in her journal:

I know, I believe the song the apostle John sang. My sins have been forgiven me. I have overcome the Evil One. I know the Father. I know I am strong. I know the Word of God abides in me.

But still it confuses her.

The moment crisis happens on any front—work, home, relationships—the instant she doesn't perform to her standard or the standard someone else sets for her, and God forbid she has a bad day, tired, irritable, sick, overstressed, pushed to the max and pushed again. Whether it's big things or small things, whatever trips her out of the God-zone and into the me-zone.

The old song comes back, haunting her.

Making her see her husband, children, friends, boss, herself, through a negative, critical eye because nothing is ever right. Nothing ever perfect. And she suddenly finds herself insisting—demanding—perfection.

Because that's what the song says.

You never get it right, little girl. You never get it right.

And she wonders when the Lord will let freedom come to her soul. When that song will have played for the last time and finally, forever . . . disappear.

QUESTIONS FOR REFLECTION

Take this song from 1 John 2:12–14 and let the Lord sing His love over you. Look at what He has done for you. Look at who you are in Him. Can you receive it? Can you let it shape how you see yourself in everyday life?

These are the songs that need to be sung in our darkest, most troubling times. It's why we need each other, as well as "parents" in the faith, who drown out all other sounds and let this be heard. Will you let others in to help you sing?

NOTE

1. Kathryn Stockett, *The Help* (New York: Penguin, 2009), 443.

20

I GOT IT, DAD, I GOT IT

Reflections on 1 John 2:15

Do not love the world nor the things in the world.
If anyone loves the world, the love of the Father is not in him.

—1 JOHN 2:15

He wakes up at 4:00 in the morning and looks at his bedside clock. The ache in his stomach swells and he knows he'll never get back to sleep. It happens nearly every day now. He doesn't want to go to work.

He slips out of bed and quietly goes down to the kitchen to make some coffee, not wanting to wake the family. He sits at the breakfast table and stares out the window. His mind is already entangled by recent events at the office. For the last six months, his life has been hell. They're after him and he knows it.

He feels trapped, cornered.

He can't leave. He and his wife need the money. They've got too much debt as it is, plus his job carries health benefits. Even as he puts out his résumé now, it'll take weeks—months—to get a new job. With one in college and another two years away, they'd fall too far back to ever catch up.

But he can't stay.

Six months ago, his boss took him aside and told him there'd be changes. Turns out, nearly half his department had been in secret meetings to reorganize the company and he knew nothing about it. The message was loud and clear: "I don't care if you've been here ten years, you're either with us or you're gone." After hearing the plan, he knew exactly why his boss had kept him in the dark.

"You know I can't do this," he pleaded back then. "It'll tear the company apart. People who work here are going to get hurt. We'll lose our client base."

"Well then, sounds like you have a choice to make," his boss threatened.

Weeks passed, months passed, and he's barely hanging on by a thread. Even though a few changes were already being implemented, he knew the secret meetings were still going on behind his back. He knew they'd already chosen his replacement. It was a matter of time before the company broke into pieces.

"What are you going to do?" a coworker asked last week.

"I don't know. I've never seen anything like it," he said. "Why would anybody destroy the very thing they've spent a lifetime building? It doesn't make any sense to me. I'm a nervous wreck. I've just started getting my résumé out."

"Me too. There's a bunch of us."

He remembers the conversation as he makes his morning commute. He thinks about all those who've loved working at the company, believed they were making a difference in people's lives, but would soon be tossed on the street.

And then, almost out of nowhere, he thinks about his dad. He'd do anything right now just to hear his voice, tell him the story, and get his counsel.

"Dad," his heart wanted to cry out, "I don't know what to do."

Do not love the world nor the things in the world. If anyone loves the world, the love of the Father is not in him.

—1 John 2:15

After work, as he was driving home, just after he safely merged onto the highway, he called his father.

"Dad, this is Mark. How are you doing?"

"Who's this?"

"It's Mark, Dad. How's the day going for you?"

"It's Mark, honey," he heard his mom say in the background. "It's Mark."

"Oh Mark, I'm doing fine today, doing fine. How's your family, Mark? Is everybody well?" he said, his voice the same as Mark had always known.

Everything inside him wanted to lay out the story, piece by piece, play by play, with every last detail. He knew his dad would see something he couldn't see. He'd say something, that perfect something, that would calm his heart and ease his mind. But he couldn't. For the last five years he couldn't.

Not since his diagnosis of dementia. The last year or so, it's gotten worse. Sometimes his dad remembers him. Sometimes he doesn't. But always, just the sound of his dad's voice gave him courage.

"I love you, Dad. You know that, right?"

"Me too, Son. Me too."

He clicked off his phone and, for whatever reason, his mind drifted back ten years—ten years almost to the month. He'd just received the offer to come join the company and he leapt at it. He was ready to quit his old job immediately and called his dad to tell him the good news. He couldn't wait to tell him.

"You're not going to believe it!" Mark said as he told him about the job: a real promotion with a senior level title and a huge jump in salary and benefits.

"So Mark, you'll take some time and pray about this with Laurie, right?" his dad said halfway through the conversation.

"What's there to pray about? This is everything we've ever hoped for, Dad."

"Not so fast, Son," said his father. "You know the hard lessons I've learned in life. We never say yes until we take it to the Lord. He has the final say, not us. And you know His kingdom doesn't revolve around titles and positions, money and big benefit packages. The world lusts for that—we don't."

"Yeah, Dad, I know. Laurie and I will pray about it first—promise."

And he did, to please his dad. But there was no way he was going to turn down this offer. He left his other company, took the job, and the rest was history. But then, three months later, it was like he hit a wall. It was the first time he saw something in his boss that just wasn't right.

"I can't put my finger on it, Dad," Mark told his father then. "He uses people to get what he wants. And then he tells us one story while others—the people getting fired—are telling us the exact opposite. It's not adding up."

"So what are you going to do, Mark?" his dad asked.

"I'm going to soldier on, Dad. I'm loyal to a fault, you know that."

"That's not what I mean."

"I'm not sure I understand," Mark replied.

"I'm asking—what are you going to do when it happens to you?"

Do not love the world nor the things in the world. If anyone loves the world, the love of the Father is not in him.

1 JOHN 2:15

Mark pulled in the driveway and turned off the engine. To this day, he remembers what his father said. It was the perfect advice back then and it was the perfect advice now.

"Mark, we're not people who belong to this world. I think you know what I'm talking about when I say that. I know you have an important job. I know you're a talented young man. I know the pay is beyond what you and Laurie ever imagined in life. But I'm going to ask you to be careful, Son.

"If this pattern continues with your boss, then what's happening around you will happen to you one day. You're going to be faced with a choice, a hard choice, that will bring you back to the only question that matters in life. Does your heart belong to the world? Or does it belong to your Father in heaven? Which is it? And it can't be both.

"You may think you know the answer right now. But it's a lot harder when the pressure is on, when people are talking behind your back, when you're not sure where the next paycheck is coming from. You know I know what I'm talking about here. It's not easy, Son. It's not easy. So I'm asking you to be careful, Mark. Be real careful."

"I got it, Dad. I got it," Mark said out loud in the car, though no one was there to hear him. For the first time in six months, with tears streaming down his face, Mark knew exactly what his Dad—his heavenly Dad—wanted him to do.

QUESTIONS FOR REFLECTION

Many Christians today do not have elders—fathers and mothers in Christ—to mentor, counsel, and bring wisdom to them. Can you? Do you have others you trust to help you?

We tend to find our love for the things of this world in conflict with the love of the Father in us. Are there real choices you need to make today?

21

TIMMY MILLSON

~~~

Reflections on 1 John 2:16

*For all that is in the world, the lust of the flesh
and the lust of the eyes and the boastful pride of life,
is not from the Father, but is from the world.*

—1 JOHN 2:16

Jack swiveled in his chair and stared out the window. A few minutes later, he said, "I can't believe you're doing this."

Scott didn't respond. He sat on the leather sofa, same seat he always sat in when he came to talk to Jack. He knew he'd said enough for now.

"You don't believe it, do you?" Jack asked, turning back. "I mean, come on, how long have we known each other, huh?"

Again, Scott didn't respond. He didn't have to. Of all people, Jack knew how these stories played out. He was a Christian counselor, full-time on the church staff. It was his job to have hard conversations with people—especially men, since he mostly counseled men. But never had the tables turned.

"Look, I know you're just doing your job, and I appreciate that," Jack said, his voice stronger, his defense mounting. "But let it go. It's not true."

"I can't do that," Scott whispered. "You know I can't."

"OK, so what's next? What exactly are you going to do?"

Scott leaned forward. He'd been the senior pastor of the church for eight years. Every time these kinds of stories came up with other men in the church, he and Jack met together. They had to, in this case, as a matter of law. And it was Jack—Jack, the trained counselor—who always gave the clear direction on what to do and how to do it.

"You know what I have to do," Scott responded gently.

At first, Jack didn't understand. He'd felt strong, confident, up to that point. He had no reason to believe any accusation against him would stand. But then it dawned on him. He put himself in Scott's shoes and the thought entered his head like a right hook to the side of his face.

"No," he growled.

"I have to," Scott said.

"I won't let you."

"You don't want to go down that path, Jack."

Jack buried his head in his hands with a deep, exhausted sigh. He shook his head in disbelief, like he couldn't imagine why he didn't foresee this moment coming and why he hadn't done something about it. He should have known. He should have been prepared. How could he have been this stupid?

"Jack," Scott said once, then twice. Finally, Jack raised his head and looked straight into the pastor's face and heard the words he never thought he'd hear.

"Jack, I need your computer."

For all that is in the world, the lust of the flesh and the
lust of the eyes and the boastful pride of life, is not
from the Father, but is from the world.

—1 JOHN 2:16

When the knock came on his door an hour earlier, Jack
was beyond excited. He'd never admit it to anyone, but he
idolized Scott. He was a great senior pastor, a giant of a
man who'd received more accolades among worldwide
Christian leaders than anyone he'd ever known. It actually
amazed him that they were good friends.

Then Scott called this morning. He'd said, "Jack, I need
some time today." Just the thought that Scott needed time
with him—time to get godly counsel and wisdom—made
his heart soar with joy. They agreed to meet at 3:00.

But from the moment Jack saw him, he knew something
was terribly wrong.

"Jack, I've got to ask you some hard questions," Scott
began after they'd spent some time talking.

"Absolutely," Jack said. And then the questions came
fast and hard.

"What comes to your mind when you think of Patty
Zorn? Have you ever spoken inappropriately to her?
Have you ever hugged her at church in an inappropriate
way? Are you aware of how you speak about her to other
men in the church? Are you aware that your jokes

recently have been offensive to some? Are you addicted to porn?"

"OK, that's enough!" Jack roared, holding both his hands in the air. "Where's this coming from? The answer is, No! No! No! No! No! No!"

"Then talk to me about Timmy Millson," Scott demanded.

And that's when Jack swiveled in his chair and stared out the window. Two weeks ago, Timmy Millson thought his appointment was at 2:00 not 2:30. He'd come early, walked into the office, like usual, but this time the door was open. Jack was at his computer, his back to Timmy. He didn't hear him come in.

Nor did he think Timmy Millson saw what he was doing.

Do not love the world nor the things in the world.
If anyone loves the world, the love of the Father is not
in him. For all that is in the world, the lust of the flesh
and the lust of the eyes and the boastful pride of life,
is not from the Father, but is from the world.

—1 JOHN 2:15–16

Scott stood up, went to Jack's desk, and unhooked his laptop. He'd intended to secure it and walk quietly out of the office but instead, he surprised himself. He turned to Jack and asked, "Would you take a walk with me?"

There was a city park three blocks from the church which was perfect for a lazy, quiet stroll, or for children to romp through the playground, or just to sit on one of the benches in front of the massive stone water fountain.

"About three years ago," Jack confessed as they stepped outside, "it escalated. I don't know why. One day I had control of it. The next day I didn't. But even then, it didn't trouble me. I thought I was still in control. I knew what to do."

"So why didn't you do it?" Scott asked.

"I guess because I was scared. I knew if I told anyone, if it ever got out, my career would be over. I'd never get a job anywhere ever again. So I kept it to myself. I took every precaution. I did everything I could to keep myself from ever being found out. I actually thought I could play this game and win."

"You dropped too many hints," Scott replied. "Some of the guys picked up on it. Patty Zorn came to me personally, in tears. She didn't want to tell me, but you frightened her. And then came the Timmy Millson story."

They walked on together in silence. They got to the fountain, sat on one of the benches, and watched the water shooting high into the air and come splashing down with the thunderous sound of a loud rain storm.

"It's just so crazy," Jack reflected. "I did everything not to be found out. And at the same time, I did everything to be found out. What is up with that?"

"May I say a few things?" Scott interrupted and Jack reluctantly nodded.

"I want to walk this journey with you. It's not going to be easy, but we're going to do it the right way, by the book, openly before the Lord, your wife, and your church family. That's where we start. Does that work for you?"

Again, Jack nodded.

"Well, I want you to hear this, I mean, really hear this. I know you know God loves you. You're a Christian man. You've ministered the gospel for years. You teach the forgiveness of sin that's found in Jesus Christ. But I want you to hear this about you, Jack." And with that, the statements came slowly.

"The love of the Father is in you. You have allowed the lust of your flesh to reign in your body. You have allowed the lust of your eyes to reign in your heart. You have allowed pride and rebellion to seep into your soul. But the love of the Father is in you. And the love of the Father is greater than the lust in you. Do you believe that?"

Tears had already welled up in Jack's eyes. He was staring at the water. Everything inside him wanted to nod. To say yes. To keep up appearances. But he couldn't. Not now. The truth was out. His heart was exposed.

"No, I don't," he said, shaking his head firmly. "How can His love be in me after what I've done? It's impossible. I can't imagine it. I can't imagine my wife loving me now. Or my kids. Or my friends. Or my church family. Or you. Let alone, God."

And with that, the tears fell freely down his cheek, the sobs began, barely heard over the sound of the crashing water in front of them.

QUESTIONS FOR REFLECTION

Do you have Timmy Millson stories in your life? People who see what we try to hide, exposing us and our sin. What lusts are in your life today—hidden, secret, and strong?

Can you see the contrast between the lusts John described (and their parallel to Gen. 3:6) and the love of the Father? Do you believe the love of the Father in you is stronger than any controlling lusts? (See Rom. 6:8–12.)

22

THE FIRST FIVE WEEKS

~~~

Reflections on 1 John 2:17

The world is passing away, and also its lusts;
but the one who does the will of God lives forever.

—1 JOHN 2:17

Scott sat on the park bench in front of the waterfall for the third week in a row. It was Tuesday afternoon, 4:45. Summer was in full swing and the city park was buzzing with activity—young and old, walkers and joggers, Frisbee throwers, rollerbladers, lovers and loners—all enjoying a lazy July day.

It seemed everybody was here—except Jack.

"Call me if you need me. But one week from today," Scott had promised him, "at this exact time, I will be here, on this same bench. I will walk this journey with you, Jack, and we will get through this mess together. But only if you want that. It's your choice."

It was the last time they'd spoken. When Jack didn't show the first week, Scott decided to come back the next, and the next, hoping against hope that Jack would surprise him with a sudden change of heart. But that hadn't happened, at least not yet.

He looked at his watch. It was nearing 5:00.

Scott had brought a book with him this week. Inside the front cover he'd folded a document that Jack had written dating back six years. As a Christian counselor on church staff, Jack had presented to Scott, his senior pastor, a step-by-step action plan in case anyone in church leadership, paid or volunteer, was ever accused of immoral, indecent, or inappropriate behavior.

"The Parish Council adopted it word for word!" Scott told him back then.

"I hope it's never needed," Jack exclaimed.

And it wasn't. Not until now.

"In all the years I've been a counselor," Jack reflected in those days, "I've found it's the hardest thing to do. We don't want to admit we're wrong. Or that we're living a secret life. Or that we're trapped in a death spiral of an addiction we can't control. It comes with too much shame, too much humiliation."

Scott remembered Jack's words like they were yesterday. He also recalled Jack saying, "At times like that, a lot of people make the wrong choices. You want to come alongside and help, but they refuse. And often, they can turn on you."

That thought made Scott shudder. "Is that you, Jack? Is that what you're doing right now?" he whispered to himself.

Scott skimmed through the document again. He'd followed it to the letter. He terminated Jack's position and placed him under church discipline. He talked privately to all parties involved. He met in closed session with the Parish

Council and mapped out a detailed plan of recovery pending investigation and treatment. All done—step-by-step—as Jack had written it.

"Lord Jesus," Scott quietly pleaded, "I ask You to please, sovereignly, intervene in Jack's life right now. Please, turn him around."

Scott stayed till 5:45, like he'd done the past few weeks. And then he decided to come back the next week.

And the next.

The world is passing away, and also its lusts;
but the one who does the will of God lives forever.

—1 JOHN 2:17

On the day Scott confronted him, Jack admitted he was caught in a web of sexual addictions he could no longer control. He promised Scott he'd go home and tell his wife; he'd put his practice on hold; he'd start treatment as soon as possible; and, with a tear-soaked face, he said he'd follow Scott's lead.

But by nightfall, that had all changed.

Seconds after Scott left him, Jack began thinking about each accusation. One by one, he picked them apart. They were weak, flimsy. None of them would stand in a court of law. The more he thought, the more outraged he became. There was no way he was going to stand back and let these accusations soil his good reputation, hurt his family, and ruin his practice.

"I'm calling a lawyer first thing in the morning!" were the first words his wife heard that night.

Jack began to strategically mount a campaign against Scott. He contacted a number of families in the church—good friends, people he could count on, couples he'd helped over the years—and spun a story that painted him to be a wrongful victim of misunderstanding. And, surprisingly, it seemed to work.

Scott got wind of it two days later. By the end of the week, he had a letter in his hand from Jack's lawyer.

The next Tuesday afternoon, at 4:45, Scott sat on the park bench and waited.

Three weeks passed, then four, then five. There were no signs that Jack's heart was softening. In fact, it seemed it was only getting worse. His friends were becoming more and more vocal both against Scott and the Parish Council. And if nothing changed, Scott now knew, this story had the power to break and divide the church.

"What are we supposed to do, Scott?" the elders asked him.

"We've done everything we can," he replied. "Unless the Lord does something outrageous in Jack's heart, we've got tough days in front of us, really tough."

And on week five, Scott made his way back to the park bench. He didn't know why. For weeks now, he'd lost all hope that Jack would ever show.

The world is passing away, and also its lusts;
but the one who does the will of God lives forever.

—1 John 2:17

When Jack saw Scott sitting on the bench, he couldn't believe it. Had he come every week? Was it a coincidence that he was here, this week, on a Tuesday at 4:45? Just the thought he'd been here, week after week, strangely saddened him.

He was far enough away. He could just leave. Scott would never know.

But that's not why he came. It was time and he knew it. He took the first step, and then the next. Big choices, each one. And he kept going—making a beeline for the bench until he stood in front of Scott. And the moment came.

Scott looked up.

"You're here, just like you promised," Jack said.

Scott nodded. "I was just thinking, before you came, that this might be my last week. I'm sorry to say I think I was about to give up on you."

"I'm glad you didn't," Jack said, sitting down next to him, a piece of paper clutched in his hand. "But I would have, if I were you. Up till yesterday, there was no way I'd ever come and see you. I was so mad at you—and what you were trying to do to ruin me and my career. My wife and I were determined to see this case through, even if it meant going to trial."

"I know," Scott said, and then again, "I know."

"A letter, a stupid letter I skimmed in ten seconds and threw in the trash. I actually thought you were behind it. That you were getting old clients of mine to write letters so I'd change my mind. I laughed at it. But in the middle of the night, I don't know what happened, I just knew I was supposed to get up and get that letter and read it again. Carefully, this time. And I did—over and over, until I heard the Lord speaking right to me."

With that, Jack handed him the wrinkled letter.

Scott read one portion out loud:

Jack . . .

You pushed me . . . and pushed me and never gave up on me. You made me see what I didn't want to see in me, and I hated you for it. I did everything to make your life miserable because you were making my life miserable. But you didn't stop. You never stopped. Because you wanted what I didn't want for me—you wanted me well. You wanted me to see Jesus. You wanted me to know that He could take this addiction deep in my soul and uproot it forever. I hated that you saw it. I hated that you made me see it. But you never gave up on me. Never. And now, it's your turn Jack. And I want you to know I'll never give up on you. I believe in you like you believe in me. And I'm so grateful to be called your friend. . . .

Kevin

Jack turned and looked Scott right in the eyes and somehow that was enough. Scott was here, on the park bench, just as he promised. Even now, he hadn't given up on him. Even now.

And for Jack, that's all it took for him to make the right choice.

QUESTIONS FOR REFLECTION

Too many of us suffer from being given up on or giving up on others. There is a pursuit, relentless and unceasing, that belongs to us in Christ. Do you have it in you? What is it that you need today?

The choice is always in front of us. Will we choose the will of God for our lives? Will we do what's right in His eyes? Will we follow Him, or will we compromise with the ways of the world? What about you, now?

23

THE OTHER CHOICE

Reflections on 1 John 2:18–19

Children, it is the last hour; and just as you heard that antichrist is coming, even now many antichrists have appeared; from this we know that it is the last hour. They went out from us, but they were not really of us; for if they had been of us, they would have remained with us; but they went out, so that it would be shown that they all are not of us.

—1 JOHN 2:18–19

Lindsey knocked on the door and stuck his head in the office.

"Pastor Scott, you got a minute?"

Scott was standing behind his desk putting the last few things into this briefcase before heading home for the night. He looked up and saw his dear old friend Lindsey.

"Not for you!" Scott teased.

Lindsey was a retired Methodist minister, having served thirty-eight years in the pastorate. Scott trusted him completely as a counselor and friend. He relied on him in more ways than he could count.

"You dodged a serious bullet today," Lindsey said, coming into the office and shutting the door behind him.

"You got that right."

"Is it true? Jack dropped all legal charges against you and the church?"

"Yeah, it's true. And he said, if it wasn't too late, he'd like to come under the discipline the Parish Council, and I outlined his recovery."

Lindsey shook his head in disbelief. "You know, in all the years I served in the church, I've rarely seen someone like Jack. He's a good counselor. You were right to hire him on staff. He's had an effective ministry here, especially among the men. He's a good man, Scott; a real good man."

"I agree, but, to be honest, I thought we'd lost him. I know all of us were surprised to hear about his addiction issues, but that was nothing compared to how he turned on us. For a while there, I actually thought he had the power to rip this church apart."

"I know. But that's not usually how it goes," Lindsey stated.

"What do you mean?"

"Well, in my experience, the Lord defends His church. In this story, He brought Jack under conviction and Jack had a choice. He could either come under the Lord's discipline or reject it. He chose to do the right thing. But a lot of people make the wrong choice." Lindsey continued, "They do what Jack tried to do. They come hard against the church. They rally support from their friends. For a while, it looks like they have enough political power to succeed. And if the church isn't strong in Jesus, they do. But more times than not, the Lord steps in, defends His church, and eventually these people leave."

"So you think Jack and his friends would have left us?"

"Yes, I do. And they'd wind up in some sorry pastor's office who'd listen to every detail of their sad, unfair story and welcome them into his church with open arms. Of course, a little while later, poor Jack and friends would do to the new church what they did to the old church. And the story just repeats."

"How do you know all this?" Scott asked, troubled by the thought.

"Because it happened to me. I've been that sorry pastor."

Children, it is the last hour; and just as you heard that antichrist
is coming, even now many antichrists have appeared; from
this we know that it is the last hour. They went out from us,
but they were not really of us; for if they had been of us,
they would have remained with us; but they went out,
so that it would be shown that they all are not of us.

—1 JOHN 2:18–19

Lindsey sat down in a winged-back chair and motioned for Scott to sit across from him, "Let me have just a minute," he said. "Is that OK?"

"Yeah, I want to hear this," Scott said, taking a seat.

"I learned a valuable lesson in those days. I'd always thought the Devil's first line of attack against the church was to twist the Bible and bring heresies into the church. So, as a pastor, I did everything I could to guard people from false teaching. I thought that was enough, but quickly learned it wasn't."

"What happened?" Scott asked.

"This group of Christians came to my office to tell me their story. I didn't have enough sense to realize I was only hearing their version. In hindsight, I should have called the pastor of the church they'd left. That was a huge mistake on my part. If I'd met with that pastor first, things might have turned out differently.

"But, you see, I was too focused on finding out whether or not they were Christians. Did they believe in Jesus Christ as the Son of God? Were they born of Him and were they committed to the creedal doctrines of the faith? Once I was convinced of this, I welcomed them into the church."

"That makes sense, Lindsey," Scott reasoned.

"But it was shortsighted. These people brought division into our church. They might have passed the doctrinal test but they failed the relational command to love each other as Christ loved us. Within six months, there was unrest in the church. Little things at first, arguments here and there. People not speaking to each other. But soon, our leadership meetings were full of debate and rancor. And, stupid old me, I had no idea why."

"So what did you do?" Scott asked.

"I prayed a lot. I believed the Lord would see us through. I reasoned the church had caught a cold that would eventually pass. But it didn't. This was no cold. This was a big old nasty virus that was attacking the body of Christ. It took me a whole year before I suddenly realized what I needed to do."

Scott now sat at the edge of his chair and guessed the ending, "You called the group into your office and confronted them?"

"No, I didn't. Not yet," Lindsey said. "I called the pastor of their former church and made an appointment to see him."

"So what did he say?" Scott urged.

"He said he was sorry," Lindsey reported. "When I told him what we were going through, he looked me right in the eyes and said, 'I should have called you. It was wrong of me not to call you. When I heard they landed in your church, I wanted to warn you. But I was afraid, afraid you wouldn't understand, so I didn't do it. Would you forgive me this wrong?'"

"I'm impressed," Scott reflected.

"Well, what impressed me more was what he decided to do. He said to me, 'Lindsey, the work of the antichrist is first relational. He seeks to divide the body of Christ. When I saw what was happening, I went to this group of people and told them it was over. They had a choice to make. They either come under the discipline of this church or they leave. And that's exactly what they did—they left.'"

"That's how they got to your church?" Scott asked.

"That's right. But, I'm telling you that pastor gave me the courage to do the same thing he did. I got them together and gave them the exact same choice."

Scott sat back in his chair and took a deep breath. He thought about Jack. He thought about all the people who had decided to stand with him. He shook his head in disbelief and said, "Lindsey, I don't think I have that kind of courage."

"But you would've, Scott, if you'd needed it. I'm 100 percent sure of that and I'll tell you why."

"OK, tell me!" Scott said, delighting in his friend's passion.

"The Lord defends His church, Scott. He always defends His church!"

QUESTIONS FOR REFLECTION

We live in a culture that has lost any sense of authority and discipline. We are tested when God disciplines us (Heb. 12:5–6). Can you feel the rebellion in you to resist that discipline? Do you know what it's like to welcome and embrace it—especially from "parents" in Christ?

The first task of the antichrist is to divide us. The remedy is simple: a passion to keep the Lord's commandment and love one another fervently from the heart. Are you able to choose to bring that love into your relationships today?

24

AMAZING US

~~~

They went out from us, but they were not really of us; for if
they had been of us, they would have remained with us; but they
went out, so that it would be shown that they all are not of us.

—1 JOHN 2:19

Us. Five times in one verse. The apostle John saw something. He knew something. We who belong to Christ are family together in Christ.

Relationships are everything in the kingdom of God.

And more, so much more. Jesus Christ has given us the most unimaginable gift possible. By what He did on the cross, He has brought us into the fellowship of the Godhead—the Father, the Son, and the Holy Spirit—one God, forever and ever. From the beginning of time, the Lord has identified Himself as the "Us."

"Then God said, 'Let Us make man in Our image, according to Our likeness" (Gen. 1:26). Later, in the days of the Tower of Babel the Lord said, "Come, let Us go down and there confuse their language" (Gen. 11:7). Again, in the presence of Isaiah, the Lord asked, "Whom shall I send, and who will go for Us?" (Isa. 6:8).

"Us" is the name of our God. "Us" is the language of heaven. "Us" is the plan of God for the people of God from the foundation of the world. And it is John who heralded this good news. In the record of his gospel, we are allowed to hear the final prayer of our Lord Jesus Christ to His Father before His death. It is here, in praying for us, that He uses the ancient, eternal language of "Us."

"I . . . ask . . . for those also who believe in Me through their word; that they may all be one; even as You, Father, are in Me and I in You, that they also may be in Us" (John 17:20–21).

This is it! This is why Jesus came. This is what His death and resurrection means to us. He is God. He is a member of the "Us" from all eternity. And He has come to bring us home. To make us members of His family again. And to grant us the gift that was intended to be ours at the very beginning of time.

We get to be part of the "Us."

We get to speak a new language. We get to live a new way of life. Once we were separated from God and lost in our sins. But because of Jesus Christ and what He has done for us on Calvary's hill, we are separated no more. We are family now.

For this reason, said the apostle John, we have a message to the world: "What we have seen and heard we proclaim to you also, so that you too may have fellowship with us; and indeed our fellowship is with the Father, and with His Son Jesus Christ" (1 John 1:3).

Us! We get to, first, be family together in Christ. He has established His church. He has called us to love one another as He has loved us. And because of that, our message is a constant invitation to anybody and everybody to come have fellowship with us and be part of His church, His kingdom family.

And this message stands the test of time—because our fellowship is with the Father and with His Son by His Holy Spirit. We have been granted the highest privilege anyone could ever know: We have been invited through Jesus Christ to enter into and enjoy the eternal fellowship of the Godhead.

Forever.

———

They went out from us, but they were not really of us; for if they had been of us, they would have remained with us; but they went out, so that it would be shown that they all are not of us.

—1 JOHN 2:19

———

I can't imagine sitting down to interview the apostle John today. I think he'd cringe at learning the present story of our church family across the world.

"Well, sir, there are a lot of churches today that barely even speak the name of Jesus. They don't talk about Him much. They speak about God, of course, and many of them are doing a great deal of good helping the poor and needy."

I need a better start.

"But there are many churches that do speak of Him and love Him. Churches that fully embrace the whole of the

Christian faith. Absolutely! And many of them are powerfully bringing the gospel to every corner of the earth."

"So," I imagine him saying, "there are believing churches and unbelieving churches? Is that what you're saying?"

Oh boy, this isn't going well.

"Yeah, well, it gets worse."

"How could it be worse?"

"So, the believing churches aren't exactly always together. Everybody does things a little differently. Some churches are traditional, more formal in style. Others more contemporary. Some focus on being evangelical. Others more Catholic or Protestant. Others more charismatic. To tell you the truth, it's kind of a mixed bag. And these churches can be right across the street from each other."

I think about explaining "denominations" but realize that probably won't help.

"You're not together?" the apostle might say.

"Um, not really."

"Brothers and sisters live near each other and they do not come together in the fellowship of the blessed Lord, Jesus Christ?"

"No, but we run into each other all the time, you know, at social events or at local markets. And every time we get together, we talk about the Lord, what He's doing in our lives, and how we can pray for each other. It works for us."

I imagine the puzzled look.

Stories come to mind of churches—gospel-preaching churches—that have split over complicated issues, but not kingdom issues. How would I explain that to him? I can't. I don't even try. I've dug the ditch too deep already.

"If you live close, you should be together as a family in Christ." I believe his first epistle actually teaches that. "It is the Enemy, the Antichrist, who divides us."

"I agree, but . . ."

"Nobody can go out from 'us' and still be 'us.' For 'us' to be 'us' we need to be together in Jesus Christ and by His Spirit. We're His family. We belong together. That's what being in the fellowship of God is all about. Why don't you know that?"

"It's different today. I can't tell you why," I'd try to argue, failing miserably.

"And what kind of message does that send to the world?" I think he'd say, outraged. "How can we invite them into 'us' when we are not an 'us' at all? And how can the fellowship of the Father, the Spirit, and the Son be divided? Answer me that!"

I can't. All I know is that it's hard reading 1 John in these days.

The lens of doing church, being church, is simple in the Bible. We're family. If we are in Christ, we belong together. The attacks against us, trying to divide us and break us apart, come from the Evil One. That's New Testament church. We're supposed to be "us."

And we're supposed to be together in the worship and fellowship of the eternal "Us." It's the story. It's what Jesus Christ came to do. It's how He designed His church.

And John knew this. John was parent. He was papa. His job was to defend the faith and guard the unity that is ours because we're together. We're "us," always "us"!

An amazing, miraculous, Father-gifted, Son-saved, Spirit-empowered "us."

QUESTIONS FOR REFLECTION

Too many Christians have no church family. They're on their own and not a part of any "us." Is that you? Do you know Christians walking alone? If God has made us an "us," we need to do something about it. What will you do?

And will you help to work against divisions in our churches? Will you help build bridges to local churches holding to the same faith in Christ? How can you make a difference?

PART 4

WE HAVE AN ANOINTING

25

I KNOW YOU KNOW

~~~

Reflections on 1 John 2:20–21

But you have an anointing from the Holy One, and you all know.
I have not written to you because you do not know the truth,
but because you do know it, and because no lie is of the truth.

—1 JOHN 2:20–21

This devotion imagines a conversation between the parents
of the prodigal son (see Luke 15:11–32). It was late at
night. They were sitting on a couch in their family room in
each other's embrace. Their son had left only hours ago.

"Why did you let him go? Why did you give him the
money?" Elizabeth groaned softly, burying her head in his
chest.

"He was gone already," Ebenezer whispered back. "We
lost him months ago. Maybe years ago. He's been here, but
he's not been here."

"I blame his friends, Jokim and Dan. They were the
ones—"

"You can't do that," Ebenezer interrupted. "Our son
made his own choice. He decided to listen to the counsel
of his peers over the counsel of his elders. He can't blame
anyone else and neither should we."

"I know," she said, her tears flowing freely. "But you and me, we could have done more. If we could go back and do the last year over again, we'd do things differently. We'd never let it get to the point where he packs up his things, takes his money, and moves to another country. Why did we let him do that?"

He held her as tightly as he could, but he wasn't much comfort. He was crying as hard as she was, the grief making his heart throb with pain.

"He's gone, Ebenezer, he's gone. When are we going to see him again? When? Ever? What if he's ambushed and killed on the highways? What if he gets a disease and dies in some God-forsaken city away from our homeland, away from God's people? How would we know? Who would tell us? The answer is, 'No one!' That's who. We never see him again."

Ebenezer nodded. He knew the risks as well as she did. There were too many stories around town of parents who'd lost their children to party cities of the present-day Sodom and Gomorrah. Children who were never heard of again.

"Not our son," Ebenezer said, sounding defiant.

Elizabeth said nothing.

"He may have decided to leave God behind. But, Elizabeth, that doesn't mean God has done the same thing. Our son is in His hands now."

"Are you sure He wants him? After what he's done?" she whimpered back.

"More than we do and a thousand times more," he assured her. "You have got to believe me when I say I am certain of this: Our son knows."

"Knows what?"

"He knows us. He knows that the God of Abraham, Isaac, and Jacob loves him. He knows the truth, deep in his soul. It is there, written on his heart. It is seared into every fiber of his soul. Think about it. Think about the times he came to us and told us he knew the Lord was with him. Do you remember, Elizabeth? He told us he loved Him and how much he wanted to serve Him all his life."

"I remember," she said quietly.

"Well, this is it. This is the test."

"What test, Ebenezer? What are you talking about?"

"If our son knows the Lord, not just in his head but in his heart, and if the Lord has put His name deep inside his soul—as I believe He has—then one day our son will turn back to Him. He may run away from Him today but he will not be able to run away forever, not if he knows Him. But if he doesn't know Him, if it's all been locked up in his head, if he's been fooling us all these years, fooling himself, then . . ."

His voice trailed off.

"The Lord promises us," Elizabeth's voice rose, wanting desperately to believe what she was about to say was true for her son, "that if we 'train up a child in the way he should go, even when he is old he will not depart from it'" (Prov. 22:6).

"You're right, Elizabeth. With all my heart, I believe that."

"So this test," she asked, "will it be done in our lifetime?"

"For this, we pray. We never stop, ever. We pray every day."

"I want to see my son again, Ebenezer. I want him home with us."

With that, he squeezed her tight. Everything inside him wanted to grant her wish. But he couldn't do that. He couldn't do anything. This was beyond their control. They'd have to wait months, years. They'd have to trust God with their son.

"Me too," he said, as he began to cry all over again.

But you have an anointing from the Holy One,
and you all know. I have not written to you because
you do not know the truth, but because you do
know it, and because no lie is of the truth.

—1 JOHN 2:20–21

Every morning at sunrise and every evening at sunset, Ebenezer went to the top of the hill behind the house to pray for their son. He studied the land, the roads, the movement of people with the precision of an eagle looking down from its nest for food. "Today," he'd think to himself, "my son comes home."

And every day, he asked the Lord to have mercy on the boy. To protect him from the forces of evil in the world and to keep him safe "in the shelter of the Most High" so that he would abide "in the shadow of the Almighty" (Ps. 91:1). And sometimes, he'd take out his pen and write to him.

My beloved son,

Today is Thursday. You've been gone six months today. We've heard nothing from you and your mother is worried sick. If I could send this letter to you, if I just knew where you were, I'd tell you to please write home. Tell us you're alive and doing well in whatever you're doing. Anything is better than nothing.

We miss you more than words can describe. And I'll tell you a secret: I think you miss us too.

It was only a year-and-a-half ago when I woke up in the middle of the night to this terrible sound of retching. I found you outside in front of the house on all fours. You were sick as a dog. You'd been out all night with your friends. You didn't come home when you were supposed to, and when you did, you went straight to your room without so much as greeting your mother. I knew you were in trouble. Your friends were the wrong friends. Your choices were the wrong choices. And later that night, as I came outside and knelt beside you, rubbing your back, you grabbed my hand and squeezed it hard until the sickness passed. And then you just fell into my arms. It was the first time since you were a boy that you let me hold you like that.

Of course, part of me wanted to give you a piece of my mind. Your behavior that night, like many nights, was atrocious. But I bit my lip and held you until you fell asleep in my arms. It was a night I will never forget, and do you know why? Before you fell asleep, you said words that pierced my heart. You gave me such strength, such hope, that I knew that night—no matter how deep the valley, no matter how long you stay in this darkness—you'd come out. You'd make it.

"Papa, I'm sorry," you said. Do you remember this? "I have sinned against heaven, and in your sight. I am no longer worthy to be called your son [Luke 15:18–19]. Papa, I love you. Will you tell mama? Tell her I love her . . ."

"You'll have to do that yourself, my son!" I said, rocking you back and forth. But I'm not sure you heard me. You fell fast asleep.

And come morning, you acted like it never happened. But, my son, it did happen. And for a single moment in time, I was given a gift. I could see your heart. From that moment on, I knew that you knew.

You know Him. You love Him. I know you do.

And you know we love you. You love us. I know you do.

And though I don't know where you are today, I know this. Soon a day will come when you will wake out of your drunken stupor and you will again see the world through the eyes of God. Just like that night I held you. But this time, it will be different. This time, you will come to God—God your heavenly Father— and you will never again leave His embrace.

This I know, my son.

And so, I put this letter in a file with all my other letters to you. I don't know if you will ever read them. But if you do, and your mama and I are not here to tell you face-to-face, never doubt what you already know in your heart.

We love you, dear boy, and always, always will.

Papa

QUESTIONS FOR REFLECTION

When we come to know the Lord, a transaction happens. By His doing, His anointing abides in us so we know we know Him. Always, trials test whether this transaction has happened. So is it in you? Do you know you know?

It's hard when this testing happens to those we love— especially our children. Will they turn to Him? Will they come back to Him? What do you do at times like this? How do you pray?

26
I KNOW YOU DON'T

Reflections on 1 John 2:21–22

Because no lie is of the truth. Who is the liar but the one who denies that Jesus is the Christ? This is the antichrist, the one who denies the Father and the Son.

—1 John 2:21–22

I saw the pastor across the room, smiling from ear to ear, as a crowd of people circled him. As I scanned the room, I couldn't quite believe it. It was like any other Sunday after church. People flooded into the reception hall, grabbed their coffee and pastry, and chatted away like nothing had happened.

But something did happen.

I was there. I saw it. I heard it. It struck me so hard I could barely breathe. Part of me wanted to stand up in protest. Another part of me was so paralyzed by fear that I couldn't move. I waited for some kind of reaction—maybe a mumbling of voices or sounds of booing or people getting up to leave—but it didn't come. Everyone seemed content to hear what they were hearing. It horrified me.

Will somebody please tell me that what just happened didn't actually happen?

Because if it did, I just lost my job.

I'd been on the church staff nearly eight months as a youth minister. I was in my mid-twenties and wanted, more than anything, to pastor a church one day.

"Father Jerry," as he liked to be called, was happy to take me under his wing. He'd been at the church nearly ten years and people adored him. He had a robust compassion that made people feel loved and special. Mix that with his professorial looks and doctoral degree, and he commanded respect. Better yet, he knew how to run a church. He was a consummate professional in leading church services, business meetings, hospital visits, fund-raisers, high-profile funerals, press interviews, and even children's sermons. As a result, the church gained stature in the community and grew in leaps and bounds.

He did it all really, really well.

At first, I was grateful he agreed to mentor me. But as time passed, I grew uneasy. I couldn't put my finger on it but I knew something was wrong. For example, he'd say things to me privately under his breath—things that questioned the existence of God and challenged key doctrines of the Bible. Other times, he'd comment on how attractive a woman looked, what she was wearing, or how she'd styled her hair. He'd tell me things about her—past indiscretions, secrets shared in the privacy of his office—things I wished he'd never said. And he always added, "Now, remember, that's just between us."

I'd nod and not say anything. He'd smile back as if this sidebar chatter was somehow normal for colleagues in ministry.

It made my heart ache.

One day we had lunch with a fellow pastor in town. "It's hard, I tell you," Father Jerry said midway through the meal. "People want to believe that God is static and unchanging so the way He was a thousand years ago is the way He is today. They don't understand that He is evolving just the like the rest of us!"

"You keep saying 'He,'" the other pastor mocked. "You mean, 'She,' right!"

They laughed, expecting me to laugh too.

But I couldn't. I looked right at Father Jerry and said, "I actually believe He is unchanging. It's what the Bible says about Him. It's how He spoke His name to the people of Israel when they were suffering. He said His name is 'I AM WHO I AM' which means He is not trapped inside time. He's both outside time in eternity and inside time with us. He is the beginning and the end. I believe that" (see Ps. 102:27; Mal. 3:6; Heb. 13:8).

The other pastor shook his head, as if sad for me, but didn't say anything.

"Please don't tell me you're a Bible thumper," Jerry said pointedly. "You're far too educated for that! You have got to know the Bible was written in primitive times by primitive people who talked about a primitive God. We've advanced. God has advanced. Times have changed and you have got to change too."

I watched the two pastors lift their drinks to toast my coming enlightenment. "Don't worry," the other pastor encouraged, "You'll get all this in seminary."

Something was wrong. Really, really wrong.

Because no lie is of the truth. Who is the liar but the one who
denies that Jesus is the Christ? This is the antichrist,
the one who denies the Father and the Son.

—1 JOHN 2:21–22

So what happened that infamous Sunday morning? Father Jerry was preaching, his voice clear and soothing. His wit and charm endearing. He told us he wanted us to live as modern Christians, think as modern Christians, and believe as modern Christians.

Modern was the word. He said it over and over again.

"And modern thinking has to replace past thinking," he said. "We cannot be locked so deep in the past that we never arrive in the present and never find courage to change the future. Things change. We change. And God wants us to change. For that to happen we need to challenge what we think we believe."

Then came the bomb.

"Today, historians and theologians are clear," he went on. "The first Christians needed Jesus to rise from the dead. It was the only way they could substantiate their claim that He was the promised Christ. Today, we know that's not true. Jesus did not physically rise from the dead. It's a myth. It's always been a myth. But He did teach us about the kingdom of God. He did teach us about eternal life. He did give us hope."

I looked around. No one moved. They sat riveted to their chairs, mesmerized by the eloquence of the preacher. I didn't understand it. I wanted someone to have the courage to stand up and shout, "No! It's a lie!" But no one did.

My heart was racing. Should I do it? Should I stand and let the church know that "Jesus is the Christ—absolutely! He died for us. He rose for us. Every Christian born again in Christ knows that." But I didn't. I was young and scared. I knew if I said anything I'd lose my job then and there. Instead, I sat frozen, unable to move, having no idea what to do next, and feeling ashamed of my fears.

But this I knew. I'd have to say something soon. I could not remain silent.

How could I stay in a church where the pastor publicly testifies that Jesus is not the Christ, nor did He physically rise from the dead? I can't. I won't.

But what about my job? What will I do? How will I provide for my family? I sat there scared and alone. I knew the elders of the church would never support me. They'd defend their beloved pastor without question. No, I knew how this story would play out. If I said anything, I'd likely lose everything.

Six months later, almost to the day, I received a letter from Father Jerry. In it was a newspaper ad sponsored by a local church that read: "We believe the cross of Jesus Christ saves!"

He'd scribbled a little note at the bottom, "See, there are others just like you!"

It was the last I heard from him. All these years later and I still remember the sequence of events as if it were yesterday. I did what I said in my heart I'd do. I went to him the day after that horrible Sunday morning and told him I utterly and completely disagreed with him. His reaction surprised me.

"I want you to preach in a few Sundays. Will you do that for me?" he asked.

In hindsight, I think he saw me as someone he could change. I accepted his offer and did the only thing I knew to do. I called our local bishop and told him my dilemma. He urged me to stay focused, be gentle, and promise one thing.

"Preach the text and tell them about Jesus," he advised.

And I did. As best I could. The next day, Father Jerry fired me. He did it nicely, compassionately, and with pity in his heart for me. He said I was narrow-minded and feared for the people who'd have to listen to me in the future.

I didn't say anything. I simply got up to leave.

But deep inside my heart, I didn't understand. How can a Christian pastor be a Christian pastor and not personally know Jesus as Lord and Christ? How can he stand in front of the church and not tell people the truth? I didn't get it.

Why doesn't he know that he doesn't know?

And with that, I left his office and began looking for a new job.

QUESTIONS FOR REFLECTION

The mark of the antichrist is all around us. John taught us to hear, learn, and be aware. How do we handle those in the church who say they are Christians but deny the very essence of our Christian faith? In love, from love, what do we do?

It's always been true: confessing Jesus—who He is, what He has done for us—can result in conflict and suffering and persecution. Is this witness strong in you? Are you ever ashamed to speak His name, and if so, why?

27

MY BROTHER'S HEART

Reflections on 1 John 2:22–23

*This is the antichrist, the one who denies the Father and
the Son. Whoever denies the Son does not have the Father;
the one who confesses the Son has the Father also.*

—1 JOHN 2:22–23

Tuesday night, September 4, at 9:15, my older brother
sent me a text: "The mystery of the Trinity is what is coming
in our conversations." I read it and agreed.

For four months, we'd been in conversation nearly every
day by phone or text. It was new for us. We'd never been
very close, but a few years back that changed for the better.
He started coming to family events. We started calling each
other more. This past year it changed again when a team
of doctors told him he had an aggressive cancer that gave
him months, possibly a year, to live.

"I want to talk Bible," he told me soon after the diagnosis.

And we did. We spent hours on the phone over the
summer—sharing our lives and moving from one passage
of the Bible to another. Sometimes he'd write, "I need time
today. Where should we go in the Bible?" Other times he'd
write, "I need to talk about these verses. Call me?" And we

did. But he had one ground rule that was nonnegotiable and he held to it with a fierce determination.

"It has to be about the heart," he demanded, "not the head."

All summer, in and out of hospitals and doctor offices, some days good, some days not, and still he texted or called. I found him as passionate in pursuing a relationship with the Lord as with me. The more he engaged, the more I did too. The more he opened his heart to me, the more I opened my heart to him.

It felt like we were young again, out for a jog, running side by side.

And now he wanted to talk about "the mystery of the Trinity." A few days prior, he'd asked me to e-mail him the ancient creeds of the church, which I did.[1] But I feared we'd end up talking about it theologically from the head and not relationally from the heart. I decided to text him my concern.

"You know, this conversation, above all others, is about profound intimacy."

He already knew that. "Agreed," he wrote back.

To me, my brother Gregor is brilliant. He's a philosopher, scholar, businessman, and visionary who believes he can change the world for the better. And he does. He has an amazing gift of challenging the ways we think—and companies think—so that we come face-to-face with how our decisions and actions affect the people around us both now and for generations to come. He does it so well.

I love him so much. He has a passion inside him like few I've ever met.

But with all his gifting, the hardest thing for him in life has been relationships. Down through the years, he suffered through a series of broken marriages and friendships that left him hurt and scarred. He has always been quick to blame himself. He spent a ton of money and years in counseling to figure it out.

And now, in the midst of this horrible disease, it's what he thinks about. He wants to get right with the people in his life. He wants to get right with God.

He wants me to help.

But all I want to do is tell him, "I'm sorry."

You see, when we were children, our family went to church pretty regularly. As part of the service, we recited the Apostles' Creed or the Nicene Creed. We said we believed in God the Father, God the Son, and God the Holy Spirit, one God yet three distinct Persons in perfect unity.[2] We never questioned it.

But one day a friend pulled me aside and asked me if I understood it. "Do you know God? Do you have a personal relationship with Jesus Christ?"

I had no idea what he was talking about.

My brother left home and tossed church aside. He had no use for it. For him, Christianity was nothing more than a set of rules and creeds that made no impact on his life. It was different for me. I stayed in church and never left because a friend came alongside and helped me understand.

He helped me step into a personal relationship with Jesus Christ. And with each step, I experienced the love of God flooding into my soul (Rom. 5:5). I knew — without knowing how I knew — that to know the Son is to know the Father and to know the Father is to know His Son. I couldn't explain the mystery of the Trinity, but I had the smallest taste of it right at the center of my heart. For the first time in my life, I knew what it meant to pray the words, "Abba, Father."

I had somehow miraculously become part of His family.

And now, after all these years, I was filled with a painful sadness. How is it possible that I never did with my brother what my friend did with me?

I say it to him over the phone. I wonder if he understands. "I'm so sorry."

This is the antichrist, the one who denies the Father and the
Son. Whoever denies the Son does not have the Father;
the one who confesses the Son has the Father also.

— 1 JOHN 2:22–23

"This isn't easy for me," I say.

He wants to know why.

I tell him not everyone in the church agrees. I explain that early on, I was reprimanded by clergy and Christian leaders. They told me I spoke too openly and too emphatically about Jesus Christ and what He'd done in my life. They said I offended them. They said I was arrogant.

I soon found out these church leaders boasted in being "inclusive." They said they believed in God. They believed in the Trinity. But at the same time, they also believed other world religions were equally right and it was wrong to think only Christians have access to God now and to heaven when we die.

It didn't matter that these same religions deny the deity of Jesus Christ.

They brand me as rigid, narrow, and "exclusive." I am labeled "evangelical," "fundamentalist," and marginalized as someone "outside the mainstream."

I try again. I tell them I believe the Bible is right. Jesus Christ is God. He came among us, died for our sins and rose for our salvation. There is, I say, by the decree of the Father, no other name that saves. It is Jesus and Jesus alone (Acts 4:12).

It doesn't work. They oppose me, and I don't know why.

"Am I telling you too much?" I ask my brother.

"No," he urges. "I need to hear this."

I tell him about the Antichrist. I tell him the Devil's work is simple. He blocks us from knowing God relationally, in our hearts, minds, and souls. He doesn't want the greatest news the world could ever hear to pierce us: We are invited into the relationship of the Trinity.

I take my brother to these verses in 1 John: "This is the antichrist, the one who denies the Father and the Son. Whoever denies the Son does not have the Father; the one who confesses the Son has the Father also" (2:22–23).

He says quietly, "This is beautiful."

And I realize a bittersweet world is opening up for him. His heart has known too many broken relationships. He has borne the guilt of it nearly all his life. He has searched long and hard for the secret of how to do relationships right. And here, in these last days, the answer comes.

It is found in God.

He sends me a text on my phone. It is short, but it is my brother's heart. "I want to know Christ."

QUESTIONS FOR REFLECTION

There is order here. Our relationship with the Father and the Son, by the Spirit, must be right for all other relationships to be right. He must be first, always first. Is He, today, for you?

It's here, in this order, that we find the power to heal broken relationships. The Devil rips apart. We end his tyranny when we ask Jesus Christ to be Lord over the brokenness. What would that look like in your life?

NOTES

1. Specifically, I sent the Apostles' Creed, Nicene Creed, and Athanasian Creed.

2. This is beautifully expressed in a portion of the Athanasian Creed:

And the catholic faith is this: That we worship one God in Trinity, and Trinity in Unity; neither confounding the persons nor dividing the substance. For there is one person of the Father, another of the Son, and another of the Holy Spirit. But the Godhead of the Father, of the Son, and of the Holy Spirit is all one, the glory equal, the majesty coeternal.

28

THE ANGEL'S SONG

Reflections on 1 John 2:24–25

As for you, let that abide in you which you heard from the beginning. If what you heard from the beginning abides in you, you also will abide in the Son and in the Father. This is the promise which He Himself made to us: eternal life.

—1 John 2:24–25

Friday night, September 7, I asked my brother, "What are you afraid of?"

He looked me straight in the eyes and said, "I don't want to die."

We were in the emergency room a half hour from his house in Vermont. The doctors believed my brother had another infection near the surgical sight where they'd removed his cancer. Thank God, they'd gotten all of it. But in the last six weeks, there'd been too many setbacks from the surgery.

It was hard to hear him say, "I don't want to die." We'd talked every day since his diagnosis back in May. Now, for reasons I couldn't explain, I was suddenly aware we'd never talked about death or the fear of what happens to us when we die. I made a mental note to do just that when he got out of the hospital.

A few weeks prior, my wife and I were vacationing in Maine. My brother called and asked, "What are you reading in the Bible today?"

"You really want to know?" I inquired. I was reading in Revelation 3 where the Christians in Laodicea—so full of pride—had cast Jesus out of the church.

As we read it together, my brother jumped at verse 20: "Behold, I stand at the door and knock; if anyone hears My voice and opens the door, I will come in to him and will dine with him, and he with Me" (Rev. 3:20).

"There's beauty here," he said, as if reading it for the first time.

I told him how hard it is to be a Christian pastor these days. We get busy with our churches. We may say the right things, do the right things, but miss what's most important. Jesus Christ wants to dine with us. He wants to spend time with us. But we push Him out the door and sometimes don't even know we've done it.

"That scares me," I admitted to him. "I get so lost in what I do that I can't hear Him knocking, can't hear Him speaking. I don't even realize He's outside."

My brother was quiet.

Finally he said, "I'm scared to open the door."

He said he didn't feel worthy of it. He'd done too many things wrong. There was too much guilt in his life, too many broken relationships, too much of his life wasted on things that, in the end, have no meaning. If he opened the door, he'd be exposed. How could he face himself? How could he face the Lord?

At the same time, this is exactly what he'd hoped for.

He knew God was bigger than what he could grasp with his mind. "Promise me it's about the heart relationship and not just knowledge for the head," he'd say to me time and time again. And now this was it. The invitation real, relational, and profoundly intimate.

The Lord Jesus Christ was knocking on his door. Calling his name.

"Dine with me?" my brother asked, amazed.

A few days passed. The words "Dine with me" had snuck deep into his heart and had become his prayer morning and night.

"I don't know how to open the door," he said, "but I want to." I did what I could to say the right things to help him open it and assure him he'd know when it happens. "You'll feel His presence," I promised. "You'll know He's there with you." The door, the knock, the voice, the invitation had somehow come to life for him.

And for a moment, it seemed it belonged only to him.

As for you, let that abide in you which you heard from the beginning. If what you heard from the beginning abides in you, you also will abide in the Son and in the Father. This is the promise which He Himself made to us: eternal life.

—1 JOHN 2:24–25

"This is going to sound nuts," he texted me. "But last night, I felt the Lord's presence. I could hear the angels singing."

"Not nuts," I wrote back. "Sounds like a door opening."

"Yeah," he said later when he called. "I actually heard their song: 'You have to tell them, you have to go and tell them. . . . We are here.'"

A rush of joy filled my heart. It was as if the angels' song wasn't just for my brother. They wanted me and my family to know too. The door had started to open. The Lord was coming in, and with Him, a host of angels bringing us assurance: "We are here!"

A little while later my brother texted, "You've got to read 1 John 4:4."

It read, "Greater is He who is in you than he who is in the world."

With that, our conversation changed. We slipped away from talking about fearing the intimacy of the Lord Jesus Christ coming in to dine with us and we with Him. We now talked about Jesus abiding in us and we in Him. My brother was suddenly aware that Christ in him was stronger than all the devils that had tormented him in the past.

And more. He now knew by experience that to abide in the Son is to abide in the Father and that this was God's plan for him from before the world began.

Oh what news, the best news ever—"We are here!"

As for you, let that abide in you which you heard from the
beginning. If what you heard from the beginning abides in you,
you also will abide in the Son and in the Father. This is the
promise which He Himself made to us: eternal life.

— 1 JOHN 2:24–25

I didn't fully understand what was going on.

My brother asked about the angels. "This is all so new to me," he said. I gave him passages in the Bible. I told him they attend the Lord and where He is, they are, and they serve as messengers at His direction. I didn't think to say more. I didn't think to tell him the angels attend the saints when they die (see Luke 16:22). Nor did I know why we never talked about death or what happens to us when we die.

I wish we had. But we didn't. And now, here I stood in the emergency room on Friday night, September 7, hearing my brother say, "I don't want to die." We should have talked about it.

"I don't want you and Kate [our sister] to suffer like this," he urged. "I don't know why it's happening to me, but I'm going to do everything I can to get better."

I grabbed his hand and said, "You've got an infection. The doctor seems confident he caught it in time. We'll get through this. It's a setback, that's all."

My brother nodded but I could tell he was afraid—really afraid.

I look back at that night and realize I had no clue what was about to happen. Some fifteen hours later, the infection would storm my brother's major organs. He'd go into septic shock, cardiac arrest, and then into intensive care where he did everything he could to get better as we prayed for a miracle.

And the miracle came . . . just not as we'd hoped.

On Wednesday night, September 26, my brother told his wife that he was ready. It was time. The fear was gone—finally, miraculously, gone. We have no idea how it happened. The fear had been so strong in him. But not now. Not anymore.

With that, a little while later the door opened. The angels came with their song. And my brother left us, holding in his heart a promise from above.

"This is the promise which He Himself made to us: eternal life" (1 John 2:25).

QUESTIONS FOR REFLECTION

So often, we run from intimacy. Are you able to hear Jesus knocking on the door? Can you open it, let Him come in, and let Him dine with you today? What are you afraid of most?

The beauty of this intimacy is that He's not only "with us" but "in us" (see John 14:17; 15:1–5). What does that mean to you? How does it affect your daily relationship with Him?

29

FREE FALL

Reflections on 1 John 2:26–28

*These things I have written to you concerning those who are
trying to deceive you. As for you, the anointing which you
received from Him abides in you, and you have no need for
anyone to teach you; but as His anointing teaches you about
all things, and is true and is not a lie, and just as it has taught
you, you abide in Him. Now, little children, abide in Him.*

—1 John 2:26–28

A friend called the other day.

"I get enough of it in the world," he said, infuriated.
"People taking sides, talking behind my back, lying to my
face. One day they're your best friend; next day they won't
talk to you, and the next, they're writing hateful e-mails. I
hate it. It hurts me. But I get it, and I expect this kind of
behavior in the world."

His voice increases in volume and intensity.

"But not here," he thunders. "Not in church. Not among
Christians."

I listen. His church is being torn apart, and he feels like
there's nothing he can do about it. He tells me story after
story of things said, things done, that we who belong to
Jesus should never say or do. He's outraged, disgusted, and
brokenhearted. He wants me to say something. Anything.
Just to ease the pain.

But how do I do that? If only I could tell him the church is a safe place, the Devil and his forces of evil only torment the world, never the church. But it's not true. Satan does everything to break in, wreak havoc, and tear us apart.

So I do the only thing I know to do. I tell him a story he already knows.

These things I have written to you concerning
those who are trying to deceive you.

—1 JOHN 2:26

"Do you remember the day he resigned?" I asked. A mutual friend of ours had surprised us both. He left his job with no job in front of him, no financial means to support his family at home let alone two kids in college.

"Yeah I do," he said, reluctant to change the subject.

It had startled us both. Our friend had what many of us long for—a Christian as a boss. He believed in him. He spent time in prayer with him. He built up confidence that his boss's single passion for excellence in the company was driven by a greater desire to bring glory to God in everything they did.

He loved his job. He spent years at the company. He'd still be there today. But something happened; he had no idea what. It was as if one day a switch went off and the boss who loved him became the boss who hated him. Not just hated him, but with force came against him.

At first, indirectly. His boss talked about him to others, saying things that were not true. Then, passively. He noticed his boss was avoiding him, unwilling to make eye contact, cancelling meetings, turning the opposite direction as he came close. And then openly, publicly, in front of others. His boss unleashed volleys of wrongful accusations that embarrassed and hurt him.

What had he done to deserve this?

He made an appointment to see his boss in private. He was confident, if they could meet face-to-face and talk it out, they'd get to the bottom of it. He knew to do what Christians do. He assumed a posture of humility. No matter what it was, he was ready to accept responsibility for the break in their relationship. Ready to say sorry. Ready to make right what had gone so terribly wrong.

Just one meeting, he thought, that's all he needed. Worst case scenario? Even if he gets fired, at least he'll know what he did. He'll have the chance to ask for forgiveness and get right with his boss. If he has to leave, then he'll leave in the peace of Jesus Christ. That's what he prayed for. But that's not what happened, His boss, fuming with anger, refused to talk and refused to reconcile.

Weeks passed. Months passed. And the story only got worse.

He went back a second time. Third time. Fourth, fifth, and sixth time. Every time, his boss refused him.

Despair quietly settled over his soul.

If only his boss was a man of the world, he'd understand. But when it happens between Christians, it's different. The pain is different. How's he supposed to go to work every day? Everyone knows the story. What kind of witness is that? What does he do? How does he act in a way that honors Jesus in the midst of it?

He spent hours with his wife talking and praying. They sought counsel from elders and friends. They fasted. They poured over the pages of Scripture. They begged the Lord to keep their hearts free from bitterness. They chose to speak well of his boss, to bless and not curse.

But despair is a horrible disease.

It steals something from us. Like a thief ransacking our hearts, hope is gone. Hope our prayers will be answered. Hope the Lord will step in and change the story somehow. Hope our suffering will soon end. Without hope, a terrifying darkness takes its place that spirals the soul into a deep, dark, black hole.

It's hard to get up every day. It's hard to do what's expected of us.

It's hard to do anything.

And, for a moment, we thought despair won. We heard that our friend had gone to his boss and resigned his position saying, "It doesn't honor the Lord for us to work together unreconciled." We also heard that his boss accepted his resignation with no attempt to make things right in Christ. It was over.

He had no job. He had no means to support his family. To make things worse, his suffering didn't come from the world. It came from a brother in Christ.

As for you, the anointing which you received from Him abides
in you, and you have no need for anyone to teach you; but as
His anointing teaches you about all things, and is true and is
not a lie, and just as it has taught you, you abide in Him.

—1 JOHN 2:27

There was silence on the other end of the phone.

"You still there?" I asked.

There was a slight pause before I heard, "Yeah, I'm here. And I get it." I didn't need to finish the story. We both knew how it ended. The Lord stood with our friend and his wife. He saw them through the worst of times. Despair did not win the day; the Lord did. And in the midst of it, our friend taught us so much.

"What happened to us should never have happened," our friend told us. "Christians are never to treat each other this way. Never! But the fact is, it does happen and it leaves us with a choice of how we'll respond. I can tell you that there were a lot of days my wife and I didn't respond well. We did our best to hold on to Jesus. But something would happen— a phone call, an e-mail, a run-in with the boss—and we'd find ourselves in a free fall, saying things we shouldn't say, doing things we shouldn't do. And every time that happened—the Lord is so faithful—we found one thing to be absolutely true. It wasn't our grasp of Him that mattered first. It was His grasp of us that made the difference."

"I love that," I said, before hanging up the phone. "The Lord abides in us. That comes first and gives us the strength to abide in Him right back. It's the perfect order."

"I agree," he said. "And it gives me the one thing I needed today. I have hope now. Even the tiniest bit. The Lord will stand with our church. He will see us through . . . no matter what happens."

QUESTIONS FOR REFLECTION

The promise is that this anointing of the Holy Spirit is going to teach us how to handle life's hardest problems (see John 14:26). How do you find Him in the midst of free fall?

This verse is also written for the Christian community. This anointing, this teaching, is found as we come together for counsel and prayer. Do you have people around you bringing faith and hope? How do you help others in free fall?

30

SHAME

Reflections on 1 John 2:28–29

Now, little children, abide in Him, so that when He appears,
we may have confidence and not shrink away from Him in shame
at His coming. If you know that He is righteous, you know that
everyone also who practices righteousness is born of Him.

—1 JOHN 2:28–29

A secret is whispered here.

If you know Him, if you're born of Him . . . those trying to deceive you won't win the day. Maybe for a short time. But they never the win the day.

Never! Not if you're truly "born of Him."

And that is Clara's story. She knows something's wrong. It's like this little window pops open and, for a split second in time, she can look out and see clearly. She can think clearly. She gets what's going on. She knows she's made the wrong decision—and why.

Bam! The window slams shut. By her own hand.

She willfully slams it, locks it, and turns away. She pushes what she saw out of her mind. She rehearses her lines. Like a lawyer training for a closing argument, she states her case. She justifies her position. She refuses to give in. She has to keep moving. Before the window opens again.

And tells her what she already knows.

Something's wrong.

If only she could slam shut the voice of her best friend, Emma.

"Come on Clara, you're walking in idolatry and you know it," Emma snapped. "Why did he choose you, can you tell me that? And why did you say yes?"

It took weeks for Clara to push those words out of her head. She had barely talked to Emma since. They'd been best friends for over a decade and now she couldn't stomach the sight of her—or even the thought of her.

Of course, Emma was partly right. The senior pastor had called Clara and asked her to chair a committee that rallied political support to keep him in office.

"You're the one I want," he said definitively, boosting her confidence. "The Lord has given you all the gifts I need 'for such a time as this'! Will you do it, Clara? Will you stand by me like you and Bill have done all these years?"

"Yes," she said at once. "Yes, I'd be honored to."

She was perfect for the job. She had her bachelor's in business, master's in public relations, fifteen years in corporate sales, and helped run a successful campaign for a state senator. A shoo-in to chair the pastor's committee.

She'd get the job done quickly, effortlessly.

After all, the pastor had been at the church for decades. He was respected and loved. At the celebration of his twenty-fifth anniversary, the testimonies that poured in were astonishing. He had faithfully preached Jesus. He had opened the Bible and made it come alive in the hearts of a generation. The applause of that night, by his own insistence, belonged to his Savior and Lord.

But things changed after that. Changed for the worse.

He didn't steal money. He didn't have an affair. He didn't do anything indecent or immoral. But what he did should never have been done.

He changed the focus. Rather than pointing to the glory of God, he began to point to himself. Slowly, almost imperceptibly, he started taking center stage. In his preaching, there were too many stories about him. In his leading, there was too much emphasis on, "This is where I want to take the church."

And somehow, in these days, he started demanding loyalty—loyalty to his vision, loyalty to him. Those who were for him found his favor. Those who were against him found his wrath.

"This is not the man we knew before," Emma insisted to Clara.

"He hasn't changed," Clara barked back. "You have."

"You know that's not true, Clara. Look around you. People are upset. They don't understand what's happening. You and me, we can't even talk to each other anymore. Do you think that's pleasing to the Lord? I can tell you, I don't!"

"Yeah, well, I'm not the one leading the rebellion against our pastor. You are!"

"Rebellion?" Emma gasped, hit by the force of Clara's words.

"Yeah, go home and think about it, Emma. You're the one causing all the problems—you and those with you—and you're too blind to even see it."

Now, little children, abide in Him, so that when He
appears, we may have confidence and not shrink away
from Him in shame at His coming. If you know that
He is righteous, you know that everyone also who
practices righteousness is born of Him.

—1 JOHN 2:28–29

It woke Clara in the middle of the night. It woke her and
scared her.

It was a dream. That's all it was. But it was more than
a dream. It felt real to her. She could hear footsteps outside
her bedroom door. Someone was there and not just anyone.
She knew who it was. She wanted to run and hide. Her
heart was racing. She had to act and act fast. But where
could she go?

She didn't want Him to see her.

She immediately sat up, fully awake, fully expecting
the Lord to open the door and come in. But He wasn't
there. She knew that now. She was dreaming. It wasn't real.
None of it was. But it felt real. She still felt scared. Scared
of Him. Scared He could see what she was doing, and she
didn't want that. She was too embarrassed and ashamed.
What she was doing was wrong. She knew that now. She
knew it in every part of her being.

It was just a dream. Thank God, it was just a dream. She
leaned back, put her head on the pillow again and realized

she was only fooling herself. He did know. He could see. There was no place to run. No place to hide.

And a blush quietly washed over her soul.

Just past 9:00 the next morning, she called Emma.

Emma heard the phone ring, looked at the caller-id and debated whether to answer it. Everything inside her wanted to ignore it but she didn't.

"Hey, got a minute?" Clara asked softly.

"What do you want, Clara? Please don't tell me you're trying to get my vote for next week's meeting."

"No, Emma, nothing like that."

"So what is it?" Emma asked, her voice sounding mad.

"I want to talk for a while, like we used to. I miss that, Emma. I miss you."

Emma took a deep sigh. There was nothing in her that trusted Clara right now. She'd done more dirty campaigning than anyone else on the committee. Still, Clara's voice sounded surprisingly good to her. Like the old Clara.

"Yeah, me too. I wish none of this had ever happened."

"Yeah, well I think a lot of it is my fault, Emma. I knew something was wrong. If it had the power to tear you and me apart, you'd think I'd be smart enough not to be part of it. But I wasn't and I'm sorry."

Emma was silent, strangely at a loss for words.

"I haven't figured it all out," Clara openly confessed. "All I know is that I've hurt my brothers and sisters in Christ. And worse, I've hurt and offended the Lord and it has to stop right now. I have to do everything I can to put things right."

With that, Clara did what she swore she wasn't going to do. She told her best friend the story of last night's dream, the feeling of shame that was still aching deep in her heart and the sense of hope she had when morning finally came. She knew—she finally knew—what she had to do.

"You're my first call, Emma. My first call!"

QUESTIONS FOR REFLECTION

Are you ready for the Lord to come today? Are you doing what you shouldn't be doing? Are there areas in your life you'd feel shame and shrink back?

The Lord is kind to bring these areas to mind. Do you have people like Emma in your life—always calling you, urging you, to practice what's right in Him? How do you do this for others?

31

MIRACULOUS CHILD

See how great a love the Father has bestowed on us,
that we would be called children of God; and such we are.

—1 JOHN 3:1

Clara stood at the window, her purse still slung over her shoulder as if she was debating whether to stay. She'd called Robbie late Friday afternoon to see if she could drop by first thing Monday morning. It seemed right then.

Not so much now.

Robbie was like her go-to mom. She'd basically raised her in Christian faith, counseled and prayed her through multiple crises, and did what never ceased to surprise her— love her through it all.

Would she love her now?

"I've totally messed up. I think you know that," Clara said, as Robbie came into the living room and handed her a cup of coffee.

"Yeah, I figured that's why you called."

In a flurry of words, Clara recounted the past months quickly—chairing a campaign at church, rallying support around a cause she fiercely believed in, feeling the rush of working with a pastor she adored and an amazing team of respected elders. She was in her sweet spot, doing what she was trained to do.

"I did it well," she stated coldly, looking straight at Robbie who had settled into her favorite spot on the sofa. "I convinced myself I was doing what was right for me, right with God, and right for the church."

Clara's voice trailed off, her bravado gone.

A comfortable silence fell between them. A few minutes passed and Clara walked toward Robbie, put her purse on the coffee table and sat next to her. With tears brimming in her eyes, she shook her head in crazed disbelief.

"I can't believe it, Robbie. I can't believe how many people I've hurt."

See how great a love.

—1 JOHN 3:1

They sat in Robbie's living room and slowly unpacked the story piece by piece. Clara was convinced she had committed the unforgiveable sin in which there is no return, no forgiveness, and no hope. She was, at times, inconsolable.

"I pushed Him away," Clara grieved.

She saw herself as an addict, racing for her substance of choice behind closed doors where no one could see.

Every time she administered the drug, she knew it was wrong. She was hurting the people she loved, hurting God, hurting herself. But she did it anyway. She didn't care. She craved the satisfaction.

"What kind of Christian does that, Robbie? Answer me that, huh?"

Robbie sidestepped the question. "Tell me more about the drug," she pushed.

As best as she could, Clara told her there was something sinister, something ugly down deep inside her begging for approval. "It's like I'll do anything to get it. It's been there as long as I can remember. So when the pastor tapped me to chair his task force, I leapt at it. It made me feel recognized and important again. I can't tell you how good it felt when he called me or wanted to meet with me. It made me want to do everything he asked. If he said, 'Go to the left!' I went left. If he said, 'Go to the right!' I went right. It didn't matter. I'd do it every time just to get his attention. And then the whole crowd around him would applaud and cheer me on. You want to know my drug of choice? That's it!"

Robbie sat quiet, nodding. She understood.

"So when my friend Emma came to me and told me I was tearing the church into pieces; I was hurting people we've known, loved, and worshiped with for decades — people who love Jesus — I turned against her. I told her she was wrong and spat out the words, 'It's over, Emma, for good. We're through.' And I didn't care, Robbie. I didn't care."

Clara stopped, the tears came rushing back. She reached over to Robbie, grabbed her hand, and said exactly what she needed to say.

"I wanted the drug more."

The Father has bestowed on us.

—1 JOHN 3:1

Clara had already taken first steps.

She had gone to the pastor, resigned her position, and removed herself from the crowd hotly pursuing his dreams. She had gone to Emma and asked her forgiveness, as well as a few others. The list would take a while. And she'd called Robbie. These were things she could do, things still in her control. It was what wasn't in her control that seized her insides and sent her into a state of panic.

"It's not the drug. It's me," she blurted out. "There's rebellion in me. Willful rebellion. How many times did the Lord tell me to stop? Stop because I was offending Him. I was hurting His people. I was tearing His church apart. And I said no to Him! For months on end, and I didn't care."

Clara's eyes were wide open, dumbfounded at herself.

"Christians don't do that, Robbie. People who love Jesus don't do that to Him. They follow Him, they don't turn away and spit in His face just to get their needs met. But that's what I did. I thought I was a Christian, but now

I know I'm not. There's something wrong with me. Really, really wrong."

With that, she fell into Robbie's arms and sobbed.

That we would be called children of God; and such we are.

—1 JOHN 3:1

As she held Clara in her arms, Robbie quietly prayed over her until her crying slowly subsided. Robbie knew it was time to speak the promises of God into her life.

"You are here this morning, Clara, and that tells me everything I need to know. You heard His voice. You heard it the whole time. And you've said yes to Him."

"No, I shut Him out," Clara lamented.

"Yeah, for a while. And every time you shut Him out, you knew you were doing it. You knew it was wrong. You knew there was no peace in your heart. And you kept going, and kept going, and all the while He was speaking to you."

Clara looked at her, puzzled, not understanding.

"You are His child, Clara. You've been born of God. You've received Him and, as the Bible says, 'As many as received Him, to them He gave the right to become children of God, even to those who believe in His name'" (John 1:12).

"No," Clara said emphatically.

"Yes," Robbie returned. "That's why you're here. It's why you resigned your post. It's why you're meeting with people you've hurt. You've heard His voice and said yes to Him. And the first thing we do when we say yes is to turn from our wrongdoing, say sorry, receive His forgiveness through the blood of His Son, and then take steps to make things right again."

"You're forgetting the rebellion in me. I knew what I was doing," Clara replied.

"I know you did. And I know you've got a drug problem," Robbie said, with a semi-teasing smile. "But that's something Jesus Christ wants to set you free from."

"I want that."

"Do you think He will do that for you?"

"No, to be honest, not after all this," Clara admitted.

"Well, I think He will. Actually, I know He will because He loves you, Clara. That's why He pursued you all these months and never stopped. You are a miraculous child of the Father, born by His saving power and He never let you go. That same power will deal with the ugly stuff inside you if you'll let Him."

Clara nodded, and took a deep breath. For the first time in a long time, she felt the peace of God well up in her heart again. It didn't make any sense to her, not after what she'd done, but somehow that didn't matter. Not now, not today. She let it come—and let it come more—and prayed it would never leave.

QUESTIONS FOR REFLECTION

Too often, we let sin reign in our lives. We push away the Father's pursuing love, which calls us to face our sin and begin real, clear steps of repentance. Can you talk about the promise in 1 John 3:1 as it relates to your quiet rebellions?

The mark of being a miraculous child of God is that we love one another. So why do we allow broken relationships to continue? How can you let this promise of 1 John 3:1 make a difference?

32

FINDING HOPE

~~~

Reflections on 1 John 3:2–3

Beloved, now we are children of God, and it has not appeared as yet what we will be. We know that when He appears, we will be like Him, because we will see Him just as He is. And everyone who has this hope fixed on Him purifies himself, just as He is pure.

—1 JOHN 3:2–3

Weeks had passed, and then a month or two.

Clara had climbed out of crisis mode and fallen back into a normal routine. Work was slow but steady, her children—both in their early twenties—were dealing with more stress at school than usual. They were calling almost daily. Her husband, Bill, continued to be her prince. He somehow knew exactly when to be at her side and when to leave her alone, giving her space to heal.

She wanted it behind her—all of it.

Days would come and go, and she'd realize she hadn't thought about it once, not once, and that gave her hope.

The only times it came thundering back is when she'd bump into old Christian friends around town who were still fiercely fighting for their pastor, friends who now felt betrayed by her. Instinctively, she'd reach out to greet them only to find them snap back in anger.

"How could you?" a woman said just yesterday in a grocery aisle. "What you've done is wrong. You're the cause of all the problems at church right now, you know that?"

"No, not wrong," her husband next to her interjected. "What you did was evil."

Every time, it took her breath away. Every time, it made her heart hurt. These were people she'd loved for years, people she'd worshiped Jesus with, prayed with, served in mission with, who now treated her as a dirty leper tossed aside in the garbage. "I can explain," she longed to say with everything inside her.

But it was too late. The time for conversation was over. The church had split, sides were taken, and blame had claimed its victims. All she could do was stand there and watch them walk away.

Beloved, now we are children of God, and it has
not appeared as yet what we will be.

—1 John 3:2

Right after the episode in the grocery store, she wanted to call Emma or Robbie or one of her close friends and tell them what just happened. A month ago, two months ago, that's exactly what she'd have done.

It was different now. People had moved on.

"What did you expect?" Emma said the last time she'd had a confrontation. "It's gonna happen. You have to get used to it and not let it upset you so much."

"Yeah, you're right," Clara had said, noting that Emma's patience with her was slowly running out. The crisis had passed and Emma—like all of her friends—needed to get on with their lives. Clara knew that. At the same time, she knew it wasn't over for her. These confrontations still ripped her heart. She was still grieving.

But why was she still grieving? Why did it hurt so much?

Over dinner, she told the story to Bill. "All our friends expect me to be better now, and I'm not. I don't know why I'm not, but I'm not. I don't mind putting on a face for them. They've been amazing these past months—all of them. It's just that I don't know what to do with myself. I don't know how to get better."

"Yeah, you do," Bill said assuring her. "You've always known."

"Have I?" she quipped, not understanding him.

"Take it to Jesus, Clara," he said softly. "He will help you process all this."

It was, for her, the perfect words at the perfect time. These past months, she'd leaned so heavily on the people around her that she'd barely written in her journal—a note here, a note there—but nothing substantial, never pouring out her heart to Him. This was it. This was exactly what she needed to do.

That night, quiet at her desk, she started.

I feel like I've only had the first round of treatment. I need more. Most of the symptoms are gone. My friends see me as being well again. But I am not. I can feel it under the surface. The disease is still there raging inside me.

Lord, I need Your help.

I felt it yesterday when I ran into Steve and Pat at the grocery story. All they could do was lash out at me and walk away. It was awful. You'd think I'd have enough sense to defend myself but I didn't. I just stood there looking ridiculous.

Everything inside me wanted to scream out, "Why don't you like me anymore?" Or, "Don't you remember? We've been on five or six mission trips together from church. Your son and our daughter dated in high school. You both were in our home group during the time Bill lost his job. You prayed us through. Just like we got to be with you when Pat's sister was dying. We saw the Lord do miraculous things together. How many years has it been? Twenty? Twenty-two? How can you just walk away from me? Why don't you like me anymore?"

I don't know how else to say it. This is the disease inside me and I can't seem to shake it. I need approval. I need to be liked, and I'll do anything for it, anything.

Beloved, now we are children of God, and it
has not appeared as yet what we will be.
We know that when He appears, we will be like
Him, because we will see Him just as He is.

—1 JOHN 3:2

I take this verse to heart. I believe I am Your child. I believe when You appear, I will see You. I will be like You. I want that with all that I am.

My problem is that I have a hard time believing You're at work in me now. I have struggled for so many years with this wretched disease. It's what drove me to do what I did these past months. I wanted the praise of my pastor more than You. I pushed You away. I pushed my friends away. I helped rip the church in two.

All because my need is so strong. Yet, You came to my rescue. You helped me see my sin. You helped me go to the pastor, resign, and step away. You helped me endure his wrath. You helped me go to those I hurt and ask their forgiveness. You helped me see a lifetime of bad decisions all because . . .

I need to be liked.

I thought I was making progress. I thought You were helping me take steps forward. And then yesterday happened. I run in to Steve and Pat and all of it comes flooding back into my soul. I hate this about me. Will it ever end?

Two steps forward. Three steps back.

What do I do next?

In the quiet of her soul, Clara felt herself release the question to the Lord. She didn't know what to do next. She was afraid there was no next, afraid she'd spend the rest of her life controlled by this horrible longing inside her.

"Is this it?" she prayed out loud. "In my past, I know You saved me. You made me Your own. In my future, I know I have the promise of what I will be when I am with You in heaven. But what about now? What do I do next?"

Over the next half hour, she filled her journal with memories of when she'd let her desire to please people get the best of her. She did exactly what Bill had said to do. She was taking it all to Jesus.

"This is me. This has been the story of my life since childhood." She no more wrote these words when she heard a familiar echo inside her.

"But this is Me. This is My story."

Her eyes fell on the next verse. "And everyone who has this hope fixed on Him purifies himself, just as He is pure" (1 John 3:3).

She read it over and over again. This was the answer to her question. This was what she needed to do next—fix her eyes on Jesus. Believe He will work in her now. Believe He will get at the root of the problem. Believe He will take a lifetime of wrong behavior and make it right.

"Yes, Lord, I believe. I believe because that's Your story."

She sat back in her chair and smiled. These weren't just words on a page. She could feel it inside her as if the Lord had just breathed hope into her soul and with it—confidence, real confidence—that tomorrow would be different.

QUESTIONS FOR REFLECTION

It takes courage to come to Jesus and let Him do His work in us today. He's in the business of making us well, "pure." Do you want it? What would it take for you to believe the promises of 1 John 3:2–3 and pursue Him?

Many Christians do not know how to spend time with the Lord, quietly, in prayer, in His Word. Will you ask Him to make these promises in 1 John 3:2–3 real and alive in you?

PART 5

PUTTING INTO PRACTICE

33

SANDY HOOK

Reflections on 1 John 3:4–6

Everyone who practices sin also practices lawlessness;
and sin is lawlessness. You know that He appeared in order to
take away sins; and in Him there is no sin. No one who abides
in Him sins; no one who sins has seen Him or knows Him.

—1 JOHN 3:4–6

He shot and killed his mother.

Then at 9:30 a.m. he shot his way into Sandy Hook Elementary School. Within seconds, someone called 9-1-1. Within minutes, sirens were heard in the distance as first responders descended on the school in force.

By the time they entered the building, the shooter had already killed himself. The school was out of danger, the rampage over. They soon found six educators including the school principal, dead. They'd been shot. No, more than shot—they'd been slaughtered. And then they came upon the unimaginable, the incomprehensible.

He'd killed children, twenty of them, first graders, six and seven years old. It was December 14, 2012. Twenty miles from our home. We will never forget.

Everyone who practices sin also practices
lawlessness; and sin is lawlessness.

—1 JOHN 3:4

There's a basic rule in life: You don't touch our children.

When a military power attacks civilians, unarmed and defenseless, we say it's wrong and cowardly. But how infinitely worse to attack our young. Our Lord has no tolerance for it: "It would be better for him to have a heavy millstone hung around his neck, and to be drowned in the depth of the sea" (Matt. 18:6).

It is sin. It is lawlessness. It is evil.

When Dan Malloy, the governor of the state of Connecticut, arrived in Sandy Hook just hours after the shooting, he said the only thing that could be said: "Evil visited this community today."

This is exactly what President Clinton said in April 1995 when he had to comfort a grieving nation after the Oklahoma bombing: "To all my fellow Americans beyond this hall, I say, one thing we owe those who have sacrificed is the duty to purge ourselves of the dark forces which gave rise to this evil. They are forces that threaten our common peace, our freedom, our way of life."[1]

The president made no attempt to explain the massacre of human lives by focusing on the mental state of the bomber himself. He went deeper. These were "the dark forces" at work in the bomber which "gave rise to this evil." Almost one hundred seventy people died in Oklahoma, nineteen of them were children in a day care.

No matter how often the secular world tosses the Bible aside, at times like these it expresses exactly what we are feeling. Our politicians, in the face of violence, especially when it's our children, rise to the microphone and say what the Bible says.

It is sin. It is lawlessness. It is evil.

Kaitlin Roig was there at Sandy Hook. She was teaching a first-grade class when the shots rang out in the classroom next door. Scared, she did what she had to do. She gave them direction. She led them into the bathroom. She told them she loved them and tried, in simple language, to help them understand.

"It's going to be OK, you're going to be all right . . . be absolutely quiet . . . there are bad guys out there now. We need to wait for the good guys."[2]

It's that simple: There are bad guys out there who have handed themselves over to the Devil to do what he tells them to do. They practice sin. They practice lawlessness. They force the rest of us to struggle "not against flesh and blood, but against . . . the spiritual forces of evil in the heavenly places" (Eph. 6:12).

There are bad guys out there. Evil guys.

You don't touch our children.

You know that He appeared in order to take
away sins; and in Him there is no sin.

—1 JOHN 3:5

The good guys came.

Without the sound of those sirens and the immediate intervention by the first responders, there is no imagining how many more teachers and children would have died that day at Sandy Hook Elementary School.

In the same way, there is no imagining what our lives would be like if the Good Guy Himself did not come to Bethlehem that first Christmas morning.

He is the sound of the siren. He is the One who has come to deal with those who practice sin, lawlessness, and evil. He has come to end the Devil's reign over us—purging us from the dark forces that give rise to evil—and usher in the day of justice.

This is exactly what we need to hear when our children have suffered. President Clinton, in the days after the Oklahoma bombing, urged this point: "Let us teach our children that the God of comfort is also the God of righteousness. Those who trouble their own house will inherit the wind. Justice will prevail."[3]

Justice always prevails in the Lord, whether now or in the time to come, and not only in the massacres of Sandy Hook and the Oklahoma bombing, but in all cases where injustice violates our children, the helpless, the poor, and the outcast.

Thank God, the Good Guy came!

Thank God that we can now see the face of the Shepherd, as described in Psalm 23, standing in "the valley of the shadow of death" (Ps. 23:4). He is there in our suffering. His hands, His feet, His side bear the marks. He died for us. He suffered for us.

The sounds of His siren are loud and unmistakable: Justice always prevails!

No one who abides in Him sins; no one who
sins has seen Him or knows Him.

—1 JOHN 3:6

The world media descended on the little town of Sandy Hook, Connecticut. The outrage over the killings could be heard from every corner of the globe. The response was immediate, the judgment decisive.

You don't touch our children.

But odd as it might sound, as the days and weeks passed after the tragedy, I found myself feeling strangely good about myself and the world I live in. The shooter had proven the point again: There are bad guys out there. This is what they look like. This is what they do. In sharp contrast, I am not like that.

We are not like that.

An avalanche of kindness burst on the little Connecticut town as people gave generously, sacrificially, to comfort the grieving families and community. The nation, the world, mourned as we watched on TV the small caskets taken to the churches and then to the cemeteries. We wept because we care.

There are good guys in this world! This horrible tragedy helped unite us in our outrage, in our fierce determination to protect our teachers and children, and in our resolve to never let this happen again.

There are forces of evil in this world.

There are bad people who do bad things, who practice sin and lawlessness and evil and they must be stopped, no matter what it takes. Oppression must stop. Violence of any kind must cease. Justice must prevail.

And it's not me.

I am no shooter. I am no bomber. I am not one of the bad guys. That's how I felt. For a brief moment in time, it made me feel strangely good about myself. I saw the world through the lens of one of Kaitlin Roig's first-grade students.

Hearing the gunshots. Huddled scared in the bathroom. Praying, waiting for the Good Guy to come from heaven and deal with the bad guy. Having no understanding, none at all, that when He came for the bad guy, the bad guy was me.

QUESTIONS FOR REFLECTION

In 1 John 1:9 and 2:1–2, we know what to do and where to go when we sin. But these verses deal with the choice to sin and keep on relentlessly sinning. Is this a choice you're making in your life?

The deeper our self-awareness in being the bad guy, the deeper our need for a Savior. How do you convince yourself you're better than you really are?

NOTES

1. William Jefferson Clinton, Oklahoma bombing memorial service address, Oklahoma City, OK, April 23, 1995, accessed June 12, 2014, http://www.americanrhetoric.com/speeches/wjcokla homabombingspeech.htm.

2. Kaitlin Roig, interview by Diane Sawyer, *ABC News*, ABC, December 14, 2012.

3. Clinton, Oklahoma memorial service.

34

BAD GUY ME

Reflections on 1 John 3:7–8

*Little children, make sure no one deceives you; the one who
practices righteousness is righteous, just as He is righteous;
the one who practices sin is of the devil; for the devil has
sinned from the beginning. The Son of God appeared for
this purpose, to destroy the works of the devil.*

—1 John 3:7–8

I'd never seen myself as a bad guy.

When I came to saving faith in Jesus Christ, it wasn't
because I was caught doing bad things. It was because my
life was a mess. My mom died when I was sixteen. I was
sent away to a boarding school and had no idea how to
cope with her death, let alone the loss of my family, my
home, and all I held dear. I was scared.

I did my best every day to push down the grief, work
hard and keep my chin up like Mom and Dad had taught
me to do. It worked some days but not very well.

A few years later, a Christian man at college befriended
me. He quickly saw something wasn't right and prodded
me to tell my story. The more I did, the more the pain came
gushing out. My heart was ravaged. I'd lost what I'd never
have again, or at least that's how it felt. I was bitter and
despairing. I had no hope, no passion for life.

It didn't seem possible, but my friend understood. He had a similar story. He knew what it was like to be beaten up and tossed aside. He also told me that he'd found help.

He shared Jesus with me.

As the weeks passed, he introduced me to other Christians. He took me to church. He taught me how to confess and repent of my sins, not just from bad things I'd done but from my sinful nature passed down from the days of Adam.

I listened, believed, and prayed for Jesus Christ to come into my life.

Slowly, He changed me. He put my shattered heart back together and breathed new life into me. The more He did and the more I sensed His presence in my life, the more I saw myself as a sinner—a real, bona fide sinner—saved by Jesus.

But even then, I was clueless.

I still saw myself as a good guy sinner who'd been messed up by life and needed a Savior. In comparison to Him and His holiness, I was a wretched, ungodly man. I knew that. But in comparison to others around me, I was a good guy.

Not a bad guy. Never a bad guy and never "of the devil." God forbid I'd ever be compared to murderers, rapists, Satanists, thieves, addicts, adulterers, cheaters, and liars. That's not me. It's never been me.

Or so I thought.

Little children, make sure no one deceives you; the one
who practices righteousness is righteous, just as He is
righteous; the one who practices sin is of the devil;
for the devil has sinned from the beginning.

—1 JOHN 3:7–8

During my years at seminary, I was sent to a mental
state hospital for three months to serve as a chaplain. I was
assigned to one particular ward that had patients, the doctors told me, who had no hope of getting better.

Most never knew my name.

I met criminals, men who'd been incarcerated for
unthinkable crimes. I met Satan-worshipers, a Juilliard
graduate, a scientist, a school teacher, mothers who hadn't
seen their children in years, and men and women who'd
once lived normal lives and worked normal jobs before
mental illness struck.

My job was to stay with them, listen to them, and pray
for them.

I soon learned to spot the ones who were violent. It
could happen in a split second. Tempers would explode,
fists would fly, people would scream, and violence would
escalate until the security team arrived and doctors were
able to administer treatment. I found myself always on
guard, always watching.

Fearing I was next.

Almost unconsciously, when violence broke out, I'd reach into my pocket and grab my key ring. The same keys that got me into the ward, got me out. I'd feel the urge to run. I'd feel the prejudice rise inside me. I wasn't like them. I was different. They were different. I never thought it, but I felt it. I was better than they were.

And with it came a rush of twisted, crazed emotion. They made me feel good about myself. I felt like I'd done a good thing for God by being with those less fortunate. I felt—in my selfish, arrogant heart—I had the favor of God on me and they didn't.

Little children, make sure no one deceives you; the one who practices righteousness is righteous, just as He is righteous; the one who practices sin is of the devil; for the devil has sinned from the beginning.

—1 JOHN 3:7–8

Near the end of my chaplaincy, a strange thing happened. The men and women on the ward rose up in unison against one of their own. They didn't like the way one of the men coughed, the way he dressed, the way he talked, or anything about him. They laughed at him until he cried, until he ran out of the room crying hysterically.

I decided to follow the man and found him in an adjacent sitting room balled up on a couch.

"Do you know what it's like to be an outcast of outcasts?" he asked me.

I pulled up a chair and sat next to him. I could see he wanted an answer.

"No, I can't imagine it," I said honestly.

"They look down on me," he went on. "They make fun of me. They make me feel like scum. Do you know what it's like to feel like scum?"

I instantly felt uneasy. He was looking at me like I was guilty of treating him the same way, but it wasn't true. I was horrified at what just happened to him.

"No, I don't. I'm sorry you had to go through that . . ."

He interrupted me. He sat up, coughed a deep guttural cough, looked me right in the eyes and said, "God doesn't look down on anyone."

It took my breath away.

"You know what?" he said once, then twice.

"What?"

"Jesus is my only friend. He's all I've got."

With that, he sat back in the couch, balled up, and cried.

The one who practices sin is of the devil;
for the devil has sinned from the beginning.

—1 JOHN 3:8

I didn't move. I couldn't.

I listened to his crying. I watched the tears fall from his eyes. I knew my part in this. I too had done this to him. I had done it to all of them. He'd said it so well.

"God doesn't look down on anyone."

It took an outcast of outcasts to tell me that. I had sinned against the people of this ward. I had sinned against God. I had looked down on them. I had thought myself better than they were. I had thought somehow—in my sinful, evil heart—that God loved me more.

What kind of person am I?

But this had been the practice all my life. There were people I looked up to and there were people I looked down on. I had done exactly what the people of this ward had done to him. I had laughed and mocked and made fun of others.

I was like them. The criminals, the Satan worshipers, the rapists.

I didn't move. I couldn't.

It was the first time I began to see the real me. Not the good guy sinner, but the bad guy sinner. And more than a sinner. The sin I'd practiced and the kingdom I'd belong to was fully and completely "of the devil."

Me? That was me? Bad guy me?

I reached my hand over to his, caught his eye, and told him I was sorry. He nodded his head and said the only words that mattered.

"Jesus is my only friend."

QUESTIONS FOR REFLECTION

Isn't it easy to be deceived—to play down the practice of ongoing sin in our lives? To take no thought of the Devil or his influence over us? John pressed this point. Can you hear it? Can you talk about it?

The deeper we understand these things, the greater we know our need of Jesus, Son of God, who destroys the work of the Devil in our lives. What will it take to ask Him to help you stop the ongoing sins capturing your heart?

35

WALKING WITH JESUS

Reflections on 1 John 3:8–10

*The Son of God appeared for this purpose, to destroy the works
of the devil. No one who is born of God practices sin, because His
seed abides in him; and he cannot sin, because he is born of God.*

—1 JOHN 3:8–9

She came to church after worship began. She left before
it was over. She came alone, sat alone, and did it for months.

"Has anybody met her yet?" I asked a few women after
the service.

"I have. She likes it here," one of them said. "She seems
really nice, very shy. I think she wants to be left alone for
now. Not sure why. She said her name is Maya. I didn't get
her last name."

"I think we give her space," another said. "Tell her we're
here and we care but not push it. Also, we pray for her. She
might be going through a tough time."

"Good plan," I nodded, and we all agreed.

The better part of four months passed. We were about
to begin Sunday morning worship when I heard a question
from behind me.

"Do I have to join this church to come here?"

As I turned to look at her, she took two steps back but she was insistent. "I need to know the rules."

"You're welcome here," I said, recognizing it was Maya. "You don't have to join unless you want to make this your church home. Stay as long as you want."

She smiled a little, turned, and left.

For the next several months she didn't come back. I figured I'd scared her off somehow. But then, one Sunday morning, she reappeared. The women who'd been praying for her went to her, excited to see her. Slowly, ever so slowly and with nearly insurmountable apprehension, Maya let them into her life.

She found shelter. Something she never thought she'd find again.

The Son of God appeared for this purpose, to destroy the works of the devil. No one who is born of God practices sin, because His seed abides in him; and he cannot sin, because he is born of God.

—1 JOHN 3:8–9

It took over two years before Maya felt comfortable telling me her story.

"I'm divorced," she said bluntly, waiting for my reaction. "My husband had God-knows-how-many affairs. After ten years of marriage, I finally took my two children and left. Of course, he blamed me for the breakup. He told me, 'God hates divorce' and, if I left him, I'd be out of God's will for our lives."

"So he's a Christian man?" I asked, puzzled.

"Who knows? You tell me," she shot back sharply. "I thought he was. The elders in the church still think he is even though they know everything."

"They know?" I said, confused. "Does the pastor know?"

"My husband is the pastor."

"What?"

"They love him. Everybody loves him. The elders don't care about his personal life as long as the church keeps filling up Sunday after Sunday. And it does. Tons of college students and young professionals in their twenties. So guess what happens when I find out my husband is sleeping with some of them?"

I don't say anything. I can't imagine it.

"They tell me to keep it quiet. The elders and my husband try to convince me not to divorce him or do anything that would make the news public. They say if it went to the media the church would be torn apart in scandal. My husband promised he'd stop. He'd get counseling. He'd do anything to make the marriage work."

Maya shook her head.

"I couldn't do it. You might not believe this, but I love the Lord. I've loved Him since I was a child. But I wasn't about to live a lie for the sake of the church or my husband's image. Why didn't they fire him when they found out? How could they let him keep preaching?"

She looked at me like she wanted answers, and I didn't have any.

"Then tell me this," she pressed harder. "Are you a Christian if you sin?"

"Depends," I said.

"Depends on what?"

"Depends on whether we stop. Yes, Christians sin. I sin. All of us sin. But the Lord is kind to show us, convict us, and correct us. That's why the apostle John said, 'If we confess our sins, He is faithful and righteous to forgive us our sins' (1 John 1:9; see also 2:1). If we are born of God, if His Spirit lives in us, if we truly love Him, then He helps us. He gives us the power to stop the wrong we're doing."

"And what if you don't stop?" she asked coldly.

"If we keep on, and keep on, and keep on, the Lord tells us we are not born of Him and we have neither seen Him nor know Him" (1 John 3:6; see also 2:29).

No one who is born of God practices sin,
because His seed abides in him; and he cannot sin,
because he is born of God.

—1 John 3:9

Maya took a deep breath and said, "I never thought I'd be part of a church family again. To be dead honest, as much as I love the Lord, I don't trust His people."

"I understand that. So why did you come back?" I asked.

"When I was in college, I developed an eating disorder. I knew it wasn't right but it gave me something I was missing inside. I had friends and family come to me and beg me to stop. I promised I would, but I didn't."

A faint smile crossed her face.

"Ironic, huh? I guess I know something about keeping on, and keeping on, and keeping on doing what I knew the Lord didn't want me doing."

"Yeah, but it sounds like He made it real clear to you," I observed.

"He did. But I refused to stop. And when I finally decided I'd had enough, I couldn't do anything about it. It controlled me."

Maya looked at me, wiping a tear from her eye.

"I needed Jesus to help me. I needed my church to come around me and get me out of it. I couldn't do it on my own. I knew that. That's exactly how the Lord rescued me. And in the same way, it's why I think I need a church family now."

I waited a minute wondering if she was thinking what I was thinking. "So, do you imagine He will do that for your husband?" I asked gently.

"I don't know. He's still sleeping around. He hasn't stopped. So you tell me."

By this the children of God and the children of the devil are
obvious: anyone who does not practice righteousness is
not of God, nor the one who does not love his brother.

—1 JOHN 3:10

Maya found her way into our church family and changed
us all for the better. Over time, she became a champion for
women who'd lost their way, been abused, been beaten
down, and been torn apart inside. She does what others had
done for her. She leads them to Jesus and stays with them
until they're whole again.

She did her best to raise her children to honor their
father. That was the hard part. Her ex-husband lived in a
confused, dark world of preaching the way of Jesus and
practicing the way of the world, flesh, and Devil.

He never stopped.

He hasn't stopped to this day, all these years later.

For Maya, as much as she grieves for the man she once
loved, she holds a gift in her heart she knows will never be
taken from her. The Lord answered her prayers and protected her children. Both of them, now in college, know
Him and love Him.

And more, to her utter delight and joy, they walk with
Him.

QUESTIONS FOR REFLECTION

How is possible to believe in Him, speak of Him, but live our lives like those who know nothing about Him? How do you deal with this?

If we are children of God, born of God, and His seed abides in us, we do not do what the "children of the devil" do. Are you walking like you're talking? Is it clear to everyone around you—by your actions—that you are born again in Jesus Christ?

36

CAIN AND ME

Reflections on 1 John 3:11–13

For this is the message which you have heard from the beginning,
that we should love one another; not as Cain, who was of the
evil one and slew his brother. And for what reason did he slay him?
Because his deeds were evil, and his brother's were righteous.
Do not be surprised, brethren, if the world hates you.

—1 John 3:11–13

I remember the day I was fired like it was yesterday.

I can still feel it, like a knife going straight into my gut. I had been on the job, working with the same team, for years. In my last few months, we'd come to a critical decision point that would set the course for the future. I did then what I'd always done. I raised my voice; I stated my position; I argued my case.

This time, my voice was the lone voice. They were done with me.

The knife slid in quickly, easily. By the time I looked up to see their faces, they were gone. Not just done with me as a worker but done with me as a person. I soon learned the hard truth my heart couldn't bear to hear.

I had value when I was of use. When I had no use, I was of no value.

Maybe it would have hurt less if they weren't Christians, if they didn't know Jesus. But they did know Jesus. He was at the center of everything we did. It's why we worked together so well. It's why we could argue and disagree. We knew the royal law that governs His kingdom and we lived that law. We loved one another. Always (see James 2:8).

Until one day, we didn't.

For this is the message which you have heard from
the beginning, that we should love one another.

—1 JOHN 3:11

I remember my first days as a Christian. Everything felt so different. It was like I'd stepped into a new country, a new culture, where the people of God knew the royal law and lived the law because it was inside them. It was inside me. Just like the Bible says it: The love of God had been poured into my heart through the Holy Spirit (see Rom. 5:5).

Because of it, I was profoundly aware that God loved me.

I knew Jesus had made that love real by what He did on the cross for me. And I knew, by the very nature of this love stirring deep in my soul that it was wildly uncontainable. It was meant for others. Family and friends, yes. Brothers and sisters in Christ, yes.

But more. A thousand times more. It was meant for every race and tribe and tongue and nation, believer or unbeliever, moral or immoral, the kind and gentle or the wicked and evil. It's this, and this alone, that drives Christians to reach every corner of the globe. The Lord has done the great and gloriously unimaginable.

He has made His heart known. We are to love one another as He loved us. That's Him, it's who He is. It's His kingdom. It's everything.

Not as Cain, who was of the evil one and slew his brother.

—1 John 3:12

My wife and I took the knife out ourselves.

It wasn't the first time but it felt like it. The wound was deeper, the pain worse. As the shock wore off and I began to slowly recover, I had every hope I'd be well again. The Lord had helped me before, I believed He'd help me now. He'd shown me what I'd done wrong in the broken relationships of the past.

I believed He'd do the same this time too.

But it didn't go that way. Something dark began to work in me. I had been wronged, betrayed by those I loved and somehow, writhing in the pain of it, I made a decision. Not a conscious, rational decision, but rather one of the heart and soul, forged in secret, a quiet vow—I'd never forgive them—ever.

I never said it out loud to anyone. I never said it to myself. But it was there as sure as the knife was still in my hand.

Without knowing it, I broke into two separate pieces. One man a kingdom man living the royal law. The other man, outside the kingdom, where the law had no rule over me. I was free to break it at will.

And I did—with my words. At first, I chose to be kind, thinking it would honor the Lord. I made a careful distinction, when speaking to others, to oppose the actions of my colleagues and not judge them as brothers and sisters in Christ.

That didn't last long.

The more time passed, the worse it became. I said things I shouldn't have thought, let alone said. I did things, like racing back to the past, digging out old stories that now, cast through the lens of my bitterness-infused pain, made them out to be monsters. The more I tore them apart, the better I felt about myself.

The better I felt about God. He was for me, not them. I was in the right, a law-abiding citizen. They were in the wrong. The royal law we've heard from the beginning didn't apply to me, not here.

And unforgiveness dug in its tentacles. A dark rage sprang up and spread to nearly every area of my life. It was me, not them, holding the knife, stabbing them with my words, hating them with my soul, and begging God not to show mercy on them, but to bestow vengeance.

I didn't understand it then, but I understand it now.

Cain and me . . . we were suddenly best of friends.

Not as Cain . . .

—1 John 3:12

A few months later, I was driving in town talking on my cell phone. I heard a police siren behind me, looked in the rearview mirror, and it was for me. In the time it took to pull over, grab my license, and car registration, and put down the window, I'd mustered my defense. I had my excuses.

"It's illegal in the state of Connecticut to talk on your cell phone while driving," the policeman stated as a matter of record, taking my information.

"I know," I said, tossing all my excuses to the wind. "I'm sorry."

He went back to his patrol car, contacted his office, wrote up the ticket, and eventually came back to me.

"You're the pastor of a church here in town, is that right?" he asked with a little more kindness in his voice.

"Yeah, that's right," I said surprised, wondering how he knew and feeling even more embarrassed. "Officer, I shouldn't have done it. I know it's illegal. Worse, I have the hands free device right here in the car," I said, holding it up for him to see. "It was stupid of me not to use it."

"Well, don't let it happen again," he said, handing me the ticket to sign. "I'm giving you a warning this time, Pastor, that's all, just a warning."

I signed it and handed it back to him.

"Officer, you shouldn't let me off the hook that easy just because I'm a pastor. We deserve even harsher treatment when we disobey the law, don't you think?"

"Maybe," he said quickly, and then left for his car.

I sat there knowing exactly what had just happened. It was wrong of me to talk on my cell phone while driving and I did it anyway. In the exact same way, it was wrong of me to hate my colleagues who'd hurt me. But I did it anyway and kept on doing it.

The siren of God had come for me countless times since I'd been fired. I pushed it away. I covered my ears. I mustered my defenses, perfected my excuses, and surrounded myself with people who let me rant in the fury of my dark, bitter rage. But it was over now. Finished and done. I'd been pulled over—finally. And I could hear the Lord as clearly as I heard the policeman.

"It's illegal in the kingdom of God to hate. It's against the royal law."

I'd known that from the first day He'd stamped His law on my heart. I also knew it came with power, power to choose to live in that love. I had it now. I had power to lay down the knife at the cross of Jesus. Power to break the reign of unforgiveness torturing my soul. Power to love those I hated.

Sitting there, in the car, I was two men, broken into two pieces, no more.

I was friends with Cain no more.

I chose then—and I choose now—the royal law today and forever.

QUESTIONS FOR REFLECTION

Are you broken into two pieces? One, obeying the royal law; the other, with specific people, strangely free to disobey. If so, what are you going to do about it?

If we are to live the royal law in His power and strength, we have to be honest about areas of anger, bitterness, resentment, jealousy, and hatred. Can you make right choices today? Can you let the power of His cross, applied by the Holy Spirit, come into each story?

37

PASSING INTO LIFE

Reflections on 1 John 3:14–15

*We know that we have passed out of death into life, because
we love the brethren. He who does not love abides in death.
Everyone who hates his brother is a murderer; and you
know that no murderer has eternal life abiding in him.*

—1 John 3:14–15

Sitting in a hotel meeting room. It's 2:45 in the afternoon.
We've been at it since 8:30. Fifty of us. I have no interest
in the present discussion. None whatsoever. I look around
the room. Some are engaged. Others are working on their
computers. Some have their head down, thinking? Sleeping?
We're out of here at 5:00.

I take out my journal and make a quick entry.

*I wonder where Mike is today. Is he well? Is his family well? Is the
Lord blessing these days for him? It seems impossible but we
haven't talked for seven months.*

The last conversation didn't go well.

*I think I started it. I wrote the first e-mail that upset him. He wrote
back furious, calling my motives into question. That angered me. I
should have picked up the phone right then and apologized. I didn't.
I sent a second and third e-mail. He did the same and it got nasty. A
little stove fire had taken flight and was now burning down the house.*

I picked up the phone—finally.

Really bad timing. I shouldn't have surprised him. Just the sound of my voice set him off. The stronger he got, the stronger I got.

We haven't talked since.

I've done nothing to reach out to him. I've pushed him out of my mind. I haven't even prayed for him. When he dissed me, I dissed him right back. Or did I diss him first? I can't remember. I miss him. I miss our friendship in the Lord. I can't imagine a kinder, gentler soul. This is my fault. I've acted badly, sinfully.

Resolve: Pray for Mike and Deborah and their kids. Send a note.

He who does not love abides in death.

—1 JOHN 3:14

About 3:15, I heard the door across the meeting room open.

I glanced up, expecting to see something familiar but I don't. I think I see Mike. I look harder, trying to convince myself it's not him. It can't be. He lives half-way across the country. Why would he come to this meeting? But it is Mike, I'm sure of it now. I watch him look for an open seat. He finds one nearby, takes off his overcoat and sits down behind a row of people, disappearing from view.

Our eyes don't meet. He doesn't know I'm here.

This is really strange. I was just thinking about him. What's even stranger is that I'm irritated. I don't want him here. I like my plan better—pray for him and send a note. The last thing I want is to casually bump into him, shake his hand, and pretend nothing happened. And I sure don't want a confrontation.

I hate this. I put my head down and dive back into my journal.

I can't believe this. He's here. Sitting across the room from me. Before, I couldn't remember why I was so mad at him. Not in detail, anyway. But now I can, like it was yesterday.

He'd made three bad decisions, one right after the other, and before he made a fourth, I stepped in. I asked him to stop what he was doing. I did it as gently as I knew how but it didn't work. He took it personally and went right for my jugular.

He called me "arrogant and self-driven." He said, "How dare you criticize me when you're the one caught up in the politics of self-promotion." Me?

His words still hurt.

I wrote him back, stunned. I thought I could ease the tension between us but instead, I made it worse. "What you've done," he wrote in his last e-mail, "has deeply hurt me. I can only hope our relationship isn't permanently damaged."

What I've done? What about what you did to me?

I can feel my heart racing. Is it possible to get out of here without him seeing me? What if he comes over? What do I say? What do I do?

Everyone who hates his brother is a murderer; and you know that no murderer has eternal life abiding in him.

—1 John 3:15

I start to doodle.

I think about various escape routes. I dream up excuses why I can't stay. I make the decision not to confront Mike. No new wounds. No opening old wounds. There has to be a way, if we do meet, to be kind but aloof, pleasant but distant.

I write down a quick prayer: "Lord, help me out of here."

But I'm not sure He hears me. Why would He?

I look back in my journal. A half hour before Mike walked into the meeting room, I wrote about him. I missed him. I missed our friendship over all these years and confessed I'd acted wrongly and needed to do something to make things right. So guess what happens? Out of nowhere, he shows up.

I get it. This is no accident.

I'm now suddenly aware there will be no escape routes. No excuses why I can't stay. No avoiding Mike. I look back across the room. I still can't see him.

But I will. I know that now.

We know that we have passed out of death into life,
because we love the brethren.

—1 JOHN 3:14

Before the meeting ended just past 5:00, I'd written one last prayer: "Lord, give me success with Mike."

I slowly made my way over to him and waited nearby until he finished a conversation. I called out his name, stretched out my hand, and smiled.

He turned and, to my surprise, grabbed my hand strong and quick.

"Incredible to see you," he said, like nothing had happened between us. I immediately asked about him, his wife, and his children. He did the same, and as soon as I could, I said, "Mike, do you think we could grab some time together?"

"I'd love to," he nodded.

And we did, later that evening, at dinner.

I leapt at the chance to say "I'm sorry"—sorry I'd hurt him the way I did. He stopped me and did the same thing right back. We took time to walk piece by piece through the events that had torn us apart. We didn't avoid it. We didn't make light of it. But it was different this time.

I knew why.

We were not alone.

The Lord was at our table and in our conversation. We'd slipped out of earth time and burst into kingdom time. The wounds that hurt didn't hurt anymore. Not like they did. The anger I felt when I first saw him that afternoon was gone. In its place, love had come, unspeakable love that surprised me, delighted me.

I had my old friend back, my brother in Christ Jesus.

As the night ended and we stood to leave, I did it again. I put my hand out. He grabbed it, pulled me in, and hugged me. For reasons I couldn't explain right then, I felt tears hit the corner of my eyes and a sadness overwhelm me. I told Mike it was tears of joy. But later, I wondered.

I wrote in my journal later that night:

O foolish, sinful heart, why did you let seven months go by?
  What kind of Christian man takes an old friend and sends him
away? Out of mind, out of heart, out of soul, without even a prayer?
  Lord Jesus, forgive me.
  Help me never pass this way again.

QUESTIONS FOR REFLECTION

John said that not to love is to abide in death, to hate is to murder, and life—eternal life—isn't in us. These are strong words. Where have you let hate and a lack of love creep into your heart?

Every time we take the leap and let the love of Christ, by His Spirit, move through us to others, we pass from death to life. Can you feel it? What holds you back? Will you initiate?

38
OFF TO RAHAB

Reflections on 1 John 3:16–18

*We know love by this, that He laid down His life for us; and we
ought to lay down our lives for the brethren. But whoever has the
world's goods, and sees his brother in need and closes his heart
against him, how does the love of God abide in him? Little children,
let us not love with word or with tongue, but in deed and truth.*
—1 John 3:16–18

Winter storms were threatening to blanket New England
in a blizzard. "If we don't fly out now," I told David, my friend
in South Carolina, "we'll be stuck." I was getting nervous. I
was scheduled to lead a three-day men's conference.

"Come early," he said. "It's perfect timing. There's
someone I want you and Erilynne to meet. You're gonna
love her!"

And we did. We met Melanie in a restaurant outside
Myrtle Beach. She'd gotten there before us and sat in a booth
next to a friend. She's an African-American woman with
bright eyes, a contagious smile, and a strong handshake.

"Tell us your story," David said to her, after we'd
introduced ourselves.

"Well, the only story I have is that I love Jesus!" she
replied without hesitating. "And I want the women on the
streets of Myrtle Beach to know Him too."

We soon learned that Melanie was the founder of Rahab's House.[1] She'd begun the work in March 2010, and that day, as we sat eating lunch, seventeen women were at the house under her care.

She said with profound passion, "We're a safe place for women. Safe when they're released from prison or rehab programs and have nowhere else to go. Safe from homelessness, addictions, and abusive relationships. Safe from a life of prostitution. That's who we are and what we do." And with a wry smile, she added. "We get 'em out of rehab and into Rahab!"

"What got you started," I asked Melanie.

"I worked as a prison chaplain and I couldn't stand watching these women get out with nowhere to go. I'd see them released with no one there to pick them up. They have no home, no way to get a job, and no hope in life. So they do what they know to do. They go back to the street and back to a life of drugs. So I prayed and asked for help.

"'Lord, what You did for me let me do for them. You laid down Your life; help me lay down my life. You gave Your all; help me give my all. They need You, Jesus, like I need You, Jesus. Show me what to do.

"I figured if these women are gonna make it, they need what I need—a personal relationship with Jesus Christ. He's the only One who can give us the dignity we deserve."

"So first, we got a home," Melanie's friend stated.

"And became a not-for-profit ministry," Melanie added.

"Then the Lord gave us provision. Pastors, churches, community leaders, and private donors helped finance us," her friend jumped in.

"We opened our doors!" Melanie beamed. "The Lord blessed us with a staff of professionals—all volunteers—to provide Bible studies, counseling, life skills training, vocational training, and community service so when our women leave Rahab's House they have a job, a home, and hope for the future."

"It sounds perfect," Erilynne said. "And I love the name Rahab!"

"Me too!" Melanie responded. "She's a woman of faith in the Bible and her home was a place of rescue. I love that she was set free from a life of prostitution and, by God's power, she became a woman of honor in Israel."[2]

"And that's your dream, isn't it?" David asked. "For these women to become women of honor."

"That's right," Melanie answered. "We get to see the Lord do miracles!"

But whoever has the world's goods, and sees his
brother in need and closes his heart against him,
how does the love of God abide in him?

—1 JOHN 3:17

For the next hour, Melanie told us story after story of women who'd made it and women who didn't. One story in particular stood out.

Pam.

She happened to be walking by at just the right moment.

Melanie had finished meeting with some of her staff in town. They were outside on the street, ready to go to their cars, when they all saw her.

They didn't let her walk by.

They went to Pam and surrounded her with the love of Jesus Christ. Within minutes, they brought her inside, fed her a meal, and listened to her story.

Thirty-seven years old. Fifteen years on crack. Three years in prison. Living a life of prostitution. No family to speak of and no home to go to.

They offered her a place at Rahab's House, and she accepted. That night, she slept safe in a bed at Rahab's House. She stayed a few days, then a week, then a month, then a couple of months.

"She's still there, nearly three years later," Melanie said, elated. "She manages the house for me. She pours her life into our women every day because she knows what Jesus Christ can do."

Melanie reached beside her and pulled out a piece of paper with pictures of Pam on it. "Here she is when she arrived and here she is now. Just look at her!"

The last picture revealed a stunning woman, radiant and beautiful. At the very bottom of the page were words written in bold: "Now I walk with Christ."

Her story is a miracle story. The Lord stepped into her life and saved her. He walked her into freedom from crack and prostitution. He gave her what no one and nothing in life could give her.

"She has dignity now," Melanie told us. "And what the Lord did for her, she's now doing for others. The love He gave her, she's giving to our women! That's Pam. And I tell you the truth, she's a woman of honor!"

Little children, let us not love with word or
with tongue, but in deed and truth.

—1 JOHN 3:18

Behind all the stories was one more story nearly missed.

Melanie was reluctant to tell it. She'd much rather talk about the women at Rahab and her dreams for the future. "We need a family house next," she envisioned. "There are too many women who have children and nowhere to go."

But slowly, over lunch, we pieced together her story.

She's only thirty years old. She lives at Rahab's House with the women. Like them, she has a roof over her head and meals on the table. The ministry provides her a car, gas money, a phone, and basic needs to run the ministry.

But she takes no salary. Like the rest of her staff, she's a volunteer. "I use food stamps like everybody else at the house," she said casually. "But the blessing is all mine! This is gonna sound crazy, but I don't think I ever knew I was a saved woman till I became a serving woman. I never prayed to Jesus like I pray to Jesus now. I need Him for everything. I need Him every day to do for these women what I can't do for these women."

Then she sat back and smiled.

And we got to see in her what she sees all the time at Rahab's House—a blessed and empowered woman who God has chosen to honor.

QUESTIONS FOR REFLECTION

John showed us this love is sacrificial love. It is tested every time we see people in need. Is your heart open? Do you love in word, or in deed and in truth?

This passage speaks of radical generosity. This agape love, if it abides in us, gives freely because we've received freely. Are you like Melanie in this story? Are you a radically generous giver to those in need? If not, do you know why not?

NOTES

1. Sadly, in the fall of 2013, Rahab's House closed due to the inability to find permanent housing. Melanie continues to live in the area and passionately serves women in need.

2. The biblical story of Rahab begins in Joshua 2. In the big picture plan of God, she becomes the great, great grandmother of King David and, with distinction and honor, is listed in the genealogy of Jesus Christ in Matthew 1:5.

39

ONE KIND ACT

Reflections on 1 John 3:17–20

But whoever . . . sees his brother in need and closes his heart. . . .
Little children, let us not love with word or with tongue, but in
deed and truth. We will know by this that we are of the truth, and
will assure our heart before Him in whatever our heart condemns
us; for God is greater than our heart and knows all things.

—1 John 3:17–20

Thad,

You asked me to write my story, and I agreed, but now I wish
I hadn't. I can't find the words to describe most of what happened
to me in those years.

So I've decided to write what I can and leave it at that.

My daughter Kristie was killed by a drunk driver in July 1982.
She was nineteen. She worked that summer as a waitress in a
restaurant out in California with a bunch of her college friends.
She finished up late one night, got in the car to head back to
where she was staying, and never made it home.

Our phone rang a little past four in the morning.

It felt like the earth opened its mouth and swallowed me alive.
Every part of my life went into free fall, spiraling deep into a darkness
I'd never known. Jules, my wife, did her best to hold our family
together, but she was falling just as fast.

We held each other tight, but we were light years apart. I
couldn't handle my own pain, let alone hers. We did what we
could, especially for the other children.

They flew Kristie's body back to Boston.

The church was packed for the funeral. For three weeks, our home was filled with people coming and going, food, friends, and our church family. And then one day it was quiet. Everybody slid back into the routines of everyday life.

And I kept falling, deeper and deeper into the dark.

I met Bucky while on vacation in Maine in the summer of 2012. He and Jules had come up from Boston and were staying a few houses down from us.

I saw him nearly every day as I walked our Old English Sheepdog past their house. At some point, I told him my brother was dying of cancer and I wasn't handling it well. I was scared. I didn't want to lose him. On top of that, in those days, I wasn't sure if he knew Jesus.

"Yeah, I get that," Bucky said. Then, to my surprise, he did the unforgettable. He gave me a glimpse of his heart.

We will know by this that we are of the truth, and will assure our heart before Him in whatever our heart condemns us; for

God is greater than our heart and knows all things.

—1 JOHN 3:19–20

I'm sorry to say this to you. My pastor and church family only added to my grief. I needed them to be with me in the pain, in the fall, in the dark.

But they were not willing.

They did a lot, mind you. They loved us, prayed for us, and were there for us anytime we had a need. They didn't mean to hurt us, but they did. They comforted us with a comfort that left us wanting.

The pastor made the funeral joyful and happy. He told us Kristie was in heaven with Jesus now and she was in a far better place. He said God decided He wanted her with Him and, though we miss her, we're happy for her. We're happy for God. All of heaven is rejoicing now that Kristie is there. He said if we surrendered our lives to Jesus today, we'd be happy too.

It felt like a dagger pierced my heart.

I fractured inside. I put on a face and nodded my head. I acted like I believed but, in truth, I did not. How could I? I'd lost my little girl. Was I to think God did this? He took her from us? He sent a drunk driver to violently end her life? All because He wanted her with Him and not with us? Is that the story, really?

It made me plummet faster.

I'd thought Jesus wept at the death of his friend. Was He not weeping with me? When we're lost in the dark, didn't He promise to be with us? I didn't understand. The God I knew and the God they knew—were they different?

It had to be me. Something was wrong with me.

And far worse, I wasn't sure about Kristie. I was sure about our other kids, but not her. Did she really know Jesus in her heart? At the end of high school and beginning of college, I could tell she was struggling with her faith in God. She told me she believed. And then later, she told me she didn't.

I shared this with my pastor, but he brushed me off. He didn't want to hear it. He assured me Kristie was in heaven with Jesus and I needed to trust that.

"You know for sure?" I asked him.

"Absolutely!" he said with a cheery smile and pat on my back.

I returned the smile on the outside but inside I died another death. If only I had the courage of Job in those days. I'd have told him he was a worthless physician doing more to condemn my soul than bring me an ounce of real comfort.[1]

Could he not see my despair? What if she didn't know Him? What then? Where would she be now? Could she be suffering in the fires of torment? I sought out other pastors but they all said the same thing. Not one of them heard my fears.

None wanted to be where I was.

Relief came in the most unexpected way.

I'd stopped praying altogether. We went to church for the sake of the family. I kept up appearances but my heart was cold and distant. In some ways, I'd say I was prayed out. I'd asked all my questions. All I needed were some answers. But would He tell me? Would He let me know Kristie was safe with Him?

All I got back was silence.

Until one day, I was driving to work. It was the strangest thing. I heard in my heart a voice as loud as if He was sitting right there in the car beside me. I didn't understand at first. It confused me. Was this really the answer to my prayers?

"One kind act!"

All day those words tumbled around in my head. I told Jules when I got home that night. I asked her what it meant, and as we were talking, the phone rang. I picked it up and heard the voice of an old friend. Calling from the ER.

Their son was dead.

We raced to the hospital to be with them. We held them. We cried with them. We stayed with them. We told them we'd be with them every step of the way. And out of my mouth I said what I didn't know was inside me to say.

"The Lord is here. He will not leave us now."

And suddenly I knew what I'd known all along. Jesus had been there, falling with me, faster and faster. With me in the dark and in the cold, in the despair and in the tears. He had never left. He had never turned away.

There, in the ER, weeping with our friends, my heart started to heal.

Jules grabbed my hand. We were no longer light years apart. We linked arms with our friends and raced off the cliff into the dark with them for we knew as sure as life was in our lungs that Jesus Christ our Lord would be with us. Grieving with us. Hurting with us. Staying with us.

And in that moment, all my questions were answered. No, not the way I wanted. But more so. I trusted Him. I trusted Jesus. Jules and I could go to Him and leave Kristie with Him assured in our hearts because we're sure of Him.[2]

He knows all things. He's greater than all things and that's enough for us. Even when fear comes raging back and I wonder if Kristie is really there in heaven with Him, I do what He told me to do.

"One kind act!"

I find someone going through what I went through and come alongside. And every time I do, my heart heals a little more.

And so it has again, in meeting you.

Bucky

QUESTIONS FOR REFLECTION

There are too many stories like this. We brush off people with simple pat answers rather than entering into their pain with them—and with Him. What does it take to trust the Lord in the deepest suffering of the soul?

How often it's in the giving of "one kind act" that we find the healing our hearts desperately need. Can you relate to Bucky's story? Will you do what the Lord has told us to do: go love with His love with all your heart?

NOTES

1. Job 13:4. I've done this myself. In my desperation to give comfort to the grieving, I've made statements in the name of God that I had no right to make. I came to realize I was doing this to protect myself. I found it easier to give a quick, gospel answer than to stay with them and enter their grief.

2. Job, in his suffering, asked so many questions. At first glance, as the story ends, it seems the Lord answered none of them. But as we look carefully, we find a great secret told. All Job's questions find their answer in the presence of God in the whirlwind. He is, for Job—and I pray for all of us—the answer we need most.

40

AND A THOUSAND MORE

~~~

Reflections on 1 John 3:21–24

*Beloved, if our heart does not condemn us, we have
confidence before God; and whatever we ask we receive
from Him, because we keep His commandments and
do the things that are pleasing in His sight.*

—1 JOHN 3:21–22

October 19, 2012
Bucky,

*Your story has meant everything to me in these sad and difficult
days. My brother died a few weeks back. I miss him more than I
can say.*

*Please keep his wife and son in your prayers. For all my family,
especially my dad. It would mean so much to me.*

God bless you and Jules, dear friend.
Thad

October 24, 2012
Thad,

*I read your letter and my heart broke. I am sorry for the depth
of pain your soul now bears. Be assured of our love and prayers
for you in the Lord.*

Always remember, I'm here. Anytime. Running beside you.
Bucky

December 18, 2012
Bucky,

I'm not doing well. I need your help.

I have memories I can't shake. They come back to me at the oddest times and frighten me. I do my best to push them away, but recently I find I can't.

There's one in particular that has a power all its own. I am back at my brother's bedside. We're in the ER, waiting for test results. We hear doctors outside the room. My brother gets anxious. He needs to know what they're saying. I try to calm him, but he's restless. He looks at me, and I can tell he's scared. He knows something's wrong, really wrong. And then he says it.

"I don't want to die."

And the memory freezes. There is fear in his eyes and, even now, I can feel it wash over my soul. I must do something to take away the fear. I can't leave him like this. But I stand there as frozen as the memory. Helpless. Scared. Knowing now what I didn't know then. It's almost over. Death is near.

The memory plays back. All I can see are his eyes. All I can feel is his fear.

And I'm scared again. It's too much for me. Just as my heart starts to spiral in panic, I remember your story. I do what the Lord taught you to do. Just "one kind act." I lift my voice in prayer, "O Lord, who can I show Your kindness to today?"

I find, to my surprise, it works.[1]

I get out of myself. I find someone in need and give, even when I have so little to give. And every time I do, almost without fail, I feel the Lord present with me. The more I give, the more He gives me to give, and I know the Holy Spirit is welling up inside me. I feel alive. I feel the love of Jesus coursing through my veins.

And somehow, I don't know how, but my heart heals a little.

Just like you said.

So I choose a life of kindness.

I've filled these weeks of grief with "one kind act" after another. I will never stop. I know that now. It's what the Lord commands us to do. It's pleasing in His sight. But I've got to be honest, Bucky. I think I'm doing it for the wrong reason. I'm not giving to give, I'm giving to get.

It's selfish love, not selfless love.

Like an addict, I need the love of Jesus inside me today. I need my heart to heal, my pain to go away, and the fear burning inside these memories to be gone. If that means "one kind act," then I'll do it but not for them. For me.

That's how it feels, Bucky—selfish, wretched, sinful me.

These days are hard days. I'm getting up in the morning and choosing a life that lives and breathes "one kind act" after another. But I feel like my heart is growing cold. For whatever reason, the memories are back in strength. I'm fighting fear nearly every day. It's getting more difficult to get outside myself.

I need help, old friend. Will you come and run alongside?
Thad

This is His commandment, that we believe in the name
of His Son Jesus Christ, and love one another, just as
He commanded us. The one who keeps His commandments
abides in Him, and He in him. We know by this that
He abides in us, by the Spirit whom He has given us.

—1 JOHN 3:23–24

Christmas Eve, 2012
Thad,

I think it's time to tell more of my story.

A few years after my daughter died, I stumbled into a world I knew nothing about. It came on me slowly, imperceptibly.

Jules saw it first. She said she saw changes in me. Little things. I was sleeping more. I was spending more time on the couch, lost in a book or the TV. She said I was rarely happy anymore, and she wanted her old Bucky back.

I didn't think much of it at the time. I promised Jules I'd do better.

Of course, I didn't. It only got worse. I'd lost my oomph. I didn't want to go to work. I didn't want to go out on Saturday morning missions with the church. I didn't want to hang out with friends. The real kicker came when I was in the middle of a business meeting and began to cry. For no apparent reason.

I told Jules and agreed to see a doctor. It was the first time I was ever diagnosed with depression.

Over the years, it's come back a few times. The story is always the same. I begin to hunker down, turn inward and isolate. Sometimes it's easy to detect because my behavior changes. Other times, it's not. I learned I could be the same Bucky on the outside and emotionally withdraw and hide out on the inside.

I don't think the diagnosis is complicated. I have never stopped grieving.

I miss my little girl, and I always will.

So I choose not to isolate. I choose not to emotionally withdraw. I choose "one kind act" because I know it holds the mystery of the kingdom of God.

This is how I wrote it in my journal: "If we believe in the name of His Son Jesus Christ, if we love one another just as He has said, then we will know He abides in us, and we in Him. And with every kind act and every gift of love the Holy Spirit Himself will come and fill our hearts, and we shall be free."

I wonder what that sounds like to you?

Is it selfless love? I think so. But is it selfish? Yes, absolutely. It's meant to be. It's how His kingdom works. He pours blessing into us as we pour blessing out to others. We get more to give more and know Him more because of it.

Do it and don't stop.

Do it selfishly if you have to. It doesn't matter, not to God.

Just don't turn away. Don't isolate yourself. Don't let the Devil steal what the Lord wants you to have. I tell you, the moment we stop loving others as He has loved us, we wither up and die inside. I don't want that for me.

I don't want that for you.

So choose "one kind act" after another and let Him heal your weary heart. Let Him take the fear embedded in these memories of your brother—let Him take your brother too—and make you safe again. He will do that, I promise you. It's what He does. It's who He is. Isn't that what Christmas is all about?

"One kind act" and He came to us.

"One kind act" and He laid down His life for us.

"One kind act" and a thousand more, He gives us a foretaste of the glories of His kingdom and tells us to go do the same.

So let's run together. Let's choose "one kind act and a thousand more" and I trust, as we run, our hearts will heal a little more along the way.

What do you think? Write me soon.

Bucky

QUESTIONS FOR REFLECTION

The Bible never separates our belief "in the name of His Son, Jesus Christ" (1 John 3:23) and our passion to love one another. Do you separate them? Can you feel life inside you as they come together?

Sometimes selfless, sometimes selfish, and yet the Holy Spirit testifies that we are His and He is ours as we do what He commands. Will you take it up? Will you commit today to "one kind act and a thousand more"?

NOTE

1. First John 3:16–24 reveals this secret beautifully. We are to love not "with word or with tongue, but in deed and truth" (3:18). So when we see others in need, we give as the Lord has given us. We serve as He has served us. We lay down our lives for others as He laid down His life for us. By this, the apostle writes—that is, by this love from God abiding in us and going through us to others in need—our hearts find the rest and confidence we so desperately need.

PART 6

LOVE
ONE ANOTHER

41

HEARTSICK

Reflections on 1 John 3:23—4:3

This is His commandment, that we believe in the name of His Son
Jesus Christ, and love one another, just as He commanded us. . . .
We know by this that He abides in us. . . . Beloved, do not believe
every spirit, but test the spirits to see whether they are from God,
because many false prophets have gone out into the world.

—1 JOHN 3:23—4:1

There are stories I'd rather not tell.

I'm a pastor. I teach the Bible; it's what I do. I've done it since I was twenty-two. But I fear there are times, way too many times, when I do it without my heart. I stay distant and hidden, not even aware of it. Nor am I aware that my soul is covered in a pride that has blinded my eyes, dulled my ears, and hardened my heart.

Some time ago, I was asked to teach on this passage of 1 John 4:1–3. So I did what I always do. I grabbed a chunk of time, a gigantic cup of coffee, and space at my desk where I could push away the world and read, pray, study, and write.

I didn't see it at first. But there, on my desk, in plain view, was a yellow sticky note from my wife: "Steve Harrelson called. He's in town. He'd love to see you. Coffee, maybe?" A telephone number followed.

Without even thinking, I took the note, crumpled it up, tossed it in the trash and went back to my work. It was as if I'd caught a mosquito in the corner of my eye, swatted it, and went back to what I was doing. A bother, that's all.

Hardly worth mentioning.

Beloved, do not believe every spirit, but test the spirits to see whether they are from God, because many false prophets have gone out into the world. By this you know the Spirit of God: every spirit that confesses that Jesus Christ has come in the flesh is from God; and every spirit that does not confess Jesus is not from God; this is the spirit of the antichrist.

—1 JOHN 4:1–3

I was enthralled by these verses. The apostle John was doing what pastors are meant to do. We warn the people of God about "false prophets." We teach them how to "test the spirits." We keep them safe and help them stay safe.

I wrote down four talking points.

1. Knowing the danger of false prophets in the church today.
2. Helping all Christians know how to "test the spirits."
3. Strengthening our confession of Jesus Christ.
4. Learning to depend on the Spirit to discern the antichrist.

Brilliant. Academic. Practical.

But one thing really bothered me. Why did John say we must confess "Jesus Christ has come in the flesh"? Why didn't he say, "Jesus Christ as Lord" or, "Jesus is the Christ, the Son of God" (see 1 Cor. 12:3; John 20:31)? I knew many scholars believed John did it to address a threatening heresy of his times. But was there more to it?

Jesus Christ has come in the flesh.

Off to the side of my notes, I wrote a quick reflection:

This is classic John. For him, relationships are everything in the kingdom of God. Always. Jesus Christ is not a doctrine. He's a person. He came to us relationally, "in the flesh," so we might know Him, love Him, and learn how to love each other.

Somewhere, deep inside me, I could hear the sound of my heart. There was more to this text, so much more, if I'd just pursue it. But no, I reasoned. Not for now. Perhaps another time.

This is His commandment, that we believe in the name
of His Son Jesus Christ, and love one another,
just as He commanded us.

—1 JOHN 3:23

The next morning, I went back to my desk to review the notes before going to church. As I sat down, I noticed a text message had come in on my cell phone from a number I didn't recognize.

"Thad, it's Steve Harrelson in the flesh! I'm in town two more days. Any chance we could get together? I think it's time to put things right? What do you think?"

The timing couldn't be worse. I needed to stay focused on teaching the Bible. I didn't need this distraction, especially from Steve Harrelson. The answer is no. No to coffee. No to time together. No to putting things right.

I decided I'd text him later. Something kind but decisive: "Steve, great to hear from you! Sorry to miss you this trip. Hope we can get together next time you're in town. God bless!"

The teaching went really well. The people responded with a genuine excitement and seemed blessed by the Lord. I gave them everything I had.

Just not my heart. They didn't seem to notice.

I didn't either.

This is His commandment, that we believe in the name
of His Son Jesus Christ, and love one another, just as
He commanded us. The one who keeps His commandments
abides in Him, and He in him. We know by this that He
abides in us, by the Spirit whom He has given us.

—1 JOHN 3:23–24

I sent the text to Steve mid-afternoon. But the moment I sent it, it didn't feel right. For some reason, I couldn't shake from my mind the words of his text, "Thad, it's Steve Harrelson in the flesh!" I had just talked about this at the Bible study.

Jesus Christ came in the flesh.

It's the whole point of 1 John, and especially the fourth chapter. He came relationally, in the flesh. He came to love us and show His love by what He did on Calvary for us. And then He taught us the same. We are to love each other.

I opened my Bible again.

For some reason, I'd missed this. I hadn't looked back at the end of chapter 3 where the words now jumped off the page. We are to "believe in the name of His Son Jesus Christ, and love one another" (3:23).

This is it, I suddenly realized.

This is how we "test the spirits" to see if we are of God or not. It's how we recognize "false prophets" and "the spirit of the antichrist." It's how we know we abide in Him, and He in us, in and through His Holy Spirit. We love one another, "just as He commanded us."

I instantly became heartsick. In my mind's eye, I saw myself sitting at my desk preparing the teaching, seeing the yellow sticky note with Steve Harrelson's name on it, and crumpling it up. Tossing it away. Moving on.

But that was it. I didn't know it then. I know it now.

That was my test.

And I failed.

I texted Steve back and apologized. I told him I wanted to meet with him, needed to meet with him, and he graciously wrote back and accepted.

But my heart still hurt.

What if Steve hadn't texted me? I'd never have known this sin of mine. I'd have gone home at night feeling good about myself, like I did a good job. I taught the Bible. I helped others. I gave praise and glory to God. When, in fact, I'd done the exact opposite. I'd betrayed the very text I taught. Romans 2:21 came to the front of my mind: "You, therefore, who teach another, do you not teach yourself?"

Right then, right there, I repented before the Lord from my proud and cold heart, my blind eyes and my dull hearing. I asked Him to forgive me and help me, and the moment I asked, I realized—He already had.

I get to meet with Steve for coffee in the morning.

I get to take the test again.

QUESTIONS FOR REFLECTION

If we disconnect the end of 1 John 3 and the beginning of chapter 4, we will not have the tools to discern the antichrist. For together, we see that what we believe and how we love are forever inseparable. Test yourself: Is your belief in Christ as right as your love for others?

Have you ever caught yourself dismissing people? Do you know why you do it? Are you willing to ask the Lord to help you see, understand, and stop?

42

STEVE HARRELSON

Reflections on 1 John 4:4–6

You are from God, little children, and have overcome them;
because greater is He who is in you than he who is in the world.

—1 JOHN 4:4

I tossed and turned all night. I couldn't believe a text on my cell phone could do this to me. But it did, and I was faced with a deep-seated ugliness inside. "Thad, it's Steve Harrelson in the flesh! I'm in town two more days. Any chance we could get together? I think it's time to put things right! What do you think?"

What do I think? I didn't think. I reacted. I brushed him off because I couldn't be distracted from my work. I was teaching the Bible. I was helping Christians know how to detect false prophets in the church. I was busy-busy-busy and couldn't be bothered.

Of course, now I know, I didn't even do that well.

Had I gone back to the end of 1 John 3, I'd have heard the thunders of John's message: If "we believe in the name of His Son Jesus Christ" then we will do the one thing He commands us to do. We will "love one another." False prophets divide the church. They tear us apart. They love only those who love them.

True prophets raise high the royal law: We must love one another (see James 2:8).

We cannot give people the brush-off.

And that's what I did with Steve Harrelson. I pushed him away. I taught against false prophets while I was, at the same time, doing what false prophets do. And now, at 9:00, I was scheduled to meet him at a local coffee shop. To put things right. To say sorry. And to ask his forgiveness for the way I treated him yesterday. Which, I'm sad to say, is exactly how I treated him all the yesterdays before that.

You are from God, little children, and have overcome them; because greater is He who is in you than he who is in the world.

— 1 JOHN 4:4

It happened all the time in school. There were children who didn't fit in. They were different from the rest of us. We talked about them, made jokes about them, and poked at them to see if we could provoke a reaction. It somehow made us feel better about ourselves.

To this day, I remember Clarence in my second-grade class. He always sat in the back row. He had the worst breath. He'd have epileptic seizures which made us call him "Freak!" when he couldn't hear.

But he heard. He knew.

Even in those early days, I knew it was wrong. I knew I had to break from my classmates and try to be his friend. If I were Clarence, that's what I'd want.

It didn't stay with me though. I grew up and discovered the world was full of Clarences. Of course, I'd never intentionally mistreat someone. Never call them names. Never speak ill of them so others could speak well of me. These are games, I reasoned with myself, I'd never play.

But what did it matter? I did what everybody else does with our Clarences. I brush them off, push them away, and make them disappear from sight.

It's what I did to Steve Harrelson in the past.

And evidently, I was still doing it.

You are from God, little children, and have
overcome them; because greater is He who is
in you than he who is in the world.

—1 JOHN 4:4

A few years ago, the Lord brought Steve Harrelson to mind. I was at a church service when a young woman with special needs came up and asked for prayer. I'll never forget it. I wrote it down later in my journal.

"Do you know what makes me sad?" she asked me.

"No, tell me."

"We push people into the shadows. That makes me sad. Why do we do that? People can be so mean."

"Did you see that happen this week?" I asked.

"I see it all the time with my friends. It's happened to me all my life. I don't like it. It makes me sad. It's not what Jesus wants us to do."

"I'm sorry," I said back.

"Yeah, but I won't let them be alone. I try to make them happy. I want you to pray for my friends and ask Jesus to make it stop. We don't want to go into the shadows anymore."

So I prayed with her. But I couldn't help feel my heart explode in pain for the people I've pushed into the shadows.

Later, out of nowhere, I thought of Steve Harrelson. I wonder how he's doing now. I've heard he's working with kids in the inner city. I never treated him well. I wonder if he ever knew.

Lord, forgive me.

You are from God, little children, and have
overcome them; because greater is He who is in
you than he who is in the world.

—1 JOHN 4:4

I opened my Bible to 1 John 4 and stared at the page. Everything inside of me didn't want to go see Steve this morning. Not because of him. Because of me.

I started thinking about what I'd do, what I'd say. I could make it easy for me. Stay superficial. Sound genuine, sincere, and real. Do most of the listening. Show compassion. Say sorry. Do whatever it takes to make things right.

Then leave. I had a busy day in front of me.

Or I could do the opposite. I could make it hard for me. I could be real with him. Real with God. There's a pattern of behavior in my life that is wrong. It's ungodly and ugly and needs to stop. But how do I do that? I know I do it. That's not in question. Steve is proof of that. And he's not the only one.

But why do I do it? Why do I show partiality? Why do I love the people that fit into my world and can't see — won't see — those who don't fit? And why do I do it so naturally? The moment Steve texted, I dismissed it without a thought. Without a prayer. It was inside me, deep inside me. And there I was, studying the Bible so I could teach it.

"What kind of Christian am I? What kind of Christian pastor?" I thought.

I looked intently at the Bible and these verses came into view: "They are from the world; therefore they speak as from the world, and the world listens to them. We are from God; he who knows God listens to us; he who is not from God does not listen to us. By this we know the spirit of truth and the spirit of error" (1 John 4:5–6).

What a mixture I am. In this area of my life, I am behaving as a man of the world. I am doing what society does — prizing those who fit "in." Dismissing those who belong "out." But that's not what God does.

Nor those who belong to God.

I am living in a "spirit of error" that has to stop. But I don't know how to do it. How do I unpack the years of wrong behavior and find out why? I need to go and meet with Steve. I suddenly want to. Really, really want to.

I wonder, will he know how to help me? Will he bring me wisdom and counsel?

> *Lord Jesus, for what I have done, for this horrible sin of partiality, for brushing people aside—tossing them into the shadows—I am truly sorry. Please have mercy and help me. I am going to hold on to the promise today of 1 John 4:4 and believe when You say, "Greater is He who is in me than he who is in the world." Be my victor and drive the spirit of error far from me.*
>
> *I ask Your forgiveness to my heart in Jesus' name and Your healing to my soul. Help me to see Steve today—really see him. And to hear him. And to love him as You have loved me.*
>
> *To the honor and glory of Your holy name, I pray. Amen.*

QUESTIONS FOR REFLECTION

The spirit of the antichrist wages war against us to separate us from Christ, from each other, and from within. We must choose different. Often that choice begins with those we toss in the shadows. Are you willing to start there?

Great is He who is in us! Greater than the antichrist working to tear us apart. Stand in His strength. Will you let Him heal any areas in your life where prejudice and error have taken hold?

43

TIME TO BE REAL

Reflections on 1 John 4:7–8

Beloved, let us love one another, for love is from God;
and everyone who loves is born of God and knows God.
The one who does not love does not know God, for God is love.

—1 JOHN 4:7–8

My own sticky note said, "Steve Harrelson, 9:00, coffee shop at exit 22." I left the house in plenty of time. About a fifteen-minute drive. I didn't want to be late. Not for him. It was time to say sorry. Time to put things right.

Time to be real.

I'd been struggling with a story I'd told a few weeks back at a men's conference in North Carolina. Driving to the coffee shop, I replayed it in my mind.

"How is it possible," I asked, surprisingly indignant, "for the most sought-after Christian marriage counselor in your town to be in the throes of a divorce? Separated from his wife? With his two older children not even speaking to him?

"These are the facts. Yet you hear it all the time—people quickly come to his defense. They say there's no one like him. He's a miracle worker. Marriages that were a complete train wreck are back together like new.

"Does that work for you? As long as our Christian leaders do their work well, does it matter how they live their lives? Do you care? Or, should I ask, does God care? I think He does. I think we should. It's time we demand more."

I begged the men to deal with this issue.

We cannot speak right and live wrong. No more—ever.

"What kind of witness is that to the world around us?" I went on. "Are they not mocking us, mocking God, every time they meet together and tell the stories of our hypocrisies? They deserve better. Our children deserve better.

"God requires more. God demands we be real," I urged, hearing myself again.

How easy it was to tell that story and thunder challenge into these men's souls. As I drove to the coffee shop, it thundered right back at me like an ache in my head. That hypocrite isn't someone else. It's me.

I told the men, "We must love one another. It's the royal law. It's the King's edict. Relationships are everything in the kingdom of God! Believe it. Live it."

While quietly, without a thought, with barely an ounce of compassion in my heart, I tossed Mr. Steve Harrelson under the bus.

And into the shadows.

Beloved, let us love one another, for love is from God; and
everyone who loves is born of God and knows God.

—1 JOHN 4:7

He was already there when I arrived, seated at a table
near the front window. He got up, stuck out his hand to
greet me, but I went right for him with a smile and a hug
that I needed, I think, more than him.

"It's been a long time," he said.

"Yeah, too long."

We went to the counter, grabbed some coffee and Dan-
ishes, and found two soft leather chairs in the back of the
cozy little shop. "I want to hear about you," I said, "your
family, your ministry. I hear you're working with inner-city
kids."

He reached into his pocket and pulled out a check.

"I want to hear about you, too. But I want to put things
right first. This is for you," he said, handing it to me.

"What's this for?" I asked, completely taken aback.

"Don't you remember?" he said, surprised by my reaction. And then he told me the story. He was part of a church
my wife and I were pastoring in Pittsburgh some years ago.
He'd fallen briefly on hard times, lost his job, and couldn't
pay his bills.

"You came to my house and prayed with my wife and
me. I asked for your help because I needed some money,

and you gave it to me. I promised I'd get it back to you and never did. I still feel awful about it. Will you please forgive me?"

I sat there speechless. It was so long ago I'd actually forgotten.

Finally, I said, "So, this is it? This is what you wanted to put right between us?"

"Yeah, this is it."

"Nothing else?"

"No, not that I can think of."

I looked him straight in the eyes and knew he meant it. I carefully put the check on the coffee table in front of us. What do I do now? Do I tell him the truth? Do I let him know why I've come here this morning? But why doesn't he know already? Isn't he aware of how I've treated him all these years?

Why isn't he offended by me? I would be—no, actually, I *am* offended by me.

Do I tell him? Or do I take the check and run?

Beloved, let us love one another, for love is from God;
and everyone who loves is born of God and knows God.

—1 JOHN 4:7

"You have to understand something," he said. "My wife and I spent the next couple of years just barely getting by.

When I heard you and your wife were leaving Pittsburgh, I did my best to raise the money, but I couldn't do it."

"Steve, really, you don't need to explain."

"No, I do. I want you to hear this. The last time I saw you, just before you left, everything inside me wanted to tell you I'd pay you back. I'd keep my promise. But I didn't say it. I was too ashamed. I didn't want that to be the last thing you'd remember me by. And plus, you made it really, really hard for me," he said with a tease.

"How did I do that?" I asked.

"You were way too kind to me. You always have been. The moment you saw me, you did what you just did here a few minutes ago. You hugged me. You told me I was your friend. You thanked me for all the time we'd spent together. You made me feel like this money wasn't between us when it was. At least it was to me.

"So then, I decided I'd write you. I'd wish you well in your new pastorate and tell you again that I'd keep my promise. I'd get you the money. But I didn't write. I decided it was best to get it as soon as I could and just send it to you. I didn't do that either.

"Then the Lord called my wife and me to move into the inner city of Pittsburgh and be part of a church that's witnessing the love of God to those in need. To do that, we had to raise support for our family. God has been so faithful.

"But I never could raise the money to pay you back. I can't tell you how this has weighed on my soul. But six weeks ago, a check came to us out of nowhere. We weren't expecting it at all. And get this—it was the exact amount!

"I called the person who gave it and told him the story of what you and your wife had done for us so many years ago. I asked if it would be alright if we used the money to pay you back. He agreed immediately, absolutely!"

He lifted his hand in a fist pump like his favorite team had just scored.

Like someone just told him he'd won the lottery.

Like two old friends—separated by time and hurt—had come home and were back in each other's arms.

"This means everything to me!" he said with sheer, unspeakable joy.

The one who does not love does not know God,
for God is love.

—1 John 4:8

Our hands met in midair with the sound of a loud clap. I thanked him over and over again. I told him how sorry I was he'd held this burden in his soul for so long. I wish I'd known. I promised him it was never wrongfully between us.

He told me he loved me. I told him I loved him.

And then sat back with a secret tucked down deep in my heart.

QUESTIONS FOR REFLECTION

Nothing in the world compares with the agape love of God. By it, we are born again; and in it, we live. How does God, who is agape and abides in the Christian heart, change you, and change how you do relationships?

It's hard being real with God, with others, and with ourselves. Do you have secrets tucked deep in your heart? Secrets blocking the agape of God to care for you and let you care for others?

44

THE CHECK BETWEEN US

Reflections on 1 John 4:8–11

For God is love. By this the love of God was manifested in us, that God has sent His only begotten Son into the world so that we might live through Him.

—1 JOHN 4:8–9

"So tell me your story. What's life like in the inner city?" I asked, intent on hearing every detail. Steve Harrelson took a sip of coffee and put down his cup right next to the check he'd just given me and began.

"Nine years this June," he said. "I can't believe it's been that long. Gabe was six and little Joey was three—now they're fifteen and twelve! But it's been the best years of our lives. We feel like what we're doing is pleasing to the Lord and strengthening the community around us. What can be better than that?"

As he said it, I watched delight spread like a sunrise over his face.

I did my best to stay focused—which wasn't easy. I was still trying to process what had just happened between us.

"Our church is involved in four areas of community life," he told me. "Each one impacting children." And then he listed them, describing each in detail: pregnancy resource center, pediatric medical clinic, tutorial program for school-age kids, and vocational training for high school dropouts.

As he talked, I listened with half an ear. I kept glancing down at the check on the coffee table. I still couldn't believe it. This is why he wanted to meet with me? We'd given him a gift—but to him, it was a debt he carried like a weight pressed down on his soul all these years. Look at him—he's free of it now.

He's happy. Everything's right again.

But it's not.

I've come here this morning to ask his forgiveness for the way I've treated him. I did what I shouldn't do to anyone. I pushed him away—unconsciously at first—then by choice. He didn't fit in my world. He's different from me. Why do I keep doing this? Does he know? I don't think he does. Can he help me?

Why didn't I ever make time for him, or space, in my schedule or my heart?

Lord Jesus, What do You want me to do here? Do I say something? Or do I let it go? He's so happy, why should I ruin this moment for him? I don't want to do that. But how can I leave without being right with him in my heart? Or is that selfish of me? And how can I take this check from him after what I've done to him, after how I've behaved? Help me know what to do. Please.

"But what I love most," he went on, my focus back on track, "is working with kids who have disabilities. My wife and I spend most days in the classroom working with students. We're able to give them the attention they deserve.

"And best of all," he said, from deep inside his missionary heart, "they know we love them. God loves them. And He sent His only begotten Son for them.

"Each one," he said and then said again slowly, "each one knows they are special to God. Made by Him, made for Him, and beautiful in His sight."

"Each one . . ." I repeated and knew he was a much better man than me.

In this is love, not that we loved God,
but that He loved us and sent His Son to be the
propitiation for our sins.

—1 JOHN 4:10

"So help me understand two things," I said, a little confused. "When we first met, you were an accountant, right? I don't remember you ever saying you wanted to be a teacher. And second, well, this is the harder question for me. I want to know how you see the unseeable. The people the world tosses aside."

His eyes shot down.

I could see I'd made him uncomfortable with my questions. I apologized and told him it was none of my business. He shook his head and looked right at me.

"No, I'm glad you asked." He motioned for more coffee and we went back to the counter, refilled, and sat back down. But the tone between us was different.

The joy gone.

"You're right, I was an accountant," he began. "It was the safest profession I could find. I was good at it and, for the most part, I could work alone—just me.

"You see, you don't really know my full story. I'm a misfit, always have been. I was the joke of my classmates. Always made fun of, always pushed aside, always called names. A couple times, I changed schools, but it didn't matter. The same thing happened. I remember one day, when I was about sixteen, I finally accepted it.

"I'm what you call one of the 'unseeables' in the world. That's me.

"Of course, that changed the day I met Lily. She was the first person in my life, outside my immediate family, who ever took notice of me. She was amazing. She went out of her way to welcome me into her circle of friends. She couldn't wait for me to meet her family or take me to her church. She saw me. She loved me.

"Eventually, I learned that God loved me too. It took a while. My self-image had spent a lifetime in the gutter. Lily kept telling me I was special to God. Made by Him, made for Him, and beautiful in His sight. But I didn't believe her. For others—yes, absolutely. But not for me. But she kept on. She wouldn't give up.

"One morning in church, she handed me a note: 'This is what love is all about, Steve. Jesus came for us. Jesus saw

us. Jesus died for us. His death, His blood, the propitiation—
the payment. Love that big. Love that real.'"

He dropped his eyes again and became quiet. I watched
as he swiped at the tears in his eyes. I wanted him to go on
with his story. But the longer we sat there, the more I realized
he'd finished his story. He'd told me everything.

The unseeable misfit had been seen by God. And loved.
And forgiven.

Beloved, if God so loved us, we also
ought to love one another.

—1 JOHN 4:11

"If I remember right," I said, breaking the silence. "Your
job moved you to Pittsburgh. At some point, I'm guessing,
you heard about the church in the inner city and its work
with kids. You knew what it was like to be unseeable. And
you knew how to see the unseeable.

"And you knew what they needed—more than anybody.
And so, you and Lily moved from a nice home in the suburbs with two young boys, a good job, a peaceful life, and
moved into the inner city where it's not safe.

"Where the pay stinks. Where you can barely afford to
take your family on a nice vacation in the summer or build
up a college fund for the boys when they finish high school.
All because you knew what He did for you. And if He did

it for you, you had to do it for others who were like you. That's what I'm guessing."

He nodded his head slowly, lifted his eyes to mine and gave me a half-smile. "Well, something like that," he mumbled, as if he needed me to know there were still mysteries about him that couldn't be figured out quite so easily.

"It's not hard, you know."

"What's that?" I asked.

"Seeing the unseeable."

I looked at him. Then I looked again, for the umpteenth time, at the check between us and told him I disagreed.

Beloved, if God so loved us, we also
ought to love one another.

— 1 JOHN 4:11

Then I looked at my watch. If I didn't leave now I'd miss my first appointment in a string of appointments that took me to the end of the day.

"Do you have a little more time?" I asked Steve. When he said yes, I texted the office, told them I'd be late and to reschedule the morning meetings.

"I can't believe a man with your responsibilities, with such a busy schedule, would take this much time for me. I wasn't expecting it," Steve admitted.

"Me either," I said, as a confession. "But, to be honest, that's the problem and I need your help."

QUESTIONS FOR REFLECTION

The story of what Jesus did for us—His coming, His death on the cross for our sins—is intended to be lived every day. We get to live that agape in His power! Will you ask Him to make it real in you right now?

So many of us live like Steve, with low self-image. Do you see how Lily lifted his head to see Jesus and how it changed him? Whose head can you lift today? Who needs to know this agape that makes all the difference?

45

SEEING THE UNSEEABLE

~~~

Reflections on 1 John 4:12–14

No one has seen God at any time; if we love one another, God abides in us, and His love is perfected in us. By this we know that we abide in Him and He in us, because He has given us of His Spirit.

—1 John 4:12–13

"I need to ask your forgiveness," I began.

Steve's face crumpled in a quizzical frown. He had no idea what I meant.

For just a moment I froze. I'd become everything I promised I'd never become. Early on, as a young Christian man, I saw something that confused me. There were too many broken relationships among us. People in Christ unreconciled with others in Christ. The command of God— love one another—meant little.

And I didn't know why.

As I started traveling in the circle of pastors, I sometimes saw the same thing. I met gifted preachers, brilliant theologians, successful men and women who lived their passion by changing their world for Jesus Christ. A few of them let me get close. Close enough to hear them say what I didn't want to hear at all.

Vision comes first. Ministry comes first.

Not people.

And in their wake, they let me see a long trail of broken relationships behind them. People crushed in heart as their pastors pursued the big things of God.

"It's part of the story," one clergyman told me. "You can't let it bother you."

"It's what our pastor does," said one of the casualties. "It's what we've come to expect."

Not me, I vowed, never me. I choose to walk a different path. We are to love one another as Jesus Christ has loved us. This is where it all begins. It is the one great nonnegotiable. Where there are bròken relationships, we mend; we forgive; we reconcile. We do everything we can for as long as it takes.

Because I knew then what I know now.

Every time we love one another as He loved us, we see the unseeable God; we experience Him in us and we in Him. Every time we love one another as He loved us, love is made perfect.

But here I sit, looking at Steve Harrelson and wonder how I ever got myself in this mess. Over and over I said it wouldn't happen. Not for me.

But it did.

No one has seen God at any time; if we love
one another, God abides in us, and His love is perfected
in us. By this we know that we abide in Him and He
in us, because He has given us of His Spirit.

—1 JOHN 4:12–13

"I don't understand," Steve whispered.

"You see, it's about those people you talked about," I started. "The ones who pushed you aside and made you feel like you didn't fit in. Well, I know those people, I know them well. I'm one of them. I've done what they've done. Not just to others, Steve, but to you. And I am so sorry.

"I'm sorry for my text yesterday. You said you were in town, asked if we could meet together for coffee, and what did I do? I texted you right back and said no—without a second thought. I pushed you away, and the moment I did, I knew it was wrong. I do it—and I know I do it—and I hate when I do it. I push people away. I pushed you away."

Steve smiled, leaned forward and grabbed my arm. "Don't be too hard on yourself. It's my fault. I should have called ahead."

"No, Steve, it's not that," I insisted, putting my hand over his. "It's me. I came here this morning thinking that this is what you wanted to talk to me about."

"Really?"

"Really. You said it was time to put things right, didn't you?"

"Yeah."

"Well, I thought this was it. I thought you saw right through me. I thought you knew I'd mistreated you all these years and you wanted to make things right with me again. So I came here expecting to look you in the eyes and say sorry."

He squeezed my arm and then sat back, looking a little surprised.

"I can't explain it very well," I went on. "I've had glimpses in my life of seeing what you've experienced. I've watched people push others down, push them away without care or kindness, like they're throwing away a piece of trash. And worse, I've seen Christians do it. I've seen pastors do it.

"A long time ago, I vowed I'd never do it. But I do. And yesterday was a perfect example. I spoke at church, teaching from 1 John where no one can escape God's word to us: We are to love one another as Jesus Christ has loved us.

"I gave a strong message. I was convincing. I gave no wiggle room for anyone."

I put my head down, ashamed and embarrassed. This was it. This was my sin. I'd become one of those preachers who got to tell others what to do—but didn't have to do it myself.

"Guess what I did right after I spoke," I said to Steve, looking right at him.

He shook his head almost imperceptibly.

"I texted you back and blew you off."

Because He has given us of His Spirit.
We have seen and testify that the Father has sent
the Son to be the Savior of the world.

—1 JOHN 4:13–14

We sat there for a few minutes in silence. Somehow I knew Steve got it. He understood as few could.

Finally, I said again, "I'm sorry."

It came so naturally to Steve. He knew exactly what to do. He stood up, opened his arms, and invited me to do the same.

One simple embrace.

One simple act of kindness and right then, in a second of time, I could feel the Lord's forgiveness—and Steve's—poured rich, full, and deep into my soul.

"Can I have more time with you?" he asked with a playful tone.

"What do you have in mind?"

"There's something I want you to see. It'll take an hour—maybe an hour and a half at most."

I looked quickly at my watch. Not that it mattered. I'd have given him the rest of the day if he wanted it. "Yeah, absolutely," I said, reaching for my phone to text the office that I'd be back sometime after lunch.

"And don't forget the check," Steve insisted, pointing to it on the coffee table. I picked it up with a lingering reluctance and put it in my shirt pocket. We left the coffee shop and decided to get into Steve's car.

"Have you ever been down to Springer Street and Lexington?" he asked as he strapped himself in. "It's where the pushers, pimps, and prostitutes hang out."

"Not exactly," I said, a little concerned. "Is that where we're going?"

"Yeah, it's the best."

As he said it, his face lit up like a child on Christmas morning, and I knew exactly where we were going.

"You're taking me to see the kids who live there?"

He gave a quick nod, and I sat there stunned. Here in my own backyard were kids in need. Kids living in the worst section of town. Kids I'd never seen or knew anything about. Kids Steve flew all the way from Pittsburgh to see.

On the corner of Springer and Lexington.

And now he wanted me to see the unseeable too.

"But there's so much more!" he said with delight. "We get to see God! Every time we hold them, every time we hug them and they hug back, we get to know the love of the Father. We get to feel the Savior's rescue. What," he asked, "could be better than that?"

QUESTIONS FOR REFLECTION

I've always found this is the hardest and best place to be: confessing our sins to each other. Getting right with each other. With whom do you need to do this? What holds you back?

It's a simple prayer: "Lord, help me see the unseeable and let me make a difference." This agape is meant to reach people around us in need. What would happen in your life if you could suddenly see the unseeable? Will you pray this prayer and get yourself ready for action?

46

SPRINGER AND LEXINGTON

~~~

Reflections on 1 John 4:15–17

*Whoever confesses that Jesus is the Son of God,
God abides in him, and he in God.*

—1 JOHN 4:15

"Our stories are so much alike," Steve said once we were on the highway. "I was as blind as you when it comes to people like me."

"That's hard to believe."

"No, it's true. It's not like people like me hang together and help each other out. At least I can tell you that wasn't my experience! Rejection tends to isolate. I lived in a very, very small world of me, myself, and I."

"So what happened?" I asked, a little surprised.

"This!" he said, pointing at the steering wheel. "A pastor from the inner city came to speak at our church. He told us all kinds of stories of what life is like there—especially how it affects kids. He said it was impossible to see it and walk away. He said he'd like our money but he'd rather we come see it too."

"So you did?"

"You bet we did and it changed everything. Lily and I went to the pastor afterwards and told him we were interested. Two Saturdays later, he came to our house, picked us up and drove us into the city. Just like we're doing now."

"The pastor came himself?" I asked.

"Yeah, I think we were the only ones who signed up." Steve tried to remember as he got off the highway, made a couple of turns until we got onto Springer. "I can't wait for to you see those kids! They're going to be happy to see you too."

"Same here," I volleyed back, intently staring at the people on the sidewalks.

He turned left onto Lexington and quickly found street parking.

"That pastor taught me a simple rule," he said. "When we're blind to others, all we see is ourselves. It doesn't matter whether we're running with the crowd or running alone. We need the Lord to open our eyes and see what we can't see."

He turned off the engine and grabbed the keys.

"And when He does, it's impossible to see—and walk away."

Whoever confesses that Jesus is the Son of God,
God abides in him, and he in God.

—1 JOHN 4:15

"This is it," Steve said, pointing to three houses inside a chain link fence. My eye caught the sign over the entrance to the middle house: Jesus, Son of God, Lord of This Home.

"Classes are still in session," Steve told me as we got out of the car and walked toward the house. "We can slip in the back and watch. Afterward, I'll introduce you to Sam Claiborne, the director. How does that sound?"

"Great," I said, stepping inside. And the moment I did, a little hand slipped into mine. I looked down and saw a five-year-old boy staring up at me with big soft eyes, light brown skin, short, curly, black hair, and an inquisitive look.

"Is this OK?" he seemed to ask without saying a word.

I nodded and smiled back.

We followed Steve through the entry room and kitchen before coming to the classroom. We took our time though. My new friend hobbled. Something was wrong with his right leg. Not like it was broken. More like it was misshapen.

Steve found some seats in the back.

The room felt small to me, too small for the thirty, maybe forty, elementary age children and the adults filling it. Up front, I saw a teacher giving a math lesson to half of them. Off to the sides, the rest of the children were huddled in groups of three or four with an instructor sitting at eye level with them.

As I took my seat, the boy—little Joseph—climbed into my lap.

Still holding my hand.

We have come to know and have believed the love
which God has for us. God is love, and the one who abides
in love abides in God, and God abides in him.

—1 JOHN 4:16

Steve leaned toward me and began talking in a low
whisper.

I tried to listen to him but couldn't—not with this little
boy in my lap. He was now leaning against my chest, his
head buried under my chin. Both his hands now fit into my
left hand as my right arm naturally wrapped around him.

A gentle, tight squeeze.

And then I saw it.

The right side of his head was indented. His skull caved
in—maybe three inches long, one inch wide. I took my right
hand and placed it on his head over the area. This wasn't
natural, I thought to myself. This was violence.

Had he been struck by a baseball bat? A broomstick?

The little boy then lifted his head and looked at me with
the biggest, brightest smile. I smiled back, pinched his
nose, and he let out the sweetest giggle ever. But his face—
I could see it up close now—a scar over his right eye. Scars
on both his arms.

"My name is Little Joe," he volunteered softly, holding
up four fingers. "I'm four-and-a-half years old." And then
he buried himself again in my arms.

From the corner of my eye, I saw someone approaching. I heard Steve say, "This is Sam. He's the director of the home." I decided not to get up—not with little Joseph in my arms. I extended my hand in greeting and saw that class was now over. The room had become chaotic with children heading off to the kitchen for lunch; others, in wheelchairs, following behind.

"Let's go in my office," Sam directed. "It'll be quieter there."

"Can Little Joe come with us?" I blurted, and received a quick nod from Sam. I stood with the little boy in my arms and wanted—more than anything—to know his story. What had happened to him? Who did this and why?

My heart—I could already feel it breaking.

We weren't in the office two minutes before a loud knock came on the door.

"Sam, Steve, we need to talk—now," the man said urgently. Within seconds, it was clear our visit was over. Steve apologized and told me he had to go.

"Bad timing," he explained, "We've got a little crisis here. I hate leaving you like this. Is it OK if I find somebody to drive you back to your car?"

"That's fine," I said, as he turned to leave.

"I'll call you when I get back to Pittsburgh," he promised and then, with a firm close of the door, Steve Harrelson was gone.

By this, love is perfected with us.

—1 JOHN 4:17

"Please don't you go too," Little Joe said, putting his hand on my cheek.

"No, not yet," I said back. "But I'll tell you what we can do. We can have some lunch together. What do you think about that?"

He clapped his hands, squealed with delight, and said, "Yeah!"

But just as I started to get up, his little hand dove into my shirt pocket and pulled out the check Steve had given me. I watched him play with it in his hands and then hold it up for me to see.

"Mine!" he said emphatically.

"Yours?" I asked, pretending to be surprised.

"Yeah, this is mine!" and with that, his giggle came back loud and strong. For whatever reason, he balled up the check, thrust it back into my pocket, threw his hands around my neck, and hugged me like I was his long lost friend.

"I guess it is, little man, I guess it is," I said, hugging him right back, and found—to my surprise—a giggle of my own.

QUESTIONS FOR REFLECTION

As we confess Jesus, Son of God, this agape love comes to abide in us and we in Him. Will you pray for the Savior, by His Spirit, to fill you with that love today—more than you've ever known? Love for Him in worship. And love for others like never before.

Too often we live in our own protected bubbles. The way this text of 1 John 4 comes alive is to burst the bubble, see the unseeable, and ask Him to help you live this agape. Are you in a bubble? What will it take to burst it?

47

LITTLE JOE AND ME

Reflections on 1 John 4:17–18

*By this, love is perfected with us, so that we may
have confidence in the day of judgment;
because as He is, so also are we in this world.*

—1 JOHN 4:17

I said good-bye to Little Joe right after lunch. His classmates were already lining up near the stairs.

"It's nap time," he told me. "I have to go now."

He hopped off my knee to join his friends. A few feet away, he turned back with a vigorous wave of his hand and a smile that had a hint of sadness.

"Bye-bye little man!" I exclaimed with a wave back. "I'll come see you again soon, OK?" He nodded, turned, and left. And I wondered if he believed me.

It hurt to see him go. It hurt more to see him limp like that. And then, my last sight of him at the staircase, grabbing the banister, hoisting himself up, one step at a time.

"What can you tell me about Little Joe?" I asked.

"What do you wanna know?" Brother Max said as we got in the car. Steve Harrelson had asked him to drive me back to the coffee shop.

"Everything."

"About eighteen months ago there was a drug bust a few blocks down Springer," he recounted. "Two people were killed. We think one of them was Little Joe's father. One officer was shot and wounded. Police found the boy hiding under the kitchen sink, bleeding something fierce over his right eye."

"I saw the scar. What about the dent in his skull?"

"Already there," Max said, looking right at me. "Domestic violence, that's what that is. Somebody hit him hard, probably when he was a baby."

I gasped at the image. "Who does that? Where is his mother?"

"Prison. She'll be in a long time. She's the one who shot the police officer."

"And his leg? Why does he limp like that?"

"Doctors call it a birth defect. They say he'll need three or four surgeries to correct it. But they say it's possible. He should be fine. I tell you, the Lord's hand is on this boy. The home he came from? His head bashed in? You'd think he'd be all messed up, but he isn't. Right there, that's one beautiful child."

"You got that right," I echoed, trying to take it all in.

"We've raised half the money for the two surgeries he needs right now," he told me, as he drove the city streets. "We're trusting Jesus for the rest."

I asked Max for details. I wanted to know exactly how much it would cost and what the surgeries would entail. He told me everything he knew and assured me, "Soon as the Lord provides the money, we can get started."

"I can't wait," I thrilled, "to see him run with his friends!"

———

By this, love is perfected with us, so that we may
have confidence in the day of judgment; because
as He is, so also are we in this world.

—1 JOHN 4:17

———

I talked to Steve Harrelson three times over the next week. I wanted to know what he thought about our plan.

"You OK if we do this?" I asked him.

"Yeah, but are you sure?"

"Really sure!" I said strongly. My wife and I agreed that Little Joe was right. The check Steve had given us was meant for him. If Steve approved, we could put it toward his surgeries and then raise the rest of the money needed.

"I want our church to help," I told him.

"Let me see if some of our staff can come—maybe bring Little Joe with them."

"No, I don't want that," I resisted. "I want to do with this church what you did with me. I want them to go and see the children right here in our own city. I'd like them to meet Little Joe on his turf, not ours."

"OK, but do me a favor. Watch your heart," he gently warned. "Not many people are going to sign up for a Saturday morning on Springer and Lexington."

"Yeah, you're right," I paused. "We'd raise the money faster if they came to us."

"But you'd win their hearts if you go to them," Steve countered. "Think about what the Bible says, 'As He is, so also are we in this world.' Who He is and what He does is who we are and what we do! If we let Him, He takes us to see the unseeable. He lets us hear the cry of those we can't hear. And then, the highest privilege of all—we get to love them in the same way Jesus loves us."

"Hey, they love us back—maybe more," I said, thinking about that little man.

"Then don't focus on fund-raising," Steve concluded. "The money will come. Instead, do what Jesus does. Take them to meet Little Joe and his friends."

There is no fear in love; but perfect love casts
out fear, because fear involves punishment, and the
one who fears is not perfected in love.

—1 JOHN 4:18

Once again, I stood in front of the church to teach on 1 John. Everything inside me wanted to press on with the lectures and not tell my story.

But I had to.

We come this morning to one of the greatest chapters of the Bible. Hear the words, dear friends, hear the words: "God is love."

Real Love—who sent His only begotten Son for us.

Real Love—who died on the cross to save us.

Real Love—who comes bursting into our hearts the moment we're born of God and He, by the Holy Spirit, abides in us and we in Him. We are loved by God and we know it at the very core of our beings.

And when that's true, when God has made His love real to our hearts, we are to make that love real to each other.

Love one another! What He did for us, we do for someone else!

And with that, I began the story.

I told them an old friend by the name of Steve Harrelson had contacted me, asked for coffee, and I brushed him off, shortly after teaching from 1 John last week and saying that "Relationships are everything in the kingdom of God!"

I did it coldly, recklessly.

A little while later, I realized what I'd done. I was deeply embarrassed. How can I stand here and teach the Bible but not live the very thing I'm teaching?

But it got worse. I started to see a pattern in my life. It's not the first time I've tossed Steve aside. He's one of those unseeable guys—the kind who hides in the shadows and doesn't run with the crowd. He's often alone, off by himself.

Fear started rising in me. Fear I'd offended the Lord. Fear not just for this time, but for all the times I'd done this. With Steve. With others. I was suddenly panicked. What do I do now? How does this sin in my life stop for good?

I told them I met Steve for coffee. I told them the Lord gave me an opportunity to ask his forgiveness for the way I've treated him all these years.

And do you know what he did? He stood up, opened his arms, and hugged the forgiveness of Jesus into my soul. I tell you, in that moment, the fear left me. It was gone as fast it came. And the saying is true, forever true: "Perfect love casts out fear."

I told them Steve taught me how the Lord taught him to love the unseeables and how he drove me down to Springer and Lexington.

I told them every detail I could remember about the home and the children. And about Little Joe who had snuck his way into my heart.

I believe the Lord has given me the task to raise the remaining funds needed for his surgeries. But I don't want your money. I won't take it. I'd rather have you. Is it possible there are some here who'd go down to Springer and Lexington with me and meet Little Joe face-to-face—and all his friends at the home?

I looked out at the congregation, said a few closing words, and then prayed: "Lord, give us eyes to see what You see. That we might love as You love."

With that, one person spontaneously stood up, raised her hand, and said, "I'll go." And to my utter, complete shock, I saw the unimaginable.

One by one, nearly half the congregation stood and raised their hands.

QUESTIONS FOR REFLECTION

Can you imagine it: As He is, so are we in this world? As we live agape love in the community of His church, love is perfected in us. We have confidence to stand before Him. How can you, and your church family, step deeper into this agape love of Jesus?

When we don't do this, fear tends to dominate. This love is the antidote—casting it out. Do you know something of this fear in your life? Are you willing, ready, to end its control over you?

48

UNLOVABLES

Reflections on 1 John 4:19–21

We love, because He first loved us.

—1 JOHN 4:19

Steve,

So much has happened since you left ten days ago.

As I told you over the phone, nearly half the church wants to go to Springer and Lexington to meet Little Joe and his friends. Sam's first response made me laugh: "All at the same time?" Clearly, a director's worst nightmare!

So we made two decisions. First, Sam invited us to come every Saturday morning from 8:30–11:30. He'll have work projects for us to do, but we can only bring fifteen at a time. At the breaks, we'll have a chance to meet and play with the kids. Second, I asked him to come speak to our church—then after, with our mission board and church elders. That happened last night. And let me tell you, it was a major home run!

What impressed me most was how Sam engaged the congregation with great questions like, "How do we build a bridge between the suburbs and the inner city? What can we do that's helpful? And what must we carefully avoid?"

Let me capture some highlights:

We agreed the Saturday morning work projects—under Sam's direction—was a great first step.

We were concerned that Little Joe was being singled out. And Sam cautioned, "We don't want the other children to feel jealous!"

We talked about ways we could develop relationships with each child.

A lot of time was spent on how we might volunteer at the home—teachers, kitchen workers, nurses, social workers, etc.

Sam asked if we'd pray for people in the congregation to move into the city, join the staff, and be there on site with the children.

Also, we offered to help with a summer VBS in the city.

We spent a long time in prayer—for the kids, the staff, for Sam and his family. We specifically asked the Lord to teach us how we might serve in the city—a prayer we've never prayed before as a church.

After that, a man got up and said, "Is it OK if I leave a check for Little Joe?"

Almost at once, an offering basket was placed in the back of the church and by night's end we had more than enough to cover both surgeries.

Can you believe that? Praise the Lord!

You've turned my little world upside down, Steve. I can't thank you—and the Lord—enough.

God bless you, dear friend.

Thad

We love, because He first loved us. If someone says, "I love God," and hates his brother, he is a liar; for the one who does not love his brother whom he has seen, cannot love God whom he has not seen.

—1 JOHN 4:19–20

Nearly three months later, I felt like I hit a wall. I called Steve and asked for some time. I didn't know who else to talk to.

"I feel like I'm telling people half the story," I confessed over the phone. He kindly listened as I rattled off a series of high points from both our Saturday morning work projects and the stream of volunteers who serve during the week.

"So, you're afraid to tell the bad stories," Steve confirmed.

"Yeah," I sighed.

"If it's any help, I hit that wall several times a month — even now."

"You're kidding?"

"No, I wish I was. Sometimes it feels like all I have are bad stories. A month ago we had shootings in the neighborhood. Three teenage boys were killed, most likely gang related, we think. One of them was thirteen years old. Thirteen!

"Then last week," Steve continued, rattling as fast as I rattled, "we lost two of our first graders. In both cases, their moms went to court and won them back. How is that possible? These are single moms who are not well. They have prison records, both drug addicts. These kids don't have a chance. We argue it in court, but we rarely win."

"I'm so sorry," I groaned, hearing the ache in his voice.

"But what really irks me are the kids themselves. I wish all of them were like Little Joe, really, I mean that. He's a thousand times better off than most."

I heard him take a long, deep breath.

"I got hit today by a nine-year-old boy, his fist right in my face. He just lost it, threw a tantrum, next thing I know— *pow!*—and blood starts gushing out of my nose. How's that for a typical day at the office?"

"That's not good," I sympathized.

"I remember his first day here. I was so angry *for* him— who beats up a five-year-old child almost beyond recognition? Who gives their child drugs? I looked at him and thought for the first time, 'Is it possible this child is damaged beyond repair?' Even now, I don't know. I think I pray for this child more than any other. I pour and pour the love of Jesus into him—and every once in a while I see a glimmer of hope. Then, like today, it's gone. And I don't know what else to do."

"I'm glad I called," I said quietly. "I needed to hear this."

"You and I talked about seeing the unseeable," Steve recalled.

"Yeah, we did."

"What we didn't talk about was how to love the unlovable. That's what I wrestle with all the time. I can actually feel hatred inside me—hatred for those who hurt these children; hatred for a judicial system that doesn't care one iota for these kids; hatred even for nine year olds when they bash me in the nose!"

With that, he laughed just a little.

"So how do you deal with it day in, day out?" I asked.

"I run to Jesus and ask Him to help me. I hold His promise in my heart that I can love these children today because

He first loved me. I give Him the hatred rooted deep in my soul knowing I can't love Him and hate others."

"That simple?" I asked.

"That simple and that hard all at the same time."

⎯⎯❧⎯⎯

And this commandment we have from Him, that the one who loves God should love his brother also.

—1 JOHN 4:21

⎯⎯❧⎯⎯

Steve,

Summer is here and VBS is in full swing.

I wish you could see this. We've taken over a huge church parking lot a few blocks down Lexington. I bet there are a hundred and thirty kids out here having the time of their lives! And get this, close to 30 percent are from the suburbs!

Right now, I'm sitting on a rickety old fold-out chair, drenched in sweat. I had to take a break from the kids to e-mail you the attached video. Can you believe this? That's Little Joe actually running with his friends! Five months ago it was a dream and a prayer—but look at him now! He's a thousand times better. A few more surgeries later in life and he'll be good as new.

Thank You Lord Jesus!

And I hope you can hear the sounds of these kids laughing and screaming at the top of their lungs. Isn't it hysterical? We're all having so much fun.

But I miss you.

My heart is full today—for you. You brought me here. You helped me see Jesus in the faces of the inner city. You taught me to love the unlovables, and it was like a door opened into the

*kingdom of God for me. This is it! This is His command—we love
each other in Jesus' name. It starts here. It ends here.*

How blind I was in my sin, even to you.

*But you loved this unlovable. Thank you. And with all my
heart, I love you.*

Thad

QUESTIONS FOR REFLECTION

We can give agape because God who is agape has given it to us in His Son. This is why His command is a nonnegotiable. Is this love inside you? How will you love the unlovable around you?

We need people like Steve in our lives, encouraging us, pushing us to get out of ourselves for the sake of others. Do you need someone to push you? Who can you ask? And who can you push and encourage today?

PART 7

MADE REAL

49

CHAP

Reflections on 1 John 5:1–4

Whoever believes that Jesus is the Christ is born of God,
and whoever loves the Father loves the child born of Him.

—1 JOHN 5:1

I arrived at the hospital late morning. Walked in, grabbed a cup of coffee in the lobby, and headed to the seventh floor.

Gabby.

She hates the hospital.

Her husband called about 7:00 this morning saying, "Her pain levels were off the charts." He'd taken her to the ER just after midnight. "We want to fight this cancer," he said, trying to rally, "but we can't keep doing this." They'd been talking about hospice for the last few days.

The door to her hospital room was half open. As I gently pushed on it, I heard the sound of voices quietly singing and instantly stopped to listen.

Blessed Assurance, Jesus is mine!
O what a foretaste of glory divine!

I peeked in and saw Chaplain Bob Kaelin sitting by Gabby's bed. Neither of them saw me and as quickly as I ducked in, I ducked out.

This is my story, this is my song,
Praising my Savior all the day long.[1]

I stayed there until the song ended and the tears began.

Chaplain Robert T. Kaelin, III, served in the Marines during the Persian Gulf War. He'd never say it himself, but he was fearless in battle, caring more for the souls of the wounded and dying than for himself. After twenty years in military service, he came to serve as Protestant chaplain of our local hospital.

All of us call him "Chap."

I made my way to the sitting room near the elevators. I was sure, after his visit with Gabby, he'd pass by.

As I waited, I pulled out my phone and brought up Chap's blog page. He'd started it a few years ago after being diagnosed with multiple myeloma. "This way," he said wisely, "I only have to tell the story once."

The last entry was two days ago. A few lines jumped out.

Hard days after chemo. Little sleep. Weak, nauseous, throbbing headache.

The good news is that Dr. Sam seems optimistic. Not sure why. The test results are not good. Marcia and I both think the treatment plan isn't working. Dr. Sam reassured me yesterday that we weren't out of options.

Now for the better news. I did wake up this morning! Another day, another battle, another chance to live for Jesus Christ and serve those He puts in my path.

What could be better than that! Pray for me . . . as I pray for you.
Chap

He's still on the front lines, still fearless, still caring more for the souls of the wounded and dying than himself.

And he's singing. How is that possible?

By this we know that we love the children of God,
when we love God and observe His commandments.

—1 JOHN 5:2

"Chap!" I called out as he passed by.

He quickly smiled when he saw me. I stood to greet him, still not used to his bald head or pale complexion, let alone his six-foot frame all skin and bones.

"Ah, you must be here to see Gabby?" he said as we embraced.

"How do you think she's doing?"

"It's not long now," he responded, "and she knows."

"Oh, Chap, I can't thank you enough for being here. I was just rereading your last blog. Sounds like you've had a hard week."

"Always is after chemo. But it's different these last few times. I don't have the stamina like I had before, that's all."

"I'm so sorry," I said, concerned for him. "That's why I was surprised to see you when I got to Gabby's room. Then, to hear you both singing . . . well, that nearly undid me. I don't know how you do it, Chap."

"I'm a military man!" he smiled, with a gentle fist pump. I pointed to two chairs and we sat down opposite each other.

"When I was in combat," he said, reaching in his back pocket for a small Bible, "not sure whether I was going to live or die, I knew one thing above all others. We do what God has commanded, and His commands are not burdensome."

I watched him flip the pages as he spoke.

"I think of myself as being under orders. For as long as I have breath, I am to love the children of God. That's what we do—it's who we are. No matter what battle we're fighting. If we believe Jesus is the Christ, if we're born of God, if we love the Father—then we're under orders. All of us."

He found the verse and read it to me.

"For this is the love of God, that we keep His commandments; and His commandments are not burdensome" (1 John 5:3).

The strength in his voice didn't match his physical appearance. He kept his focus fixed on the page, quiet, almost as if discovering something new.

"This is the love of God," he slowly repeated, nodding his head. And then he looked at me, his eyes moist. The very same eyes, years ago, the marines of Operation Desert Storm saw as they lay dying on foreign soil.

The same eyes Gabby just saw.

As much as I understood that Chap was a man under orders, sent by God to love the children of God, I also knew it went deeper than that. His heart had been taken captive by the love of Jesus Christ. It's what got him up and dressed this morning. It's who he is; it's what he does.

And clearly, he wasn't done.

"Now tell me," he said sitting back in his chair, trying to get comfortable, "I want to know what's going on with you. How are you doing?"

Gabby's eyes were closed by the time I went to her room. As quietly as I could, I sat in the chair next to her bed. After some time passed, she turned and saw me.

"Hey," she said in a whisper.

"Hey to you," I said back.

"Oh, you just missed Chap," she frowned.

"Saw him on the way in. I got here in time to hear you both singing. Made me hope you'd do it again at church this Sunday. What do you think?"

"I'll check my schedule," she teased and then winced with pain. As it eased, the song came back to her and, ever so beautifully, she spoke the words:

Blessed Assurance, Jesus is mine!
O what a foretaste of glory divine!

Her eyes closed as she fell back into sleep. I saw her Bible on the bedside table and decided to open it to the passage Chap had just read to me. As I did, I found myself reading the next verse.

"For whatever is born of God overcomes the world; and this is the victory that has overcome the world—our faith" (1 John 5:4).

"How is it possible," I thought, "to sing in the face of death? Who does that? Who cries out, 'Blessed Assurance!' as cancer waves its flag of victory over what remains of our disease-ravaged bodies? Chap and Gabby, that's who. Overcomers, who know by faith what the world can never know.

"Jesus is mine!"

"So tell me," I heard her say softly, and I half expected what she was about to say, "how are you doing? And how's your family?" And then she reached for my hand and squeezed.

QUESTIONS FOR REFLECTION

When we believe Jesus is the Christ, we are born of God. This puts us under orders to obey His command to love the children of God. Do you see yourself as under orders? Or does it feel more optional?

This agape love indwelling us by the Spirit and then through us to others is the victory that overcomes the world. No matter what trials we face, this is our faith. Can you feel its strength? Have you seen it in others like Gabby and Chap?

NOTE

1. Fanny Jane Crosby, "Blessed Assurance," 1873, public domain, accessed May 27, 2014, http://cyberhymnal.org/htm/b/l/e/blesseda.htm.

50

GABBY

~~✍~~

Reflections on 1 John 5:5–8

*Who is the one who overcomes the world, but he who
believes that Jesus is the Son of God?*

—1 JOHN 5:5

I looked quickly at my watch. It was time for the service to begin.

"Chap, where are you?" I mumbled to myself.

One of the ushers came up behind me, "He's not here." I looked around the church one more time. It was already full. Gabby's family was seated up front. The pianist and choir were nearing the end of the prelude.

Chap had called three days before from Gabby's home.

"She's gone to be with Jesus," he informed me quietly. "I was here when she passed." He didn't hold back one detail. He told story after story of their last conversations, what she wanted at her funeral, and what her last few moments were like "as the Lord swept down and took her to Himself."

"Chap, I think you should speak at her funeral."

He didn't respond.

"She told you what she wanted you to say," I replied. "I can do it but I think it would be far better if you did."

"Yes," I heard him finally say but there was hesitation in his voice and I knew it had nothing to do with speaking at the funeral and everything to do with "this stubborn, old, unreliable, chemo-battered body" of his.

"But you be ready just in case," he insisted.

I told him I would be, but I was sure—a little too sure—he'd be there.

Who is the one who overcomes the world, but he who believes that Jesus is the Son of God? This is the One who came by water and blood, Jesus Christ; not with the water only, but with the water and with the blood.

—1 JOHN 5:5–6

Halfway into the service, I caught his figure in the shadows at the side entrance of the sanctuary. He looked frail and tired. He saw me catch his eye and nodded ever so slightly with a less than robust thumbs-up sign. He was here, just in time. Then, right on cue, he began his walk to the front of the church. With every step, it seemed like his body gained strength. His stride oozing gentle confidence. And his face had a brightness in it.

He walked straight for the casket positioned at the head of the aisle in front of Gabby's family.

He stopped, turned with military precision to the cross suspended near the front wall of the church and bowed. With one more turn he faced the people, his hands resting on top of the golden funeral pall draped over the casket.

"Let us pray," he said, his voice filling the sanctuary.

"Lord Jesus Christ, Son of God, Lamb of God, did You not come down from heaven for such a time as this? Be with us now. We need Your comfort. This we ask in Your holy name. Amen."

Everything then became quiet as Chap stood there in silence, his hand tracing an emblem stitched into the pall of a lamb embracing a flag of victory.

And then he started.

It may not surprise some of you to learn that Gabby gave me orders on what to say here this morning. She was most emphatic: "Don't speak about me. Speak about Him. This is His day. Not mine."

In our last conversation together, she was concerned about two things. She said, "I don't want my family to miss me so much they turn away from the Lord. You mustn't let that happen, Chap. And another thing, help them not to be afraid of death."

"How do you propose I do that?" I asked her.

"Tell them the story of the sea captain," she instructed. "Do you remember that one, Chap? That should do just fine."

I'd told her that story soon after she'd been diagnosed with cancer and was shaken by the news. She had no idea how to navigate the rough seas in front of her: The chemo, the surgeries, the radiation, and all the side effects. And that's exactly how it felt—like her ship had hit a storm bigger than she could handle.

"What do I do?" she asked me.

"I look to the sea captain," I told her.

She scowled at me, not understanding. I assured her that
military chaplains are asked this question all the time. The
wounded and dying need answers. They need something to hold
onto—something strong and reliable.

That's where the sea captain comes in.

What does he do when land is out of sight, when endless
seas surround? How does he find his bearings? How does he
know where to go? It's quite simple. He looks up. He finds what's
fixed and unmovable. He sees the sun by day, the moon and stars
by night, and he knows exactly where to steer his ship.

Of course, it's different when clouds come: winds pick up and
toss the ship here and there. It's more difficult when night falls
and thunderous storms beat down on him with waves cresting
taller than mountains. He looks up but he can't see anything. Still,
even then, he knows what to do.

He reaches for his compass and holds it firmly in his hand.
He knows the same God who stretched out the heavens and the
earth also gave us magnetic north and south. He can find his
bearings. He can take the helm and steer the ship. His God has
given him help. He can find his way, even in the worst of storms.

He's never lost, never.

The same is true for us.

God has given us help. All we have to do is look up. We find
what's fixed and unmovable. We look to Jesus Christ who is our
sun by day [Luke 1:78] and the morning star by night [Rev. 22:16].
And when the clouds come, the storms of life roll in, and we are
beaten down by the wind and waves, He's still there. He's our
compass. He's our north and south. We are never lost, never.

We find ourselves when we find Him.

And what did He do? He gave us two signs. The first is water,
said the apostle John. He went down into our baptism, though
He didn't need it Himself, and made a way for us—a physical,
real way to enter His kingdom. When we look to Jesus, when we

believe in Him and go into these waters, He grabs the helm of our ship. He stands as the Sea Captain Himself in our lives. We are never lost, never.

But He didn't come by water only. He also came to us by blood. When He died on the cross, He went into every storm we'd ever face. He took to Himself all our sins and sufferings, our pains and sicknesses, our fears and torments. His cross, His blood, is strong and reliable, fixed and unmovable.

Hold onto Him! He has risen triumphant. He reigns over every storm. Death cannot have us. The Devil cannot have us. No thunders of hell, no raging seas or driving winds can ever take us off course. We are never lost, never.

Just look to the Sea Captain. Hold onto Him, and He will see us through.

It is the Spirit who testifies, because the Spirit is the truth.
For there are three that testify: the Spirit and the water
and the blood; and the three are in agreement.

—1 John 5:6–8

Chap stopped and looked down at the casket. Once again, he traced his hand over the emblem on the pall. Sitting so close, I could see the tears in his eyes.

He saw Gabby through. Just as He promised.

I asked her, a few hours before she died, if she was ready. She nodded, took her hand and patted her heart gently. "He's here," she said. "The Holy Spirit is here. I'm not afraid." And she wasn't, right up to the time she died.

I can tell you this; I've rarely experienced the presence of the Lord so fully, His love so strong, as I did that afternoon with her family at her bedside. At one point, I took her hand. She looked at me and said, "It's time."

"Would you like me to go with you," I asked.

A little smile came across her face and she said, "Not yet, Chap. Soon."

When she said, "Soon," I knew she was right. I don't have much time left. I can feel the winds picking up and the seas beginning to churn. I can hear the distant thunder and see the clouds darkening overhead. It's coming, I know that, like it comes for all of us. And sometimes, I feel afraid.

But we don't need to be, do we? Not if the Sea Captain is at the helm. Not if the Holy Spirit has taken up residence in our hearts. He will see us through. We will find our way home.

And you and I will hold His promise, then and always, deep in our hearts—just like Gabby: Never lost, never.

QUESTIONS FOR REFLECTION

How do we know this faith that overcomes the world is in us? John gave us assurance by pointing to the water, the blood, and the Holy Spirit who testifies within us. Do you have this assurance of faith in Jesus Christ?

How do we help each other turn to Jesus and let Him be our strength, our refuge—fixed and unmovable—to see us through even to the end?

51

MARCIA

Reflections on 1 John 5:9–12

*If we receive the testimony of men, the testimony of God
is greater; for the testimony of God is this, that
He has testified concerning His Son.*

—1 John 5:9

We were on a mission trip in Africa when the news
came from Marcia, his wife.

Thad,

Sorry to tell you this over e-mail.

*Chap died last Wednesday in the hospital. He'd slipped into
a coma two days before and died peacefully. The funeral service
was held on Saturday at Christ Church and Chap would have
been so pleased. You know how much he didn't want people
speaking of him and all his achievements. They didn't. Instead,
they did what Chap did for them—they testified of Jesus.*

*The biggest news of that service was Robbie, Chap's
nephew. Hellion from birth, that boy. We prayed for him every
night of our married life. And wouldn't you know, at Chap's
funeral, he went up to the minister and gave his life to Jesus.
Pastor Dave promised me he'd follow up and take Robbie under
his wing.*

I found such comfort in this news.

Many who served with Chap in Desert Storm couldn't be here with such short notice. So I told them I'd have a memorial service at the Cathedral in six weeks' time. This has met with a great response. I know you'll want to be there.

When you get home and settled, will you and Erilynne come for a visit? Can't wait to hear about your trip. Safe travels home.

Marcia

The one who believes in the Son of God has the testimony
in himself; the one who does not believe God has made
Him a liar, because he has not believed in the testimony
that God has given concerning His Son.

—1 John 5:10

We connected by phone while still in Africa but it was far better when Erilynne and I saw Marcia face-to-face and talked endlessly of Chap.

We attended the memorial service. It was breathtaking as fellow marines and military and government dignitaries rose to give tribute to their fallen comrade. This man, they said with one voice, had run the race well. "He deserves the honor given him here today," one chaplain remarked, "for God's promise always stands. 'Those who honor Me I will honor'" (1 Sam. 2:30).

A few minutes after the service, a man in his late forties came up to me, shook my hand and said bluntly, "For the longest time, I didn't like him one bit."

"Excuse me?"

"I'm Colonel Mike Bowman. I served in Desert Storm with Chap."

I motioned to the front pew and we both sat down.

"In my opinion anyone who went crawling to Chap had no business being a marine. It was a sign of weakness and fear, like someone running to Mommy or Daddy the moment they skinned their knee. We are men. We are US Marines. We depend on no one. We get the job done."

I listened, wondering where this conversation was going.

"On my first tour, I went to chapel once. A buddy in my regiment took me. He said, 'When you hear Chap, you'll want to go back.' He was right, part of me wanted to. I still remember Chap saying, 'You either live for God or you live for yourself. Which is it?' And I chose to live for me, simple as that.

"My second tour, we saw a lot of combat. Chap spent a lot of his time in the medical unit. But just as often, he'd go straight into the gunfire with us."

Mike quickly looked away, like a memory had taken hold.

"When I got hit, Chap was right there. He stayed with me till I got back to the base. It took two days for the docs to stabilize me before they shipped me off to Europe to recover. Before I left, Chap came by and asked how I was doing.

"'Good sir,' I said. 'It'll take some time but I'll be back.'

"'Mind if I pray for you before you go?' Chap asked me.

"'I'd rather you not, sir,' I said. 'I can handle this.' And I watched as he nodded out of respect for my wishes but he couldn't leave it at that.

"'God saved you for a purpose out there, Mike. I think you know that. Some of the men didn't make it. You did. Always remember that.'

"Those words made me so angry. When I got back to my regiment four months later, I wanted nothing to do with him, chapel, or God. I mocked the guys who read their Bibles and talked about Jesus. To me, they were cowards, all of them."

I sat there, fascinated. I couldn't help but ask. "So what changed your mind about Chap?"

"He told me I called God a liar."

"Chap did?"

"Well, sort of," Mike backpeddled. "Six weeks later, my best friend was killed in action. Chap did the funeral before his body was shipped back to the States. I took it hard and what Chap said at the service that day really struck me:

If you don't believe the testimony God has given us, you call Him a liar. If you don't believe the testimony God has given us concerning His Son, Jesus Christ, you call Him a liar.

Is that you? Why are you doing that?

These are the facts. If we believe God, He puts that testimony into our hearts so we can face anything—even death itself.

When we believe God, He gives us eternal life and that life is found in His Son.

This fallen marine believed in Jesus Christ. Today he has what one day all of us who believe in Jesus will have—life, real life, eternal life!

Believe, dear friends, believe.

"I never forgot that. Fifteen months later, I was stateside holding my newborn daughter and all I could think about was Chap's words: 'You call Him a liar. . . . Why are you doing that?' I knew it was time to give my life to Christ. So I called Chap, left a message, and asked if he'd call me back and pray with me."

"And did he?"

"Yes sir," the colonel said, "and every year, on the same day, my phone would ring and I'd hear Chap say, 'Hey Mike, guess what today is?'"

And the testimony is this, that God has given us eternal life, and this life is in His Son. He who has the Son has the life; he who does not have the Son of God does not have the life.

—1 JOHN 5:11–12

After Mike left, I looked around and saw that most people had gone to the reception. I sat back in the pew and grabbed a small pocket Bible next to me.

Marcia had slipped it into my hand before the service began. "Chap carried it with him everywhere," she told me. "I want you to have it. A little something to remember him by." Now, for the first time, I opened it and saw Chap's handwriting:

Robert T. Kaelin, III / Chaplain in the Marines, 1987
"He who has the Son has the life" (1 John 5:12).

I flipped slowly through it, occasionally seeing verses he'd underlined, hand-written notes in tiny print, and little pieces of saved paper tucked between the pages. I eventually found my way to 1 John 5:12 and found a note written to Marcia—one I supposed she hadn't read yet—dated February 27, 1991.

One last gift from Chap's heart to hers.

Marcia,

Sometimes I wake up in the middle of the night in a cold sweat—afraid. All I can think of is you. All I can see is the military car pulling up in front of our house and you—and the kids—standing at the front door as they walk toward you bearing the news of my death.

If that happens, maybe this Bible will make it back to you. Maybe this note will still be in it.

I love you fiercely. Do you know that, Marcia? From the first day I laid on eyes on you until today—and always. I pray we live a full and long life together. I pray we will see our children grow and hold our grandchildren tight in our arms. But I fear you're reading this and I am gone. My heart swells with a cry for you.

I love you so . . .

I will see you—not stateside as we'd hoped—but heavenside. For I know we hold the promise of God firm. We have the Son; we have the life—always.

Chap

QUESTIONS FOR REFLECTION

God has made Himself clear: He has testified about His Son. When we believe, we have life. When we don't, we call Him a liar. Do you believe fully? Are you in need of this life coursing through your veins today?

To have the Son, to have Jesus, is to have eternal life in you now! There is no greater gift, no greater promise, than this. What does it mean to you to have the Son—and to have the life? Will you ask the Lord to help you know this deep in your soul?

52

HARRY

Reflections on 1 John 5:12–15

He who has the Son has the life; he who does not have
the Son of God does not have the life.

—1 JOHN 5:12

A few weeks after Chap's memorial service, a box was sitting outside our front door. I opened it and found a note from Marcia.

Thought you might like to see a few of Chap's journals. They date back to his early days in college. Every once in a while I pick them up and find myself transported back in time. I hear his voice. I remember the people, places, stories of our past. And—does this seem odd to you?—I feel like he's close again. Just a random few here. I'd like them back sometime, but no rush. Love—M

I lifted three spiral notebooks out of the box. One dated 1974, another 1981, and the last 2002. Each had the same handwriting on the top upper right of the opening page. Only the date differed:

Robert T. Kaelin, III / Chaplain of the Marines, 1974
"He who has the Son has the life" (1 John 5:12).

The next Saturday morning I sat in my study, grabbed the journal from 2002, and began to skim the pages. It was classic Chap! I saw sermon notes, Bible passages, to-do lists, prayer lists, private confessions, calendar events, quotes from the day, doodling that looked like a first-rate cartoonist, and then stories.

So many stories.

They'd start on one page, marked with the date and time, and then pick up pages later, as Chap recorded his interactions with the people he served.

I flipped to October and found one called "Harry." I could see Chap was stateside, serving at the hospital here in town and visiting a former marine.

~~*~~

These things I have written to you who believe in the name of the Son of God, so that you may know that you have eternal life.

—1 JOHN 5:13

~~*~~

7:10 a.m. / October 22

Oncology wing. Marine's name is Harry Kimball, 53, Methodist pastor of a local church since 1992.

Diagnosis: Metastasized melanoma.

Private room. Found him sitting in a chair next to his bed, reading. He greeted me like an old friend. Except for his hospital gown, I could barely tell he was a patient. He looked fit, healthy, with good color in his face.

He took the lead, asking, "What's it like to be a marine chaplain?" We talked for the better part of a half hour before I could change the subject.

"Now tell me about you. I understand you've got melanoma."

He nodded and said, "Stage 4. The doctors say, in my case, it's best to operate first, and then talk about chemo." With candor, he admitted, "I'm still in shock. My wife and I both are." Then, with great ease, he assured me of the strength of his faith in Jesus Christ as the Son of God and His gift of eternal life.

"Down through the years," he told me, "the Lord has met us in every situation. He's always been faithful and we know, even now, He's faithful still."

We talked. We prayed. Harry did more for me, I fear, than I did for him.

October 23, the next day, the entry was brief:

Harry's waiting for lab results. Surgery, scheduled November 5. Should be released tomorrow morning.

October 24, Chap was there for Harry's discharge and wrote the following:

9:45 a.m. / October 24

Harry stood to greet me—dressed, with an overnight bag on the hospital bed. I could tell something was bothering him.

"You OK?"

"Not really," he said. "Got a call last night. The elders of our church want to plan a healing service the night before I go into surgery."

"Is there a problem with that?"

"No, I think it's great."

"So, what's going on?" I asked.

"I just don't know if God wants to heal me or not. What if this is my time?" He turned, picked up his Bible and sat down. "I read a lot of passages this morning. Like this one, in John 14:14: 'If you ask anything in My name, I will do it.'"

He then turned to Mark 11:23–24 and read it out loud.

"Truly I say to you, whoever says to this mountain, 'Be taken up and cast into the sea,' and does not doubt in his heart, but believes that what he says is going to happen, it will be granted him. Therefore I say to you, all things for which you pray and ask, believe that you have received them, and they will be granted you."

These were familiar texts for both of us, and we said so. There is mystery here, unexplainable mystery. We shared stories of people the Lord healed and those He didn't. As Harry said so well, "They have the same faith, just different outcomes."

His question lingered between us, "What if this is my time?"

"You see," he went on, "I don't want people disappointed if I die. If that's what happens, I want their faith strengthened in Jesus Christ—not hurt."

Again, we told stories of people who'd "claimed" these Scriptures for loved ones, "claimed" the healing, only to find the person die and their faith crushed. He didn't want that. Not for him. Not for his family, friends, or church.

I watched in silence as he stared out the window.

"Everything inside me," he said, his voice strong, "wants to say to this cancer, 'Be taken up and cast into the sea!' But if that isn't the Lord's plan for me, I need to accept that. I need to help others accept it and walk with me into my dying."

We talked, we prayed. I read from 1 John 5:14: "This is the confidence which we have before Him, that, if we ask anything according to His will, He hears us." I repeated the phrase, "If we ask according to His will."

"That's my prayer, Chap. 'Lord, give me faith for healing. If that's not Your will, then give me faith for dying. And help me help others whichever You choose."

I followed the story in Chap's journal. He noted phone calls to Harry. He attended the healing service at Harry's church. He was there on the morning of surgery to pray for him. A few days later, Chap made this entry.

7:45 a.m. / November 8
Harry's in good cheer today. The surgeon gave a good report. Not sure the course of treatment yet. Another day or so, Harry will be discharged.

From that point on, Chap recorded weekly calls to Harry. In mid-December, he wrote,

Harry's progressing well. The Lord has been kind to him.

I couldn't find anything else. I called Marcia and asked if she'd ever heard of Harry Kimball.

"Yes," she remembered, "but it's been a while. Maybe ten years or more? Chap and I used to go out to dinner with him and his wife occasionally."

"Do you know what happened to them? Is Harry still alive?"

"As far as I know," Marcia thought. "He took a church in Florida, near Tallahassee somewhere. I'm sure we got a Christmas card last year but, now that you say it, I don't think I heard from him after Chap died."

I thanked her, got on the Internet, found his church and decided to call. "Is Pastor Kimball there?" I asked, as someone answered at the church.

"Yes, may I ask who's calling?"

"A friend," I said, then corrected myself. "Well, a friend of a friend."

As I waited to hear his voice, I couldn't believe it. All these years later, Harry Kimball was alive! The Lord had heard the prayers of His people and, according to His will, had decided to heal him of stage 4 melanoma. The excitement in my heart turned quickly to a longing for Chap. I missed him so much I actually said the words out loud, over the phone, "Oh, Chap, I wish you were here."

To my surprise, a voice answered back.

"You know my friend, Chap?"

QUESTIONS FOR REFLECTION

The Lord has entered into relationship with us. As we talk to Him, as He talks to us, we come to the great topic of prayer. Do you have confidence in this relationship? Do you know He hears you? And do you know, better through the years, how to hear Him too?

It's in the context of this relationship that we seek His will and counsel for all situations. As hard as it is sometimes, we offer ourselves to Him when we pray, "Lord, teach me to pray according to Your will." Can you offer that prayer today, fully trusting Him?

53

M

Reflections on 1 John 5:16–17

*If anyone sees his brother committing a sin not leading to
death, he shall ask and God will for him give life to those who
commit sin not leading to death. There is a sin leading to
death; I do not say that he should make request for this.*

—1 John 5:16

I was startled to open Chap's 1981 journal and find a dark,
ominous drawing of a man's face and, overtop, a demonic
figure hovering—wings outspread.

The caption under it read ominously:

Having done all for M—is rescue possible?

A few pages later, Chap wrote,

*All attempts have failed. Most think M won't be back. We've
agreed to stop communications—doing more harm than good.
We continue to pray for him in all chaplain meetings. Remember
Matthew 18:15–20.*

The quote from Matthew made me think M did something
horribly wrong, was disciplined, and refused it. The journal

recorded prayers for M but little else. Then in March, Chap wrote:

> *Bumped into M at a retirement party. Avoided me all night. I opted not to torment him by initiating a conversation. His wife was cordial but distant. If only his heart would turn back. He belongs in Christian fellowship with us . . .*

By June, prayers for M were sporadic. After that, there was nothing until mid-September when it picked up again. I found this entry on December 27:

> *Slipped in my prayers for M. I say again, in all my years, I've never witnessed anything like this. If this is the "sin leading to death," how then do I pray?*

There is a sin leading to death.

—1 JOHN 5:16

I called Chap's wife.

"We were living in Beaufort, South Carolina, at the time," Marcia began telling me. "Chap was stationed at Parris Island. One day, orders came down the chain of command for Chap to 'fix the problem' with one of his fellow chaplains who, I believe, was five years Chap's senior."

"What kind of problem?" I asked.

"You know, I can't remember the details. All I know is it scared Chap. He'd never seen defiance like that before. This man M basically spat in his face, resigned his chaplaincy, and walked away. It was awful. I'll never forget Chap quietly telling me, 'I feel like I'm witnessing the unforgiveable sin.'"

I asked if I could see the 1980 journal.

"Sure," she replied, "but if I were you, I'd call Bradford Sparks. He went through it with Chap. Did you meet him at the funeral?"

I did, but only briefly. He'd flown in from Jackson, Mississippi. A retired marine chaplain who was now serving as a Methodist pastor. I went online, found his number, and made the call.

There is a sin leading to death.

—1 JOHN 5:16

"Remember him? How could I forget?" Sparks laughed when I asked about M.

I'd called the church to make an appointment with Pastor Sparks. As it turned out, he answered the phone and was more than happy to talk with me. "You have no idea how I miss my old friend," he said about Chap. "We were twenty-three when we first met—both of us! Did you know that?"

The stories came freely, one after the other.

I told Sparks I was reading some of Chap's journals. I'd stumbled on this man called M and wanted to know more. "Marcia suggested I call you."

"M was our code name."

"I figured that. In what I've read so far, Chap never used his real name. Nor have I found out what he did. I'm guessing he preached heresy of some kind?"

"No," Sparks said definitively. "He was a solid preacher of the Bible."

"So, what was it?"

"A woman."

"Excuse me?"

"A half-dozen eyewitnesses reported inappropriate conduct with a woman on his staff. Senior military officers assigned Chap to the case. Of course M denied any wrongdoing; so did the woman. But the more Chap investigated, the more eyewitnesses surfaced. M was in serious trouble, and he knew it."

"Sounds pretty straightforward," I commented.

"It wasn't that easy. M had friends higher up, both in the military and in political office. Plus, he had money. The combination proved deadly."

"What do you mean?"

"Powerful friends in powerful places did his dirty work for him. The case was dismissed. M was never disciplined. He stayed in office and so did the woman. A senior officer called Chap and told him to back off the investigation. Chap contested, naturally, but there was nothing he could do."

I sat back in my chair, trying to take it all in. "I'm guessing that's not the end of the story," I reasoned.

"No, it's not," Sparks replied.

"So what happened next?"

"Chap and I went to M's house, unannounced. We met with him and his wife. We confronted him as a brother in Christ, urging him to separate from this woman completely, admit his wrongdoing, and then publicly stand down from his office. We begged him to do what was right before God and His church."

"How did he react?"

"He laughed at us and told us to leave." I heard Sparks take a deep breath over the phone and groan.

"All we could do was pray for him. We got three other chaplains to meet with us weekly for prayer. It lasted a couple of months or so. After that, we didn't know how to pray anymore. Then, in a strange twist of events, M resigned the military and became pastor of a church nearby."

"Let me guess," I said. "The woman went with him."

"She did," Sparks said. "It was like nothing we'd ever seen before. Defiance, brash, in-your-face rebellion to God. It scared us, really scared us. Still does."

———

There is a sin leading to death; I do not say that he
should make request for this. All unrighteousness
is sin, and there is a sin not leading to death.

—1 JOHN 5:16–17

Chap's 1980 journal came in the mail. I skimmed through it and found the first entry on M dated September 5:

Assigned to investigate M today. Need tactical wisdom. This won't be easy.

I quickly noticed Chap didn't use his journal to gather and assess data. He did, however, record dates and times of meetings, phone calls, to-do lists, prayers, and occasional observations, like one dated on October 9:

Met with M this morning. He's confident, controlled, at times patronizing. As I presented my findings, he became angry, defensive, and threatened me. I am sure this has little to do with the woman and everything to do with his heart.

The entry on Monday, December 8 read simply:

Sparks and I met with M and his wife at their home. Mission failed.

Then, on the last day of the year, Chap wrote these final thoughts.

The Lord Jesus speaks of the blasphemy of the Holy Spirit—a sin that is never forgiven either in this age or in the ages to come. This has always been a mystery to me. The apostle John called it the "sin leading to death."

And tells us not to pray. Is this it?

I had thought it was reserved only for heretics, wolves dressed as sheep who come to hurt, divide, and destroy the people of God by their twisted words which deny the faith of our Lord Jesus Christ. But now, I'm not so sure.

There are others.

Their hearts are calloused and hard. Their ears are closed so they cannot hear the counsel of God. There is no humility in them. No fear of God. No ability to see their wrong and repent. Their feet walk in defiance. Their heads are lifted high in arrogance. They are sinning against the Holy Spirit, but they don't know it.

So they laugh.

And I am left scared.

QUESTIONS FOR REFLECTION

It is our job in the body of Christ to come around those committing sin. We take initiative. We pray, discipline, and love. We do our best to recover them. Do you have this passion in you for others? Has anybody modeled this in your life?

What do you think this "sin leading to death" means about which we do not pray? Is there any defiance in you to godly counsel? Any rebellion which needs to be confessed before God?

54

SPARKS

Reflections on 1 John 5:16–18

And there is a sin not leading to death.

—1 John 5:17

Marcia sent me another batch of Chap's journals.

"His story should be published," I suggested to her on the phone. "His biography would impact a new generation of military chaplains."

"Funny," she replied. "Sparks said the same thing."

"Do you think he'd write it?"

"He might. Call and ask him!"

So I did. I left a voice message on his phone and asked him to call back.

If anyone sees his brother committing a sin not leading to death, he shall ask and God will for him give life.

—1 John 5:16

In the meantime, a journal entry in May 1986 caught my eye.

Once again, I saw a drawing of a man, this time from the waist up, his face dark and brooding—much like Chap's 1981 drawing of M. But this was different. Three angels stood around, as if protecting him, each with their eyes lifted to heaven. The caption underneath looked almost playful.

He thinks he's M!

The story began on the previous page where, in the upper left corner, I saw the words: "Wed., May 14: B in trouble," followed by a series of bullet points.

B's wife came to my office at 12:35, her eyes red from crying. She stood in the doorway and quietly announced, "He's having an affair."

I assured her it wasn't true.

She handed me a piece of paper with B's handwriting: "Call S. for lunch Weds. Needs to end—but how?" She said she found it on his desk this morning and knew she had to go to his office and find out who S is.

I asked why she was suspicious. She said there'd been calls. When she picked up, the other person hung up. When B picked up, he'd go off by himself saying, "It's confidential." She shrugged and said, "A wife knows . . . "

Then came the hard evidence. "I just saw them together. They came out of his office building and got into his car. They didn't see me. I didn't know what else to do but come here." I listened, prayed with her, and promised I'd do what I could.

The entry ended with an arrow pointing to the bottom right corner of the page where I found a large B and another entry.

> *Went straight to B's office and waited for him there. He came in at 1:25, took one look at me, and asked, "What's going on?"*
>
> > *"She knows," I said.*
> >
> > *Poor B, it was like I hit him across the face.*

We know that no one who is born of God sins.

—1 JOHN 5:18

I flipped the page and saw, just right of the drawing, the story continue.

> *B broke instantly, collapsing into a chair near the door. There were no words between us for quite a while. He was sobbing uncontrollably.*
>
> > *Finally, I asked, "Did you end it?"*
> >
> > *He nodded.*
> >
> > *As I stood up to go, he panicked, "Please, don't go. Help me."*
> >
> > *"Be at my office at 4:30," I said. "You know the routine." He nodded, slumped forward in the chair with his head in his hands, and continued to cry. I had no doubt he'd come—and he did, 4:30 on the nose. He looked terrible, disheveled, like he'd lost a barroom fight.*
> >
> > *"Nothing happened between us," he insisted.*
> >
> > *"I don't believe you," I said sharply. "You look guilty. You act guilty. Why else would you be here unless you are guilty?"*

"I mean, nothing physical. You have to believe me."

"You sound like M," I punched back.

"I'm not M!" he thundered, but it didn't work. Their stories had too many parallels, and he knew it. I watched him walk over to my office window and stand there in silence. A few minutes later, he turned to me with fear in his eyes.

"It's true, isn't it? I'm just like him."

We know that no one who is born of God sins; but He who was born of God keeps him, and the evil one does not touch him.

—1 JOHN 5:18

On the next page, 10:45 at night, Chap wrote one last journal entry for the day.

B is not M. It's just that he doesn't know it yet.

Here's what I know: Six months ago, S cried out for help and B responded. All done above board. The calls, however, didn't stop. He began seeing her in remote places—a town park, a city diner. Even to the end, he justified these meetings, "as long as it wasn't physical." But inside, all along, he knew he'd crossed the line.

And he couldn't stop.

A fire had lit inside his belly that raged beyond his control. He loved the secrecy; he craved the attention; he wanted more of her. For days and nights on end, he told me, S was all he could think about, dream about.

Seeing her again. Talking to her again.

It had to stop. But how? When? He knew full well he'd slipped into the Enemy's camp and, if he wasn't careful, there'd be no way out. "I dreaded meeting with her today," he admitted. "Nothing in me wanted to end it with her—but I did."

It was one day too late.

And so, tonight, B went home to talk to his wife. We will meet in the morning. We will meet for as long as it takes to get this wretched addiction uprooted from his soul and cast forever into the eternal fire where it belongs.

He is not M.

He is teachable, and that's all I need to know. It's the mark of the true Christian. We who are born of God may sin. But if we do, we do not continue in our sins. When we come under the conviction of the Holy Spirit, we are teachable. Always teachable. And Jesus Christ—who, for our sake, was also "born of God"— keeps us.

Keeps us safe.

So the Evil One cannot have us.

All wrongdoing is sin, but there is sin that does not lead to death.

—1 JOHN 5:17 ESV

Sparks called back.

"You and I have our work cut out for us old boy!" I said, laughing. "What do you think about writing Chap's biography? I'll do the research, you do the writing."

"Deal!" he said, surprising me.

"Really? You mean it?"

Sparks said he'd already contacted a friend in the publishing business who knew Chap. "He loved the idea. He wants to know how fast we can write it!" And off we went, talking a mile a minute, planning how we'd write this book together while, at the same time, working our regular jobs.

"Oh, by the way Sparks, I have a question for you. From what I can gather, you and Chap were still working together in 1986. I found this story about a man named B who, I believe, was a colleague of Chap's. Do you know him?"

"Why are you interested in B?" Sparks said, his tone changing.

"I'd love to find him, talk to him, see how he's doing. Seems Chap really helped him through a dark time in his life—what Chap called a 'wretched addiction.' I'd love to know what happened to him and if the addiction ever came back."

"I know B well. In fact, I see him every day. And no, it never did."

"You're kidding? Tell me about him!"

"What would you like to know?"

"Let's start with his name. What's the B stand for?"

He hesitated a moment. Then, in almost a whisper, he said, "Bradford. That's his first name. But most people just call him 'Sparks.'"

QUESTIONS FOR REFLECTION

There is a great chasm between the sin leading to death and the sin *not* leading to death. All of it rests on the mark of the Christian soul. Are you teachable? Open to correction? Do you welcome discipline with delight (note Heb. 12:5–11)?

Addictions that dig deep into the soul require us to come alongside as Chap did with B. Do you try to handle your sins alone? What would it take for you to ask for help? How about being a help to others?

55

MY DEAR JOHN

Reflections on 1 John 5:19–20

*We know that we are of God, and that the whole
world lies in the power of the evil one.*

—1 JOHN 5:19

A little later that day, Sparks sent a text: "What you don't have are my journals. It's time you hear some of my story. Here's a glimpse of what happened next."

I got home that night and Cindy was gone. She'd left a note on the kitchen table: "The kids and I are staying at the Coopers' for a few nights. Don't contact me."

I stood there frozen—note in one hand, flowers in the other. I was planning on taking her to dinner, just the two of us. I'd made arrangements for a babysitter. We'd talk it out like we always do. Stupid, stupid me. I never dreamed she'd get hurt like this. Not by me. And now, I was face-to-face with the bitter poison of my sins. My wife and kids were gone. I was in control of nothing.

The next morning, I went straight to Chap's office. "You have to talk to her."

"What happened last night?" he asked.

"They're gone. They're staying at a friend's house." I showed him the note and told him I'd do anything to get her back. I

begged for his help, desperate for Chap to pick up the phone, call her, and get this mess fixed. But he said, and said forcefully, "No, I'm not doing it. I'm not interested in your marriage right now. I'm interested in you."

I stood there stunned. I couldn't understand why my best friend refused to help me. I exploded in anger and headed for the door. Chap calmly reached for his Bible, pointed to the chair and ordered me to sit down.

"Chap, I don't have time for this. I've got to get Cindy back."

"She doesn't want you back, Sparks. Not like this. Now, sit down, we've got work to do." I banged the door with my hand and screamed, "No!"—as the realization hit me hard. I'd lost her. I'd lost the kids. I'd lost me. And there was nothing I could do about it. Nothing.

"Eyes on Jesus, Chaplain!" he bellowed. "You want this mess fixed, you turn to the One who'll fix it. Not me. Not you. Him! You got that?"

"Yes, sir," I said reflexively. I went back, grabbed a Bible off his desk, fell back into the chair, and felt my world collapse into a blaze of fire.

Right underneath the entry, Sparks had written in big, bold caps "1 JOHN 5:19–20" and drew a thick black box around it. On the next page, he'd written out verse 19 before continuing to write his story: "We know that we are of God, and that the whole world lies in the power of the evil one."

I promised Chap I'd give full attention to these two verses. "You dig into them until they dig into you," he prescribed. I agreed but saw no hope in it.

Two days later, I met with him again. 11:00 sharp. Most of those two days, I cried, wallowing in self-pity. At some point, I began to repeat verse 19 over and over again, "I know I am of God. The Evil One has no power over me. Not now, not ever. Why? Because I know I am of God . . ."

Slowly, it made sense.

I'd slipped into Enemy camp and allowed lust for S to take me captive—lust I thought I could control, play with, enjoy for a time, and never get caught. But I did get caught. So what do I do now? How do I escape the Devil's hold?

I knocked on Chap's door. I needed answers.

"Cindy?"

She opened the door and rushed into my arms. "It's going to be OK," she said. "We'll work it out." I couldn't believe this was happening. I held her in my arms as tight as I could and cried like a baby. I kept saying, "I'm sorry. I'm so sorry." She held me right back and whispered, "I know. Chap told me."

Then she pulled away, looked me straight in the eyes, and said, "We've got a long road ahead." I nodded, eager and ready. "Then tell me why this happened, Sparks. Tell me why I'm not enough for you."

"No!" I reacted. But her face, her words—I could see it now—the pain of what I'd done to her. I reached out, but she took a step back and turned toward Chap.

"She's coming home tonight with the kids," I heard Chap say, meeting my eyes. "But you're on the couch for the next few weeks. That work for you, Sparks?" I turned to Cindy to see if it was true.

"Only if you promise you'll work with Chap," she said.

"I promise," I swore, and then watched her quietly slip out of the office.

And we know that the Son of God has come, and has
given us understanding so that we may know Him who is true;
and we are in Him who is true, in His Son Jesus Christ.

—1 John 5:20

*Chap was relentless. For the next few weeks, I met him every
other day at his office, 11:00 sharp. He'd always start with the
same annoying question.*

"Have you had any contact with S?"

"No, sir," I'd say, hating the reminder. "It's over between us."

"Are you sure?"

*"I'm sure," I'd respond quickly, and then we'd begin. First, in
prayer. Then, in conversation. We'd talked about two verses in
1 John which, he kept telling me, had power to end my addiction to
lust. I followed his lead but, to be honest, all I wanted to do was talk
about the guilt I felt for using and hurting S, for profoundly dishon-
oring my wife, for sinning against God. Chap would hear none of it.*

*"I don't want to hear about you quite yet," he'd say. "I want
to hear about Him." So, I'd pull out my Bible and read the sticky
note I'd written next to 1 John 5:20:*

*Today, I put my eyes on Jesus Christ, Son of God.
I take them off S, off me, off Cindy.
He has come to give me understanding.
He has come that I might know Him.
He is true. The Evil One is not true.
The lusts I followed are not true.
I am in the Father who is true.
I am in His Son, Jesus Christ, who is true.
Today, I put my eyes on Jesus Christ, Son of God.*

"Getting right with Him," he'd say, "is how we get right with others. That's how it works. The world out there doesn't get it. People long for real love, but they can't find it because they can't find Him. Real love—and not the evils of lust—comes from the Father. This, and only this, makes relationships with others possible."

"I want that," I told him.

And slowly it happened. As I turned my heart to the Lord, He let me see me why I'd let this lust for S take control of my life. The more I saw, the more I confessed, the more I felt the Evil One lose his grip over me. "That's why I gave you these two verses," Chap kept saying. "They tell us the truth. You belong to another."

Forgiven. Little by little.

Until, at last, I was free.

"I was thinking of using this story in the biography," Sparks told me a few days later, "What do you think?"

"It's Chap—every bit of it. You made me miss him."

I heard Sparks chuckle over the phone. "He made me sleep on that stupid couch for six weeks! I'd complain about how much my back hurt, and he just didn't care. 'Try sleeping on the floor, Sparks. That should help!'"

"You were expecting mercy?" I chided.

"Yeah, right? He knew exactly what to do. I remember the day Cindy and I renewed our marriage vows, I couldn't thank Chap enough. All I could say was 'Chap, you're my apostle John and you always will be.'"

"What did you mean by that?" I asked.

"For six weeks, he talked and prayed 1 John into my life. I soon saw John's passion for the church to be right with God and right with each other was the same passion

Chap had for me. And all he did was step into John's shoes and trust the Holy Spirit would bring His Word alive in my heart and rescue me—rescue our marriage."

"So, how did Chap react?"

"With a smile, a hug, like you'd expect. But over the years, I kept it up. On the anniversary day when Cindy and I renewed our vows, I'd write Chap a note. Same thing every year:

My dear John,
I'll never forget.
Sparks

QUESTIONS FOR REFLECTION

The strength of godly counsel always rests on a good mentor, prayer, the application of Scripture by the Holy Spirit, and faith to believe God will step in and heal the soul. What can you do to have these strengths in your life?

We tend to focus first and always on the problems we're suffering. These verses, 1 John 5:19–20, refocus us on our first relationship with the Father and with His Son. Can you put your eyes on Jesus today—He who is always true—no matter your situation?

56

JESUS, MY LORD

Reflections on 1 John 5:20–21

This is the true God and eternal life.
—1 John 5:20

I sat in my office researching Chap's early years through college. Marcia had sent me everything she had, and Sparks was breathing down my neck to get my work done. "We've got deadlines," he urged me last night, worried. "Fast as I can," I said, knowing I was way behind with four interviews still to conduct.

As I reached for another pile on my desk, I saw a note from Marcia.

T—I never showed you Chap's final journal. You need to see the last few entries before he died. I think it'll be a good way to end his biography. —M

I knew better not to open it then. There was too much to do and too little time to do it. But still, I couldn't help myself. Three times I tried to ask Marcia if I could see

Chap's final journal but never found the courage. Part of me wanted to read it, part of me didn't. And now, here it was, in my hand.

I flipped to the last ten pages. As always, I saw his signature verse: "He who has the Son has the life; he who does not have the Son of God does not have the life" (1 John 5:12).

I started reading and couldn't put it down.

> *Marcia and I drove away from Dr. Sam's office about 11:30 and headed for the coast. We have a restaurant there we love to go to—The Captain's House. Wouldn't you know it, a table by a window overlooking the ocean opened up just as we walked in. The timing couldn't have been better.*
>
> *We sat there a little while staring at the view we love so much. It was a perfect summer day—not a cloud in the sky, the sunlight sparkling on the water for as far as the eye could see with a shimmering brilliance almost too bright to look at. The beach was a sight all its own, people of every size and shape imaginable playing, swimming, laughing. We saw it all and, I think, saw nothing at all.*
>
> *I reached over and grabbed Marcia's hand. She did her best to smile back at me as she took her napkin and touched the corner of her eyes.*
>
> *The news was about an hour old.*
>
> *Dr. Sam said it kindly, gently, "I think we're done, Chap. The lab results show you're no longer responding to treatment, and I have nothing left to give you."*
>
> *"How much time does he have?" Marcia asked.*
>
> *"Few weeks, maybe more. That's my best guess."*
>
> *Before we left his office, as always, Dr. Sam prayed for us. Sometimes I think it was his prayers—not the treatment—that bought me as much time as I got. I'm indebted to that man. He's been more than a doctor to me. He's been my friend.*

Neither of us ate very much. . . . Neither of us wanted to leave. We kept ordering more food just to keep our seats! Somehow Marcia—I'm not sure how she did it—found the spunk to perk right up, remember a thousand and one stories from our past, and make the afternoon thrill with joy.

I don't think I looked out the window again.

She is—always has been—the view I love best.

This is the true God and eternal life.
Little children, guard yourselves from idols.
—1 JOHN 5:20–21

The next few pages of his journal were filled with notes on daily activities. He recorded names of people he talked to on the phone or who came by to visit. I looked for and found our names. I remember our last time together like it was yesterday. He wrote,

Lovely visit with T & E today. Off to Africa soon.

I saw Scripture verses, prayers, complaints on new aches, bad night sleeps, things Marcia had said, memorable one-liners from his grandchildren—"Pappy, I swam underwater for the first time today!" and stunning one-liners like, "Pain meds come from the pit of hell" and "Dying, I don't recommend it." Typical Chap, he had a cartoon face looking just like him, bald and bug-eyed.

A few pages later, his handwriting still strong, I saw one last entry, long and substantive. After that, his penmanship started to change, his thoughts less cohesive and more random, prayers begun but not finished, sentences soon unreadable, unintelligible until, at last, the writing was done.

The entry was dated just five days before he died.

I have long wondered why the apostle John ended his letter with the words, "Little children, guard yourselves from idols." Why not leave it with the great climax, "This is the true God! This is eternal life"?

I know now.

We have idols in this life. I have idols.

Preachers, poets, hymn-writers have often described this moment before death as if we've come down to the banks of the river Jordan. Soon enough, the waters will part, we will behold the appearing of our blessed Savior, and we'll make the crossing into the Promised Land with songs of unspeakable joy and praise.

I've spent most of my adult life here at the Jordan, helping others die.

"Don't look back," I'd say. "Remember Lot's wife. Forget what's behind you. Reach for what's ahead. Press on toward the goal for the prize of the upward call of God in Christ Jesus. It's not far now. Fix your eyes on Jesus . . ."

And I'd stay with them, reading the promises of God until they crossed.

"For I consider that the sufferings of this present time are not worthy to be compared with the glory that is to be revealed to us" (Rom. 8:18).

"For to me, to live is Christ and to die is gain" (Phil. 1:21).

"I am the resurrection and the life; he who believes in Me will live even if he dies" (John 11:25).

"And it has not appeared as yet what we will be. We know that when He appears, we will be like Him, because we will see Him just as He is" (1 John 3:2).

Now it's my turn and, I find, my head keeps turning back.

I don't want to go.

My heart is flooded with grief. Not for here. Not for things, or places, or anything in life I've held dear. No, not that. But for Marcia, my kids, my family, my sisters and brothers in Christ—these are my people. God, by His sovereign power, has bound us together in a covenant of love. He has made us one. I don't want to go without them. They belong to me. I belong to them. Don't make me leave.

Don't make me turn my head, say good-bye, and cross alone.

I've said it once, I've said it a thousand times: Relationships are everything in the kingdom of God. He made us for Himself, yes. But by His eternal decree, He has bound us together—forever inseparable—that we love each other as He has loved us. So why must I go alone? How can my heart bear leaving them behind?

Marcia.

I don't know how to let go. Are these idols? Is this wrong of me?

Everything in me wants to cross. I want to be home with Jesus. I want to run through the streets of the City of God and leap with joy on the mountains and hills of Eden. I have family there, family I've never met—as many as the stars in the sky and sand on the seashore. But how can I enjoy any of that?

While I am far from those I love. My heart is split in half.

I see myself getting to the other side and turning around, watching, waiting. My tears will not dry, my heart will not stop its grieving, until those God has given me have crossed safely too. How can we rejoice in full until that day has come? Is not the entire company of heaven, from all generations, standing on the other side, waiting for the last of us to come up from the Jordan?

Then there will be singing! Then every tear will be wiped away. No more sorrow. No more pain. The kingdom of real love will have come and we who have the Son will be swallowed up by life, real life, eternal life.

Jesus, my Lord.

Forgive me, but I'm not ready to go.

QUESTION FOR REFLECTION

When we love deeply, we hurt deeply when death comes and separates us. Yes, we have all the promises of God, fulfilled in Christ, who rose triumphant over the power of death. But is Chap right? Is it wrong to grieve as he did? Are those we love idols in our hearts? In yours?

There is surrender here, as our Lord modeled on an infinitely greater scale: "Father, if You are willing, remove this cup from Me; yet not My will, but Yours be done" (Luke 22:42). Yes, He loved to the end (John 13:1). Will we? With all our hearts? And when it's time, will we ask Him to help us when death comes to separate us from those we love? Will you?

PART 8

REAL
IDENTITY

A sampling of four devotions from another
book in Thad Barnum's Deeper Devotion series.
(Available for purchase at bookstores or at wphonline.com.)

57

MAKE ME REAL, LORD

Introduction

I lead a Bible study at the local rescue mission with fifteen guys who've come off the streets. Every week they show me what it means to daily choose Jesus Christ. They say it a thousand times, "I can do all things through [Christ] who strengthens me" (Phil. 4:13). And they believe it. They won't do life without Him.

We open with prayer. We turn to the Bible, and I feel the challenge. They don't want just an academic study; they want connection. The crossings that connect the mind and heart. The truth of God's Word to my life and theirs. They need the gospel to be what the gospel really is, "the power of God for salvation" (Rom. 1:16).

They need more than true. They need practical. They need real.

A staff member comes in. He asks if anyone has seen Joe. They say he was at breakfast an hour ago but no one has seen him since. They're concerned for him. He'd been at the mission a few months and made great strides.

The men pray for Joe. They ask the Lord to help him. "If he's back on the streets, Lord," one of them prays, "help him make right decisions and keep him safe."

They finish their prayers, open their Bibles, and look at me like they don't want me to mess up. They need the truth of God's Word today. Truth they can understand. Truth that's real manna feeding their souls. Truth that comes in the strength and power of the Holy Spirit to live life today.

I have to make the connection. I have to be real so they can live real.

We start at the beginning. Back to Genesis. Back to when God created the heavens and earth in perfection. Back to when we were made in His image and created, not for corruption and evil, but for God and His glory. We deal with the entrance of sin, evil, and corruption. The reign of the Devil and death.

"If we're going to know Him, if we're going to serve Him," I tell the men, "we have to hear the whole story. He made us for good, and He wants good for us. We're the ones who sinned. We did that. Not Him. And in His kindness, He did something about it. It's why He sent His Son. He wants good for us."

Good is hard to hear when you've been lost in a world of bad.

They push me. They want to know how I know. They want stories—real stories—from when I first crossed over from my bad, my sin, my real sin, to when His good first touched my heart and soul. Not just my mind. Me.

And they push. They want to see my crossings.

I resist. I always resist because I hate exposing me. I'd rather keep things in the realm of concept. Thoughts. Principles. So I can protect my heart.

But they push because their lives aren't lived there. They need *His* good. They need it to grab their minds, hearts, and souls and give them the power they need to choose good today in Jesus' name. Real good. Real power. Filling their souls.

Especially today. Though no one knows for sure where Joe is, they all know where Joe is—he's back on the street. And they don't want that. Not for him. Not for them. Not today. The streets cannot have them today. They choose to stay together. They choose Jesus.

And so do I.

Sitting in that room, in a big circle, we are brothers in Christ. They suffer from years of drug enslavement. I don't. But I suffer, like them, from my slavery to sin and the power of that sin trying to control my life.

I choose Jesus today, like them. I need Jesus today, like them. I need to hear the Word of the Lord to my soul. And I need it to be "the power of God for salvation" that saved me once, that saves me now.

So we build and cross our paths together. Starting in Genesis, moving to Exodus. Pointing to the day when Jesus Christ comes and makes all things real. He's the One who deals with our sins, addictions, pride, and rebellion by what He did on the cross. He's the One who makes it possible to live today.

We build as we go, crisscrossing paths, roads, and highways together—all of them, our crossroads, captured in the book you now hold, inviting you to go, inviting you to pray with us. Lord, take us to where Bible and life meet.

58

THE CROSSING

Reflections on Mark 4:1–20 and Matthew 7:24–27

*And the rain fell, and the floods came, and the winds
blew and slammed against that house; and yet it did
not fall, for it had been founded on the rock.*

—MATTHEW 7:25

Here I stand. At the crossing.

Sometimes I wish it wasn't so hard to find. That what
we see on the outside is what's real on the inside. Just that
simple. But too often the chasm between the two is huge.

And I forget about the crossing, where the outside and
inside meet.

Sam taught me that years ago. He was the perfect
testimony. He came to faith in Christ through the witness of
Christian men in our church. And Sam jumped in—Bible
studies, home group, ministries in the church and our local
community. He gave time, which in his profession he had little
of. He gave money to the church and beyond . . . way beyond.

Because he cared for the needy. It hurt him to see people
suffering. Off he went on mission trips to remote parts of the
world, wanting to help, needing to serve, having a big heart.

Sam.

His name came up to serve in church leadership. Who could be better? He met all the criteria: strong in belief, in conduct, in service, in leadership.

Sam.

Until the testing came, and it came hard. By the time we heard about it, it was too late. Sam had left his job, left his wife, left his teenage kids, left his church family. Sam was gone. The guys closest to him at church pursued him. They still do, even to this day so many years later.

Some said it was an affair. Others said something big happened at work. Was he caught doing drugs? Smuggling money? A cover-up of some kind? It almost doesn't matter. Whatever it was, it was big enough to expose his heart.

And that's what testing does.

In the parable of the sower, the seed of God's Word has to land in the heart—the good soil. If not, when testing comes, we fall away (Mark 4:17).

In the same way, the foundation has to be on rock, not sand. So when the storm comes, we stand strong, unshaken (Matt. 7:25).

Jesus taught us this. The world is full of trial and trouble. What matters is that we're ready for it—that what He has done in us is real. To the heart. And what He will do for us is see us through the storm. He will give us what we need to endure. To persevere.

That's His promise (John 16:33).

James said it. All we have to do is ask. In the midst of the mess of this world, we ask the Lord "who gives to all generously and without reproach," and He gives us the wisdom we need in the moment (James 1:5). As long as we ask in faith. And from faith.

Because our faith is real. He has penetrated our hearts.

But that's the problem, isn't it?

Sam looked so real. He said the right words. He did the right things. He leapt beyond himself for the sake of others. He wept at the reading of Scripture. He showed us what it means to have a passion for the things of God. He testified in- and outside church. He looked so real.

None of us dreamed that he lived in two worlds. One on the outside. One on the inside. And the one on the inside was so dark and secretive, controlled and well-protected, that none of us saw it coming. A big storm. Bigger than him. Exposing him. Tearing his two worlds apart.

Double-minded, that's what James called it (James 1:8). A word meaning "two-souled," it's deeper than being two-faced—hypocrites with an image on the outside that betrays the heart on the inside.

It goes to the breaking of the soul. As if, deep in our cores, we can be two.

And we can't. Not before God. Never, never can we serve two masters and get away with it (Matt. 6:24). No matter how in control we think we are.

Because storms come. Storms expose.

Sam became exactly what James said: "Like the surf of the sea, driven and tossed by the wind" (James 1:6). The storm hit and he was gone. His wife, teenage kids, and church family bereft without him. His kids ached for their dad. One of them wondered if being a Christian was really even worth it.

Sam.

He taught me to stand at the crossing.

He taught me that it's not enough, as a Christian leader, to help people believe in Jesus Christ, know the Bible, learn to pray, belong to the church, grow in service and ministry, give from our resources, and serve the poor, the needy, the voiceless.

All of it can be done and the heart never touched, the gospel never made real. The salvation given us in Jesus Christ never known in the depths of who we are. Outward Christians: right words, right deeds, playing games, two-souled.

So I make myself stand at the crossing.

Between the outside and the inside. And I beg the Lord to have mercy on us. To help us cross. So that Jesus Christ is real to our hearts, in the depths of our souls, before the storms come.

So we're not like Sam—disciples on the wrong foundation, rooted in the wrong soil, double-minded, two-souled, rudderless at the time of testing. But just the opposite. We know Him. He knows us.

We've made the crossing. We've found real.

QUESTIONS FOR REFLECTION

Can you talk about what it's like to stand at the crossing between the image you project and who you really are?

Is Jesus Christ real for you? Is He the foundation on which your life is built?

59

HELP ME STAY HERE

~~~

Reflections on Luke 9:18–27

*If anyone wishes to come after Me, he must deny himself,
and take up his cross daily and follow Me. For whoever
wishes to save his life will lose it, but whoever loses
his life for My sake, he is the one who will save it.*

—LUKE 9:23–24

It's hard to stay here—at the crossing.

Just like it's hard to be in battle, on the front lines, and suddenly find I have no shields. No lines of defense. Nothing to protect me, my heart, my soul.

And here I stand. Exposed. Vulnerable. Helpless. Way out of control.

Some people call it hitting bottom. I call it the crossing, where what we project on the outside meets who we are on the inside. Of course, most of us don't know who we are on the inside. We've guarded our hearts for so long that we've come to believe we are what we know—deep down—we're not.

And we don't want to go there. We don't want to be exposed. We don't want to stand at ground zero and face the stuff of life. The real stuff we've been avoiding and neglecting. Because we hate to confront. We *won't* confront.

Who wants to be like Adam and Eve and suddenly find the tree we're hiding behind is gone? And there we stand in the presence of the Lord, in the light of His glory, with fig leaves in our hands crumbling to dust.

Exposed.

It's hard to stay here.

I remember the summers during seminary when I had to do chaplaincy work. The first was at a hospital and it was hard for me. I'd go to be with a patient suffering in pain and wouldn't know what to do. So out came my rescue mode: "How can I help? What do you need? I'll get the nurse. I'll get the doctor. They'll get meds to ease your pain."

"Whose pain?" my supervisor asked. "Sounds like the one in pain was you. Sounds like you couldn't just be there with them. Pray with them. Suffer with them. Be an ambassador of Jesus Christ to them. You wanted to go for meds?"

I had to *do*. I couldn't just *be* there. It's the crossing again. Let me do, and I'm somehow still be in control. Force me to just be there in their suffering, and I risk that. I risk me entering their world. To be with those in pain and do nothing? Just be there? Just feel it? Feel what it's like to cry out completely helpless, alone, afraid? And then stay there, as long as it takes?

No thanks.

Who can stand with someone at bottom and not be at bottom too? Who can weep with those suffering and still stay in control?

Don't teach me to be. Let me do. Get the meds. Numb them out. While we're at it, numb me too. Because it's true. I don't want to be here.

Of course I want to say I was there. Past tense. I've been at bottom. That's the incredible power of Christian testimony. I personally love the sheer joy of brothers and sisters in Christ getting up in the church and sharing what the Lord has done for them. They've been there. Their worlds have been torn apart. Helpless, hopeless, unable to do for themselves. Vulnerable to the forces of evil. At the very edge of despair. Suffering hardship and affliction. Feeling the hot breath of the Devil on their faces. Running deep into the valley where fear and death overpower the soul.

And then the Lord meets them, rescuing from bottom, making them safe.

And the church roars with applause. Praise to the Lord for what He has done! Yes, He allows us to be here, at the crossing, fully exposed and helpless. For it is here where we meet Jesus Christ. Where He changes lives. Where the cross is. Dug into the earth's soil. It's the only place to go to be saved, forgiven, and set free.

But we don't stay here. We never stay here.

That's the whole point, isn't it? He rescues us from places like that. He would never make us stay there. Not there. Doesn't He want us to be like we were? Shields up, defenses in place, back in control, guarding the heart? This is the Christian message I like.

The one I don't like goes like this: We never leave here. We stay here. We build our homes here. We build our churches here. Why? Because this is where Jesus Christ is. At ground zero. Where *real* is. No more Eden trees to hide behind. No more fig leaves. No more dividing walls between what we project and who we are. No more games pretending we are what we know we're not. No more meds or drink to numb out. No more busy-busy doing so we don't have time to face ourselves. No more running from the call of Jesus Christ.

He said it plain. Clear. Unmistakable. Unavoidable.

"If anyone wishes to come after Me, he must deny himself, and take up his cross daily and follow Me. For whoever wishes to save his life will lose it, but whoever loses his life for My sake, he is the one who will save it" (Luke 9:23–24).

Stay here. Where we are exposed. Vulnerable. Helpless. Way out of control. Where we have to depend upon the Lord, trust in the Lord, every day. Where in our weakness, His grace is sufficient. Because it is. Where we can be with others who suddenly find themselves here. In the terrifying sufferings of this world. Ambassadors of the Holy Spirit.

Here we are.

Where the Lord Jesus Christ presides. Where disciples are made. Where the kingdom of God is made real.

O Lord, help me stay here.

QUESTIONS FOR REFLECTION

How good are you at staying in places where you feel out of control?

Do you know something about meeting Jesus at ground zero?

I KNOW I SAY NO

Reflections on Psalm 23

Even though I walk through the valley of the shadow of death, I fear no evil, for You are with me; Your rod and Your staff, they comfort me.

—PSALM 23:4

Testimonies are born here—where it hurts, where people suffer, where all we can do is cry out to God for help because there's nowhere else to go. Here. Stand here. Never leave here.

It's where our Lord is.

Listen to the stories. They are all the same. Every one of them gets to Easter morning the same way—through the cross. We can't avoid suffering, not in this world. Eventually, we're going to find ourselves here in need of a Savior. Because we're lost. We're scared. We need help. We need Him.

Here. He meets us here.

Even our children who grow up in Christian homes know the story. They say their prayers. They live the life. But eventually a day comes and they do what we all do. They enter the "valley of the shadow of death" (Ps. 23:4).

They know about evil, but suddenly they feel it. They feel the fear of it. The power of it.

The rod, the staff, the Shepherd—no longer just a story in the Bible.

It's real. In a place called real. Where we find inside us the deepest cry the soul can ever cry: Are you real? Really real?

Testimonies are born here.

But not just testimonies. This is the exact place where discipleship happens. Where we grow up in Christ day by day, all our days. It's here where we don't play games. Where we keep our hearts open to Him. Our minds set on Him. Our wills given, in full surrender, to do what He's calling us to do.

Discipleship.

I sat across the table, sipping my coffee. The pastor and I went out for breakfast to catch up. I was visiting his church and this gave us an opportunity to enjoy each other's company and talk openly about the stuff of our lives. Inevitably, we stumbled into one of the most pressing theological issues of our day.

At some point, I shook my head and laughed a little. He asked why.

"Because it's amazing to me," I said, "what seminary did to us. We become doctors of the mind and not the soul.

We forget that the truth of God's Word is intended to move from the mind so as to touch the heart. To impact us. To bring us to the place where we meet Christ and He meets us."

"It's my biggest defense!" he crowed.

"What is?"

"My mind. I thank God for seminary. It taught me how to build a fortress around my heart so I never have to deal with it. Or with anybody else's for that matter. It's how I protect myself when I'm in the middle of people's suffering. I pull out the right quote from the Bible. I tell the right story from Christian history. I give them the right answer."

"Well done us," I lamented, admiring his honest sarcasm.

"But it's all too true," he confessed. "It's how I preach. It's how I lead Bible classes. I find myself discipling Christians in just the same way. Building fortresses. Stockpiling right answers. Filling the mind with all kinds of great knowledge but never speaking to their hearts. Never entering into their pain."

And with that, somehow, we were there. At that place.

He opened up. For just a moment, the fortress walls came down. His heart was a mess. And there was good reason for it. Things of the past were crushing him, controlling him, dictating every part of his life. And he knew it. He knew it was the cause of his physical and emotional issues. He knew it was affecting his wife, his kids, and the church. But more, so much more, it distanced him from the Lord.

"It's been this way for years," he said.

"So why don't you do something about it?" I asked.

"Don't need to. I'm so good at what I do, no one really knows. Not really. Except my wife. And it's easier this way. To be honest, I'm afraid of what would happen to me if I go there. I'm afraid I'll lose my job. Afraid people will find me out. Afraid of what people will think of me."

And then he paused. Like he knew he had no choice.

"But I'll do it," he promised.

"What do you mean?"

"I mean I'll go there. I know I've been avoiding it. I know it's what the Lord wants me to do. A couple of times in my life I've sought counsel from people I thought could help but it just didn't work. So I stopped. I didn't press it. But I should have. Especially me."

"Why especially you?"

"Because I'm a pastor. My job, like you said, is to be a doctor of the soul and not just a doctor of the mind. But look at me! I pay no attention to my soul. I spend all my time avoiding the very thing I know I need to do and it's killing me inside. It's killing my relationship with the Lord. And I know it."

"Can I help?" I asked.

"Yeah. Call me in a month. Call me in two. Ask me if I've started. I know I say yes to this today, but I know myself well enough that tomorrow morning nothing will change. That's my fear. So call me."

"But why won't things change?" I asked, puzzled.

"Because I know I say yes to the Lord today. Yes to you. Yes to my wife. But when it comes time to actually do it?"